5th International Workshop on Computational Terminology (COMPUTERM 2016)

Osaka, Japan
12 December 2016

ISBN: 978-1-5108-3327-2

Printed by Curran Associates, Inc. (2016)

For permission requests, please contact the Association for Computational Linguistics
at the address below.

Association for Computational Linguistics
209 N. Eighth Street
Stroudsburg, Pennsylvania 18360

Phone: 1-570-476-8006
Fax: 1-570-476-0860

acl@aclweb.org

Additional copies of this publication are available from:

Curran Associates, Inc.
57 Morehouse Lane
Red Hook, NY 12571 USA
Phone: 845-758-0400
Fax: 845-758-2633
Email: curran@proceedings.com
Web: www.proceedings.com

Introduction

Computational Terminology covers an increasingly important aspect in Natural Language Processing areas such as text mining, information retrieval, information extraction, summarisation, textual entailment, document management systems, question-answering systems, ontology building, etc. Terminological information is paramount for knowledge mining from texts for scientific discovery and competitive intelligence. Scientific needs in fast growing domains (such as biomedicine, chemistry and ecology) and the overwhelming amount of textual data published daily demand that terminology is acquired and managed systematically and automatically; while in well established domains (such as law, economy, banking and music) the demand is on fine-grained analyses of documents for knowledge description and acquisition. Moreover, capturing new concepts leads to the acquisition and management of new knowledge.

The aim of this fifth Computerm workshop is to bring together Natural Language Processing to discuss recent advances in computational terminology and its impact in many NLP applications. The topics addressed in this workshop are wide ranging:

- term extraction, recognition and filtering, which is the core of the terminological activity that lays basis for other terminological topics and tasks;

- event recognition and extraction, that extends the notion of the terminological entity from terms meaning static units up to terms meaning procedural and dynamic processes;

- acquisition of semantic relations among terms, which is also an important research topic as the acquisition of semantic relationships between terms finds applications such as the population and update of existing knowledge bases, definition of domain specific templates in information extraction and disambiguation of terms;

- term variation management, that helps to deal with the dynamic nature of terms, their acquisition from heterogeneous sources, their integration, standardisation and representation for a large range of applications and resources, is also increasingly important, as one has to address this research problem when working with various controlled vocabularies, thesauri, ontologies and textual data. Term variation is also related to their paraphrases and reformulations, due to historical, regional, local or personal issues. Besides, the discovery of synonym terms or term clusters is equally beneficial to many NLP applications;

- definition acquisition, that covers important research and aims to provide precise and non-ambiguous description of terminological entities. Such definitions may contain elements necessary for the formal description of terms and concepts within ontologies;

- consideration of the user expertise, that is becoming a new issue in the terminological activity, takes into account the fact that specialized domains contain notions and terms often non-understandable to non-experts or to laymen (such as patients within the medical area, or bank clients within banking and economy areas). This aspect, although related to specialized areas, provides direct link between specialized languages and general language;

- systematic terminology management and updating domain specific dictionaries and thesauri, that are important aspects for maintaining the existing terminological resources. These aspects become crucial because the amount of the existing terminological resources is constantly increasing and because their perennial and efficient use depends on their maintenance and updating, while their re-acquisition is costly and often non-reproducible;

- monolingual and multilingual resources, that open the possibility for developing cross-lingual and multi-lingual applications, requires specific corpora, methods and tools which design and evaluation are challenging issues;

- robustness and portability of methods, which allows to apply methods developed in one given context to other contexts (corpora, domains, languages, etc.) and to share the research expertise among them;

- social netwoks and modern media processing, that attracts an increasing number of researchers and that provides challenging material to be processed;

- utilization of terminologies in various NLP applications, as they are a necessary component of any NLP system dealing with domain-specific literature, is another novel and challenging research direction.

In the call for paper, we encouraged authors to submit their research work related to various aspects of computational terminology related approaches, ranging from term extraction in various languages (using verb co-occurrence, information theoretic approaches, machine learning, etc.), translation pairs extracting from bilingual corpora based on terminology, up to semantic oriented approaches and theoretical aspects of terminology.

Besides, experiments on the evaluation of terminological methods and tools are also encouraged since they provide interesting and useful proof about the utility of terminological resources:

- direct evaluation may concern the efficiency of the terminological methods and tools to capture the terminological entities and relations, as well as various kinds of related information;

- indirect evaluation may concern the use of terminological resources in various NLP applications and the impact these resources have on the performance of the automatic systems. In this case, research and competition tracks (such as TREC, BioCreative, CLEF, CLEF-eHealth, I2B2, *SEM, and other shared tasks), provide particularly fruitful evaluation contexts and proved very successful in identifying key problems in terminology such as term variation and ambiguity.

This workshop is a continuation of previous Computerm workshops. The last Computerm was joined to the previous COLING conference in 2014.

The Computerm 2016 workshop received 28 submissions from 12 countries and 4 continents addressing issues on 9 languages. Further to a double-blind peer-reviewing process, 5 papers were accepted as long oral presentations, 1 as short oral presentation and 8 as posters. The acceptance rate for oral presentations is 21% and the overall acceptance rate is 50%. The selected papers tackle various terminology related problems such terminological resource evaluation, semantic relation acquisition and, above all, extraction, recognition and filtering of terms, with classical ruled-based methods or statistical approaches as well as word embeddings. The domain of application of the proposed approaches is varied, going from Mathematics and Art to Environment. We believe this workshop will be a great place for fruitful research discussions, and the emergence of new research topics and collaborations. The objective of the combined oral and poster presentations is to strengthen this point.

Acknowledgements

First of all, we would like to thank the members of the program committee for the quality of their reviews. We are particularly grateful to Professor Min Song from Yonsei University, Seoul, Korea to be our invited speaker. We are grateful to the COLING organizers, in particular Monica Monachini, Key-Sun Choi and Yusuke Miyao for their help in the workshop organisation. We also would like to thank all the authors for the quality of their submission and their hard work. We are also grateful to the Faculté des arts des sciences and the Vice-rectorat à la recherche of the University of Montréal, the laboratory Savoirs, Textes, Langage of the university of Lille and the Computational Linguistics lab of the Okayama University, for sponsoring the venue of our invited speaker.

Without all of them, this 5th workshop on Computational Terminology would not take place.

Organisers

Patrick Drouin, Observatoire de linguistique Sens-Texte, Université de Montréal, Canada
Natalia Grabar, CNRS UMR 8163 STL, France
Thierry Hamon, LIMSI-CNRS & Université Paris 13, France
Kyo Kageura, Library and Information Science Laboratory, University of Tokyo, Japan
Koichi Takeuchi, Graduate School of Natural Science and Technology, Okayama University, Japan

Programme Committee

Lynne Bowker, University of Ottawa, Canada
Béatrice Daille, University of Nantes, France
Louise Deléger, INRA, France
Gregory Grefenstette, INRIA, University Paris Sud, France
Yoshihiko Hayashi, Waseda University, Japan
Olga Kanishcheva, Kharkiv Polytechnic Institute, Ukraine
Georgios Kontonatsios, NaCTeM, University of Manchester, UK
Marie-Claude L'Homme, University of Montréal, Canada
Philippe Langlais, RALI, Canada
Veronique Malaise, Elsevier BV, the Netherlands
Elizabeth Marshman, University of Ottawa, Canada
Fleur Mougin, University Bordeaux, France
Agnieszka Mykowiecka, IPIPAN, Poland
Rogelio Nazar, University Pompeu Fabra, Spain
Goran Nenadic, University of Manchester, UK
Fabio Rinaldi, University of Zurich, Switzerland
Selja Seppälä, University of Florida, USA
Karine Verspoor, University of Melbourne, Australia
Jorge Vivaldi Palatresi, University Pompeu Fabra, Spain
Pierre Zweigenbaum, LIMSI, France

Invited Speaker

Min Song, Text and Social Media Mining Lab, Yonsei University, Seoul, Republic of Korea

Table of Contents

Workshop Program

Monday, December 12, 2016

9:00–9:15   **Opening Remarks**

9:15–10:45   **Invited Speaker: Professor Min Song**

9:15–10:45   *Analyzing Impact, Trend, and Diffusion of Knowledge associated with Neoplasms Research*
Min Song

10:45–11:10   *Coffee Break*

11:10–12:00   **Session 1**

11:10–11:35   *Local-Global Vectors to Improve Unigram Terminology Extraction*
Ehsan Amjadian, Diana Inkpen, Tahereh Paribakht and Farahnaz Faez

11:35–12:00   *Recognition of non-domain phrases in automatically extracted lists of terms*
Agnieszka Mykowiecka, Malgorzata Marciniak and Piotr Rychlik

12:00–14:00   *Lunch Break*

Monday, December 12, 2016 (continued)

14:00–15:15   Session 2

14:00–14:25   *Contextual term equivalent search using domain-driven disambiguation*
Caroline Barriere, Pierre André Ménard and Daphnée Azoulay

14:25–14:50   *A Method of Augmenting Bilingual Terminology by Taking Advantage of the Conceptual Systematicity of Terminologies*
Miki Iwai, Koichi Takeuchi, Kyo Kageura and Kazuya Ishibashi

14:50–15:15   *Acquisition of semantic relations between terms: how far can we get with standard NLP tools?*
Ina Roesiger, Julia Bettinger, Johannes Schäfer, Michael Dorna and Ulrich Heid

15:15–15:30   Boosters

15:30–15:50   *Coffee Break*

15:50–17:00   Poster Session

Evaluation of distributional semantic models: a holistic approach
Gabriel Bernier-Colborne and Patrick Drouin

A Study on the Interplay Between the Corpus Size and Parameters of a Distributional Model for Term Classification
Behrang QasemiZadeh

Pattern-based Word Sketches for the Extraction of Semantic Relations
Pilar León-Araúz, Antonio San Martín and Pamela Faber

Constructing and Evaluating Controlled Bilingual Terminologies
Rei Miyata and Kyo Kageura

Providing and Analyzing NLP Terms for our Community
Gil Francopoulo, Joseph Mariani, Patrick Paroubek and Frédéric Vernier

Evaluating a dictionary of human phenotype terms focusing on rare diseases
Simon Kocbek, Toyofumi Fujiwara, Jin-Dong Kim, Toshihisa Takagi and Tudor Groza

Monday, December 12, 2016 (continued)

A semi automatic annotation approach for ontological and terminological knowl-edge acquisition
Driss Sadoun

Understanding Medical free text: A Terminology driven approach
Santosh Sai Krishna and Manoj Hans

17:00   **Closing Remarks**

Analyzing Impact, Trend, and Diffusion of Knowledge associated with Neoplasms Research

Min Song
Dept. of Lib. and Info. Science
Text and Social Media Mining Lab
Yonsei University, Seoul, Republic of Korea
`min.song@yonsei.ac.kr`

Abstract

Cancer (a.k.a neoplasms in a broader sense) is one of the leading causes of death worldwide and its incidence is expected to exacerbate. To respond to the critical need from the society, there have been rigorous attempts for the cancer research community to develop treatment for cancer. Accordingly, we observe a surge in the sheer volume of research products and outcomes in relation to neoplasms.

In this talk, we introduce the notion of entitymetrics to provide a new lens for understanding the impact, trend, and diffusion of knowledge associated with neoplasms research. To this end, we collected over two million records from PubMed, the most popular search engine in the medical domain. Coupled with text mining techniques including named entity recognition, sentence boundary detection, string approximate matching, entitymetrics enables us to analyze knowledge diffusion, impact, and trend at various knowledge entity units, such as bio-entity, organization, and country.

At the end of the talk, the future applications and possible directions of entitymetrics will be discussed.

Proceedings of the 5th International Workshop on Computational Terminology,
page 1, Osaka, Japan, December 12 2016.

Local-Global Vectors to Improve Unigram Terminology Extraction

Ehsan Amjadian[1,2], Diana Inkpen[2], T. Sima Paribakht[3], and Farahnaz Faez[4]
[1]Institute of Cognitive Science, Carleton University, Canada
[2]School of Electrical Engineering and Computer Science, University of Ottawa, Canada
[3]Official Languages and Bilingualism Institute, University of Ottawa, Canada
[4]Faculty of Education, Western University, Canada.
`ehsan.amjadian@carleotn.ca, diana@site.uottawa.ca`
`sima.paribakht@uottawa.ca, ffaez@uwo.ca`

Abstract

The present paper explores a novel method that integrates efficient distributed representations with terminology extraction. We show that the information from a small number of observed instances can be combined with local and global word embeddings to remarkably improve the term extraction results on unigram terms. To do so, we pass the terms extracted by other tools to a filter made of the local-global embeddings and a classifier which in turn decides whether or not a term candidate is a term. The filter can also be used as a hub to merge different term extraction tools into a single higher-performing system. We compare filters that use the skip-gram architecture and filters that employ the CBOW architecture for the task at hand.

1 Introduction

The terminology of a domain encodes the existing knowledge in that domain. Hence understanding and interpreting a message belonging to a domain cannot be fully achieved without knowing its terminology. This makes Automatic Terminology Extraction (ATE) an important task in Natural Language Processing (NLP). ATE methods have been conventionally classified as linguistic, statistical, and hybrid (Cabre-Castellvi et al., 2001; Chung, 2003). Linguistic methods implement formal rules to detect terms; statistical methods exploit some measures based on relative frequency of terms in general and target corpora by means of which they can tell apart a term from a word in its generic sense; and, the hybrid methods combine the advantages of both of these techniques (Frantzi et al., 1998; Park et al., 2002; Drouin, 2003; Chung and Nation, 2004; Yoshida and Nakagawa, 2005; Vu et al., 2008; VRL, 2009; Yang et al., 2010; Zervanou, 2010; Broß and Ehrig, 2013; Conrado et al., 2013). These methods often regard words in a document as atomic elements; that is, they are manifested as their symbolic alphabetical form in the algorithm (such as in 'a' below) and/or as some measure of their relative frequency (as in 'b' below). But, in a distributed approach (as in 'c' below) each word has tens or hundreds of real-valued components, as opposed to a single linguistic form or a termhood score[1]. The idea is that such finer-granularity may grant more access to the information that a word contains, potentially resulting in a better detection of terms in a document.

(a) apple

(b) 0.0003654

(c) $[0.54407, 0.9233, 0.50644, 0.46454, -0.62015, -0.35166, ... -0.93253]_n$

where n is often between 50 and 1000 for different types of word embeddings, almost similar to other vector space models such as Latent Semantic Analysis (LSA) and Latent Dirichlet Allocation (LDA). In addition to the richer representation, the rise of distributed methods in NLP, especially the recent word embeddings surge, makes it relevant to explore the ways current model architectures may fit into the

---

[1]Termhood is the degree of a linguistic unit being related to a domain-specific concept (Kageura and Umino, 1996)

Proceedings of the 5th International Workshop on Computational Terminology,
pages 2–11, Osaka, Japan, December 12 2016.

automatic terminology extraction picture. However, the fact that makes them particularly appealing is their computational efficiency and scalability as compared to the available alternatives, including LSA and LDA (Mikolov et al., 2013).

We present a simple method that harnesses the rich distributed representation acquired by a log-bilinear regression model called GloVe (Pennington et al., 2014), as well as the efficiency of log-linear models with CBOW[2] and skip-gram architectures (Mikolov et al., 2013), which is a step forward towards language-independent ATE. In our method, the GloVe model is used to preserve the global[3] scope of a word in a general corpus (i.e., its general sense(s)) and the CBOW or the skip-gram model is used to capture the local scope for a word in a technical corpus (i.e., its technical usage).

Currently, we use our method as a filter on top of a previously-developed hybrid term extraction algorithm, namely, TermoStat (Drouin, 2003; Serrec et al., 2010) along with two simpler methods (refer to section 4 for further details) and focus on the unigram[4] term extraction. TermoStat has been previously tested on mathematics domain where it performed well on the extraction of multi-word expressions, but lower on unigram terms (Inkpen et al., 2016), hence the present work is an attempt to improve unigram term extraction for the same domain.

As mentioned, the target domain of the present study is mathematics textbooks. A significant component of any academic subject is its terminology. Knowledge of the terminology of a field enables students to engage with their discipline more effectively by enhancing their ability to understand the related academic texts and lectures, and allowing them to use the subject-specific terminology in their discussions, presentations, and assignments. Therefore, generating lists of terms specific to various fields of study is a significant endeavor. However, these lists have often been generated manually or through corpus-based studies, which are time consuming, labor-intensive, and prone to human error. This can be facilitated by a great extent with high-performance automatic term extraction.

To the best of our knowledge, the present method is the first to successfully apply neural network word embeddings to the terminology extraction task. This method can be combined with any term extraction algorithm for any non-polysynthetic[5] language and any domain.

2 Related Work

As described in section 1, ATE approaches traditionally fall into three categories, namely, linguistic, (unsupervised) statistical[6], and hybrid methods (Cabre-Castellvi et al., 2001; Chung, 2003). These TE methods have been applied to both monolingual and multilingual corpora (Ljubešić et al., 2012). Linguistic methods apply hand-coded rules to the target corpus to extract technical terms. Statistical methods are often unsupervised and apply some measure of relative frequency to a technical target corpus, a reference (general) corpus and sometimes a (contrastive) corpus from another domain, to identify the existing terms in the technical corpus (Frantzi et al., 1998; Chung, 2003; Vu et al., 2008; Conrado et al., 2013). Hybrid methods combine statistical and linguistic methods to extract terminology from a target corpus and often perform well (Drouin, 2003; Serrec et al., 2010; Ismail and Manandhar, 2010; Vintar, 2010). The above-mentioned approaches, in contrast to the method put forth in this paper, regard words as atomic units represented by their linguistic forms and their statistical scores that indicate their likelihood to be terms. They may, however, implement rules associated with some linguistic features (e.g., their POS tags, their position in the POS sequence, their position in the parse tree, phrase, and/or in the sentence). These linguistic rules make an algorithm language-dependent and even sometimes to some degree domain-dependent. On the contrary, our method, if used independently, can be used for any non-polysynthetic language and for any domain as long as domain-specific and general corpora are available.

---

[2]Continuous Bag Of Words. See section 4 for further details.

[3]We use the terms "global" and "local" with a different sense from Pennington et al. (2014). They used "global" to denote a model that captures a wider set of co-occurrence statistics being computed globally (e.g., document-wide) such as in LSA, as compared to the "local" methods that use a relatively small context window for co-occurrence computation such as CBOW and skip-gram (Mikolov et al., 2013) or similarly vLBL and ivLBL (Mnih and Kavukcuoglu, 2013).

[4]Singe-words

[5]A polysynthetic language has a richer morphology than syntax, where the words are much longer and can convey full sentence-like messages

[6]These statistical methods are distinct from statistical learning approaches.

In this study, we do not use our method independent of other methods, but it can still be regarded as a step towards a language independent ATE algorithm that benefits from latent linguistic information encoded in the vectors used (see section 4 for further details on the method) in comparison to purely statistical methods that do not capture such information.

Supervised methods have been recently[7] designed for terminology extraction. Nazar and Cabré (2012) used examples of terms from the domain of interest and a reference corpus of general language, which represent positive and negative examples of terms, and a three-level (i.e., syntactic, lexical, and morphological) learning algorithm to detect the terms. They used the frequency distribution for POS tag sequences at the syntactic level. At the lexical level, they accounted for the frequency of the lexical units within the terms (word forms, as well as lemmas). Finally, at their morphological level, from each word type they extracted initial and final character n-grams where: $1 \leq n \leq 5$ (Nazar and Cabré, 2012). Their term extractor is an online web-based system that is constantly being updated when used by terminologists. More recently, Conrado et al. (2013) achieved state-of-the-art performance for unigram term extraction in Brazilian Portuguese using supervised learning algorithms and a rich feature set. They used eight linguistic features, seven statistical features, and four hybrid features in their method. The present work would be the next phase for these supervised methods, since we move closer to a rich, language-independent, resource-independent, and fully data-driven representation. It is worth noting that modern word embeddings have been successfully employed in many tasks, including the related areas of keyphrase extraction (Wang et al., 2015) and aspect term extraction[8] (Yin et al., 2016); nevertheless, this is the first time they are leveraged for the general terminology extraction task.

3   Corpus

The domain corpus that we used for the purpose of this study is comprised of 5 English high school mathematics textbooks used in Ontario, Canada (Small et al., 2005; Small et al., 2007a; Small et al., 2007b; Kirkpatrick et al., 2007; Crippin et al., 2007), which were concatenated into a corpus consisting of 1,127,987 tokens.

4   Methodology

In this study, we merged the results of three tools (see below) that we used for terminology extraction. We improved the performance of these tools by adding local-global distributed word representations coupled with a classifier as a filter. The basic idea is if a candidate term in a technical corpus is being used in a distinctly different manner and context than in a general corpus, then it is likely to be a term[9]. For each Candidate Term (CT) extracted by TermoStat, two separate embedding vectors are constructed and then concatenated. One is a global vector pre-trained on general corpora, and the other is a local vector trained on the target corpus from which the terms are extracted. Each of these two vectors portrays distinct regularities about the CT at hand, as discussed below.

The idea behind using a general global vector is to encapsulate the behavior of the CT in its generic sense(s), the intuition being that the generic sense(s) have a predominant presence in general corpora and will, therefore, dominate the vector. We use the pre-built GloVe vectors as our global vectors, created by Pennington et al. (2014)[10]. These global vectors are of 50 dimensions and were built on Wikipedia 2014 + the Gigaword 5 corpus; that is, approximately 6 billion tokens. GloVe is a log-bilinear regression model. More specifically:

$$J = \sum_{i,j=1}^{V} f(X_{ij})(\mathbf{w}_i^T \tilde{\mathbf{w}}_j + b_i + \tilde{b}_j - \log X_{ij})^2 \tag{1}$$

---

[7]There has, however, been earlier supervised work in keyword/keyphrase extraction such as Turney (2000), as opposed to terminology extraction which is the topic of this paper. While Keyword extraction is the task of extracting only a few keywords in a text, terminology extraction needs to detect all the terms, usually from a large domain corpus.

[8]Aspect term extraction is the task to identify the aspect expressions which refer to a products or services properties or attributes, from customer reviews (Pontiki et al., 2014; Pontiki et al., 2015; Yin et al., 2016).

[9]This is similar to the premise of traditional statistical ATE methods except that those models carry less local information such as syntactic behavior.

[10]Available at: http://nlp.stanford.edu/projects/glove/

where V is the size of the vocabulary, $f(X_{ij})$ is the weighting function, w_i and w_j are two separate context word vectors and their sum constructs the final GloVe vector, and finally b_i and b_j are biases for their corresponding word vectors. GloVe has been shown to adequately reflect both semantic and syntactic regularities in the data (Pennington et al., 2014); we require both for our global embeddings.

In contrast to global embeddings, technical local embeddings are built on the domain corpus. These vectors are valuable since they capture the behavior of the candidate terms in the technical domain. To construct the local embeddings, we use two neural network architectures introduced by Mikolov et al. (2013) on our corpus (discussed in section 3 above), namely, the CBOW and the skip-gram architectures shown in Figure 1. CBOW and skip-gram are efficient algorithms trained by stochastic gradient descent and backpropagation. Below are their complexities, respectively:

$$Q_{CBOW} = N \times D + D \times \log_2(V) \tag{2}$$

$$Q_{skipgram} = C \times (D + D \times \log_2(V)) \tag{3}$$

where N is the number of context words, D the vector dimensionality, V the vocabulary size, and C is roughly the maximum distance for the context from the target word. CBOW is trained to predict a target word based on its surrounding words, and the skip-gram model is trained to predict the surrounding words given a single word. The CBOW architecture tends to have better performance in discovering syntactic regularities as compared to semantic regularities, whereas the skip-gram architecture tends to have a higher performance in finding semantic regularities rather than syntactic ones (Mitkov et al., 2012; Pennington et al., 2014). Because we are dealing with unigram terms and not multi-word terms at this stage, we expect a skip-gram filter to outperform a CBOW filter. We used the gensim[11] implementation (Řehůřek and Sojka, 2010) of word2vec[12] to build vectors of 100 dimensions with context window of size 5 and minimum frequency of 5. The rest of the parameters were left with their default values.

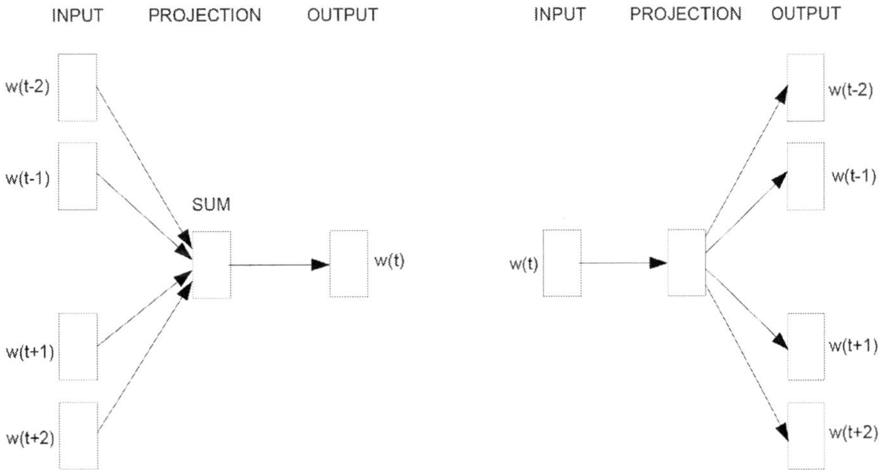

Figure 1: The CBOW architecture predicts the current word given the surrounding words, and the skip-gram predicts the surrounding words given a word (Mikolov et al., 2013).

After having the local and global vectors ready, they are concatenated and the resultant local-global vector is fed to the classifier to make the final decision. We experimented with several classification algorithms. Following Conrado et al. (2013) (see section 2 for more details), we used JRip[13], Naïve Bayes, J48[14], and SMO[15](Platt, 1998). We also tested a few other classifiers of our choice to find the

---

[11] Available at: https://radimrehurek.com/gensim/models/word2vec.html

[12] Available at: https://code.google.com/archive/p/word2vec/

[13] A rule induction classifier

[14] A decision tree algorithm. We used it with confidence factor of 0.25.

[15] A Support Vector Machine classifier from Weka

most suitable ones for the task, including logistic regression, multi-layer perceptron and PART[16]. Default parameters were used for these classifiers. We employed the Weka implementation of all the above-mentioned classifiers. We tested all the classifiers for both the CBOW and the skip-gram architecture.

As mentioned above, our method operates on the results of three other term extraction tools. The first is a full-fledged hybrid ATE tool called TermoStat[17] (Drouin, 2003). It statistically computes the specificity of a word in a multi-word expression with reference to a general corpus and uses POS-tag patterns to detect head nouns and term phrases. The second term extraction tool is called Topia[18]. We augmented it by a filter that removed all the candidate terms that had less than 3 letters and took out numbers or special characters from candidate terms. Topia uses the majority POS tag for each word, and applies only a frequency threshold to extract terms. Third, we extracted most frequent unigrams using AntConc[19][20] (Anthony, 2012), and filtered out all the stop-words.

Figure 2 illustrates our overall system. First, the term extraction tools operate on the target corpus. Then, the resultant TC's from all of them are pooled together (with no repetition) and fed to the filter. The filter uses the local vectors trained on the technical corpus as well as the global vectors trained on the general corpus to represent the received CT's in 150 dimensional vectors. These vectors are then forwarded to the classifier to tell apart terms from non-terms. The highest-performing classifier is then found and used to initialize the system. We compare the results of our system with the results received from each of the term extraction tools used in isolation.

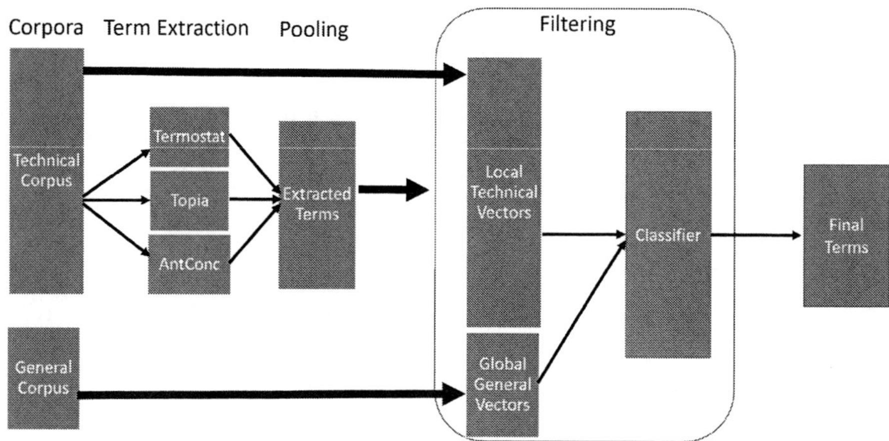

Figure 2: The figure depicts the overall system architecture of our method.

5   Annotation

To evaluate the performance of our system and compare it with the ATE tools used in isolation, two human annotators judged the terms extracted by the term extraction tools. The annotators used Term Evaluator[21] (Inkpen et al., 2016), a software program for annotating and evaluating terminology extraction, to judge the results. The annotators were asked to use their background knowledge of mathematics as the primary source of their judgment. In case of confusion, they could consult a mathematics dictionary of their choice. The annotations had kappa agreement scores of k = 0.70 for Topia, k = 0.84 for AntConc and, k = 0.53 for TermoStat. The annotation resulted in a dataset consisting of 954 instances with 325 positive and 629 negative cases, by which we assess the performance of the systems used in

---

[16] Another rule induction algorithm

[17] Available at: http://termostat.ling.umontreal.ca/

[18] topia.termextract 1.1.0 library available at: https://pypi.python.org/pypi/topia.termextract/

[19] Available at: http://www.laurenceanthony.net/software/antconc/

[20] AntConc has a keyword extraction module but no term extraction module.

[21] Available at: https://sourceforge.net/projects/termevaluator/

this study.

6 Experiments and Results

First, we aim to find the best-performing classifier(s), out of the ones tested, to be used in our system for each of the two architectures (CBOW and skip grams). We noticed that three classifiers, namely, SMO, logistic regression, and the multi-layer perceptron consistently outperformed the rest of the classifiers we examined (the full list is provided in section 4). JRip performed well, but its performance was consistently lower than the above-mentioned three classifiers. It should be noted, however, that we also have a greater dimension size for our vectors than Conrado et al. (2013), that is, 150 versus 19. Also the nature of the vectors is different in that they used feature vectors but we used embeddings. Nevertheless, we only show the results for these three classifiers. Figure 3 depicts the classifiers' performance with local-global vectors (LGVs) where the local vectors are trained with the CBOW architecture, and Figure 4 depicts the classifiers' performance with local-global vectors where the local vectors are trained with the skip-gram architecture. The classifiers' performance is presented as a function of the number of observed instances[22] (the amount of training data used), and the classifiers are tested on the rest of the instances (954 minus the number of observed instances). Instances are chosen randomly for training with a positive/negative ratio proportional to the dataset (i.e., 1/2 respectively). All of the instances in the entire dataset are unique candidate terms. The performance is measured by F-measure in the figures. We compute only relative recall[23] throughout the experiments at this stage.

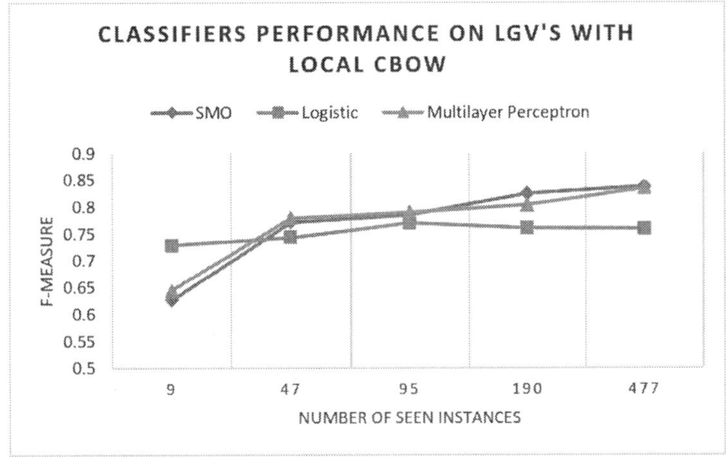

Figure 3: The figure displays the performance (F-measure) of the classifiers on local-global vectors with CBOW local vectors as a function of number of observed instances.

As shown in Figures 3 and 4 the CBOW architecture with the logistic regression classifier generalizes really well with as little data as only 9 instances. However, as soon as we add more instances, the multi-layer perceptron and SMO take the lead, outperforming one another in the process. However, the logistic regression classifier shows less improvement when subjected to more training data. Overall, we did not notice any considerable difference between the skip-gram and the CBOW architectures across the classifiers used for the purpose of unigram term extraction.

In practice, we prefer to show the system as little data as possible since extracting a few high-precision terms is relatively easy in real-world ATE; hence, we choose the local CBOW architecture with logistic

---

[22]The numbers shown on the X axes of Figures 3 and 4 (i.e., 9, 47, 95, 190, and 477) are the results of splitting training and test data such that the training data is approximately 1%, 5%, 10%, 20%, and 50% of the entire dataset respectively. The most notable improvement is when we increase the training set from 9 to 47 and that is only 4% variation in the size of the test set but 10% improvement of performance on average for LGV's with local CBOW (Figure 3) and an average of 13% improvement of performance for LGV's with local skip-gram (Figure 4).

[23]The reason for resorting to relative recall is that having annotators go through the entire corpus to compute recall is time-consuming and labor-intensive at this phase of the project.

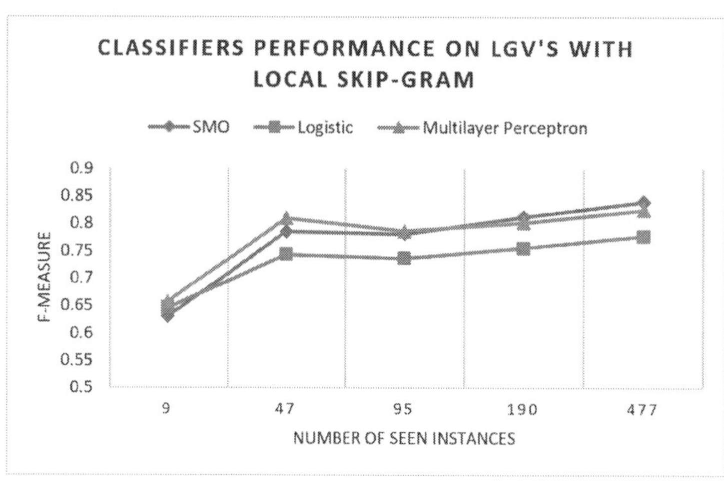

Figure 4: The figure displays the performance (F-measure) of the classifiers on local-global vectors with skip-gram local vectors as a function of number of observed instances.

regression classifier (trained on only 9 instances) as one configuration (our quickest learner), and the local skip-gram architecture coupled with multi-layer perceptron as the other configuration of our system (performs best among those trained on up to 47 instances) for the next experiment. We compare these two system configurations with a baseline and the initial term extraction tools, all tested on 907 (i.e., 954 - 47) remaining instances that are unseen to all of the systems under experiment. Table 1 compares the results of our system in unigram term extraction with individual term extraction tools and a frequency baseline that uses a stop-word filter (refer to section 4 for further details on the tools and the baseline). The results show that both of our system configurations achieve a substantial improvement over the other tools.

Method	Precision	Recall	F-Measure
TermoStat	0.371	0.528	0.436
Improved Topia	0.426	0.702	0.552
Frequency + Stopword Filter	0.407	0.514	0.454
LGV9 (CBOW) + Logistic	0.728	0.734	0.728
LGV47 (skip-gram) + Multi-layer Perceptron	**0.809**	**0.811**	**0.810**

Table 1: The table compares the results of two configurations of our system, LGV9 (using CBOW local vectors) and LGV47 (using skip-gram local vectors), with the term extraction tools used in isolation and with a frequency baseline.

7   Conclusion & Future Work

This paper offered a new ATE method that uses the distributed representation of words as a filter for the task of unigram term extraction. To do so, we leveraged the local-global embeddings to represent a term, its senses, and its behavior. The global word embeddings GloVe were pre-trained on general corpora, and we used the skip-gram and CBOW architectures to train local vectors on a technical domain corpus. This was done in order to preserve both the domain-specific and the general-domain information a word may possess, including its syntactic and semantic behavior. We showed that such a filter, with only as few instances as 9, can substantially improve the output of the three ATE tools in unigram term extraction. This indicates that with a) any high-precision (even with very low recall and F-measure) term extraction tool that outputs a few terms, b) a few random generic words in a language, and c) our filter, one can create a high-performance term extraction system for that language. Our method can also be used as a way to combine different tools to benefit from the advantages that each can offer, resulting in gain in performance. The use of the filter is not restricted to multiple term extraction tools and it can be applied as feasibly to any individual term extraction method. It is important to note that in our study the improvement in performance is not due to the merger of different tools but to a richer, more elaborate, and more informative representation of candidate terms. It was observed that the two local architectures, CBOW and skip-gram, do not show a considerable difference in capturing the technical sense and behavior of a word for unigram term extraction.

In future work, we plan to apply our local-global vectors directly to the corpus as a standalone term extraction tool. We also plan to extend the algorithm to detect multi-word terms in addition to unigram terms. It would be worthwhile to investigate if skip-gram and CBOW architectures can diverge in performance in extraction of terms that contain more than one word. Polysynthetic languages have a high morpheme-to-word ratio, that is, most of the grammatical and semantic information of a sentence is carried inside individual words, but continuous distributed models, including our LGV's, predominantly disregard word-internal structures. A very recent method based on the skip-gram architecture captures subword information in its word vectors (Bojanowski et al., 2016). We will address polysynthetic languages using enhanced LGV's as a next step. We further intend to compare our method with more available term extraction tools and methods. Applying our method to other domain corpora and datasets is another future direction for this research.

References

L. Anthony. 2012. AntConc (Version 3.3.0) [Computer Software] http://www.laurenceanthony.net/.

Piotr Bojanowski, Edouard Grave, Armand Joulin, and Tomas Mikolov. 2016. Enriching word vectors with subword information. *arXiv preprint arXiv:1607.04606*.

Jürgen Broß and Heiko Ehrig. 2013. Terminology extraction approaches for product aspect detection in customer reviews. In Julia Hockenmaier and Sebastian Riedel, editors, *Proceedings of the Seventeenth Conference on Computational Natural Language Learning, CoNLL 2013, Sofia, Bulgaria, August 8-9, 2013*, pages 222–230. ACL.

T. Cabre-Castellvi, R. Estopa, and J. Vivaldi-Palatresi. 2001. Automatic term detection: A review of current systems. In D. Bourigault, C. Jacquemin, and M. LHomme, editors, *Recent Advances in Computational Terminology*. John Benjamins.

Teresa Mihwa Chung and Paul Nation. 2004. Identifying technical vocabulary. *System*, 32(2):251 – 263.

T. M. Chung. 2003. A corpus comparison approach for terminology extraction. *Terminology*, 9:221–246.

Merley Conrado, Thiago Pardo, and Solange Rezende. 2013. A machine learning approach to automatic term extraction using a rich feature set. page 16–23, Atlanta, Georgia, June. Association for Computational Linguistics.

P.W.D. Crippin, R. Donato, and D. Wright. 2007. *Calculus and Vectors*. Nelson Education Limited.

Patrick Drouin. 2003. Term extraction using non-technical corpora as a point of leverage. *Terminology*, 9(1):99–115.

Katerina T. Frantzi, Sophia Ananiadou, and Jun-ichi Tsujii. 1998. The c-value/nc-value method of automatic recognition for multi-word terms. In *Proceedings of the Second European Conference on Research and Advanced Technology for Digital Libraries*, ECDL '98, pages 585–604, London, UK, UK. Springer-Verlag.

Diana Inkpen, T. Sima Paribakht, Farahnaz Faez, and Ehsan Amjadian. 2016. Term evaluator: A tool for terminology annotation and evaluation. *International Journal of Computational Linguistics and Applications*, pages –, December.

Azniah Ismail and Suresh Manandhar. 2010. Bilingual lexicon extraction from comparable corpora using in-domain terms. In *Proceedings of the 23rd International Conference on Computational Linguistics: Posters*, COLING '10, pages 481–489, Stroudsburg, PA, USA. Association for Computational Linguistics.

K. Kageura and B. Umino. 1996. Methods of automatic term recognition: A review. *Terminology*, 3(2):259–289.

C. Kirkpatrick, B. Alldred, C. Chilvers, B. Farahani, K. Farentino, A. Lillo, I. Macpherson, J. Rodger, and S. Trew. 2007. *Nelson Advanced Functions*. Nelson Education.

Nikola Ljubešić, Špela Vintar, and Darja Fišer. 2012. Multi-word term extraction from comparable corpora by combining contextual and constituent clues. In Reinhard Rapp, Marko Tadić, Serge Sharoff, and Pierre Zweigenbaum, editors, *Proceedings of 5th Workshop on Building and Using Comparable Corpora (BUCC 2012)*, Istanbul, Turkey.

Tomas Mikolov, Kai Chen, Greg Corrado, and Jeffrey Dean. 2013. Efficient estimation of word representations in vector space. *CoRR*, abs/1301.3781.

Ruslan Mitkov, Richard Evans, Constantin Orăsan, Iustin Dornescu, and Miguel Rios, 2012. *Text, Speech and Dialogue: 15th International Conference, TSD 2012, Brno, Czech Republic, September 3-7, 2012. Proceedings*, chapter Coreference Resolution: To What Extent Does It Help NLP Applications?, pages 16–27. Springer Berlin Heidelberg, Berlin, Heidelberg.

Andriy Mnih and Koray Kavukcuoglu. 2013. Learning word embeddings efficiently with noise-contrastive estimation. In C. J. C. Burges, L. Bottou, M. Welling, Z. Ghahramani, and K. Q. Weinberger, editors, *Advances in Neural Information Processing Systems 26*, pages 2265–2273. Curran Associates, Inc.

Rogelio Nazar and Maria Teresa Cabré. 2012. A machine learning approach to automatic term extraction using a rich feature set. page 209–217, Madrid, Spain.

Youngja Park, Roy J. Byrd, and Branimir K. Boguraev. 2002. Automatic Glossary Extraction: Beyond Terminology Identification. In *Proceedings of the 19th International Conference on Computational Linguistics*, pages 1–7, Morristown, NJ, USA. Association for Computational Linguistics.

Jeffrey Pennington, Richard Socher, and Christopher D. Manning. 2014. Glove: Global vectors for word representation. In *Empirical Methods in Natural Language Processing (EMNLP)*, pages 1532–1543.

J. Platt. 1998. Fast training of support vector machines using sequential minimal optimization. In B. Schoelkopf, C. Burges, and A. Smola, editors, *Advances in Kernel Methods - Support Vector Learning*. MIT Press.

Maria Pontiki, Dimitris Galanis, John Pavlopoulos, Harris Papageorgiou, Ion Androutsopoulos, and Suresh Manandhar. 2014. Semeval-2014 task 4: Aspect based sentiment analysis. In *Proceedings of the 8th International Workshop on Semantic Evaluation (SemEval 2014)*, pages 27–35, Dublin, Ireland, August. Association for Computational Linguistics and Dublin City University.

Maria Pontiki, Dimitris Galanis, Haris Papageorgiou, Suresh Manandhar, and Ion Androutsopoulos. 2015. Semeval-2015 task 12: Aspect based sentiment analysis. In *Proceedings of the 9th International Workshop on Semantic Evaluation (SemEval 2015)*, pages 486–495, Denver, Colorado, June. Association for Computational Linguistics.

Radim Řehůřek and Petr Sojka. 2010. Software Framework for Topic Modelling with Large Corpora. In *Proceedings of the LREC 2010 Workshop on New Challenges for NLP Frameworks*, pages 45–50, Valletta, Malta, May. ELRA. http://is.muni.cz/publication/884893/en.

Anna ch Le Serrec, Marie-Claude L'Homme, Patrick Drouin, and Olivier Kraif. 2010. Automating the compilation of specialized dictionaries Use and analysis of term extraction and lexical alignment. *Terminology*, 16:77–107.

M. Small, C. Kirkpatrick, D. Zimmer, C. Chilvers, S. D Agostino, D. Duff, K. Farentino, I. Macpherson, J. Tonner, J. Williamson, and T. A. Yeager. 2005. *Principles of Mathematics 9*. Nelson Education Limited.

M. Small, C. Kirkpatrick, B. Alldred, S. Godin, A. Lillo, and A. Dmytriw. 2007a. *Functions 11*. Nelson Education Limited.

M. Small, C. Kirkpatrick, and A. Dmytriw. 2007b. *Functions and Applications 11*. Nelson Education Limited.

Peter D. Turney. 2000. Learning algorithms for keyphrase extraction. *Inf. Retr.*, 2(4):303–336, May.

Špela Vintar. 2010. Bilingual term recognition revisited: The bag-of-equivalents term alignment approach and its evaluation. *Terminology*, 16(2):141–158.

NICTA VRL. 2009. An unsupervised approach to domain-specific term extraction. In *Australasian Language Technology Association Workshop 2009*, page 94.

Thuy Vu, Ai Ti Aw, and Min Zhang. 2008. Term extraction through unithood and termhood unification. In *In Proc. of Intl Joint Conf on Natural Language Proc.*

Rui Wang, Wei Liu, and Chris McDonald. 2015. Corpus-independent generic keyphrase extraction using word embedding vectors. In *Deep Learning for Web Search and Data Mining*.

Yuhang Yang, Hao Yu, Yao Meng, Yingliang Lu, and Yingju Xia. 2010. Fault-tolerant learning for term extraction. In Ryo Otoguro, Kiyoshi Ishikawa, Hiroshi Umemoto, Kei Yoshimoto, and Yasunari Harada, editors, *PACLIC*, pages 321–330. Institute for Digital Enhancement of Cognitive Development, Waseda University.

Yichun Yin, Furu Wei, Li Dong, Kaimeng Xu, Ming Zhang, and Ming Zhou. 2016. Unsupervised word and dependency path embeddings for aspect term extraction. *CoRR*, abs/1605.07843.

Minoru Yoshida and Hiroshi Nakagawa, 2005. *Natural Language Processing – IJCNLP 2005: Second International Joint Conference, Jeju Island, Korea, October 11-13, 2005. Proceedings*, chapter Automatic Term Extraction Based on Perplexity of Compound Words, pages 269–279. Springer Berlin Heidelberg, Berlin, Heidelberg.

Kalliopi Zervanou. 2010. Uvt: The uvt term extraction system in the keyphrase extraction task. In *Proceedings of the 5th International Workshop on Semantic Evaluation*, pages 194–197, Uppsala, Sweden, July. Association for Computational Linguistics.

Recognition of non-domain phrases
in automatically extracted lists of terms

Agnieszka Mykowiecka
Institute of Computer Science
PAS
Jana Kazimierza 5
01-248 Warsaw, Poland
`agn@ipipan.waw.pl`

Małgorzata Marciniak
Institute of Computer Science
PAS
Jana Kazimierza 5
01-248 Warsaw, Poland
`mm@ipipan.waw.pl`

Piotr Rychlik
Institute of Computer Science
PAS
Jana Kazimierza 5
01-248 Warsaw, Poland
`rychlik@ipipan.waw.pl`

Abstract

In the paper, we address the problem of recognition of non-domain phrases in terminology lists obtained with an automatic term extraction tool. We focus on identification of multi-word phrases that are general terms and discourse function expressions. We tested several methods based on domain corpora comparison and a method based on contexts of phrases identified in a large corpus of general language. We compared the results of the methods to manual annotation. The results show that the task is quite hard as the inter-annotator agreement is low. Several tested methods achieved similar overall results, although the phrase ordering varied between methods. The most successful method with the precision about 0.75 at the half of the tested list was the context based method using a modified contextual diversity coefficient.

1 Introduction

Automatic term recognition (ATR) can be applied to achieve concept names which might be included in a domain ontology. However, lists of terms obtained in this way should be filtered to exclude terms belonging to different specialized domains which occurred within the text only by coincidence (e.g. citations); terms which are general, such as *low level* used in many different domains; and discourse markers like *point of view*. It is difficult to consider that phrases such as *low level* or *left side* are domain specific, but they play an important role in several domains, e.g. medicine or technology. Phrases like *turning point* or *difficult question* should be excluded from terminology lists. While identification of domain terms has been addressed by several researchers, the problem of general terms identification has not been studied greatly, although it poses a much harder task to cope with. We propose identifying such phrases and building a separate resource to be combined with other domain specific ontologies.

The filtering out-of-domain terms has been the subject of several studies. Most typical approaches are described in (Schäfer et al., 2015), other attempts include (Navigli and Velardi, 2004)) or (Lopes et al., 2016). Discrimination of in- and out-of-domain terms was based on identifying terms occurring more frequently in the given domain related data than in other corpora. Most of these approaches looked for terms which are more salient in particular corpora than in others and work relatively well for selecting specialized terms. In this paper we focused our attention on terms which are nearly equally frequent in many corpora and thus are hard to classify either as domain specific or general. We decided to focus on multi-word terms as most of them are not present in general wordnet-type datasets. They are also easier to classify as either domain specific or general. Thus, the evaluation of the proposed methods is more reliable.

2 Terminology extraction

We used the TermoPL program (Marciniak et al., 2016) for the ATR task. It consists of standard phases of candidate selection and ordering. TermoPL accepts morphosyntactically analyzed texts and calculates the C-value (Frantzi et al., 2000) for phrases recognized using either a built-in or customized grammar. The ATR based on the C-value coefficient allows extraction of one-word and multi-word phrases, as part

Proceedings of the 5th International Workshop on Computational Terminology,
pages 12–20, Osaka, Japan, December 12 2016.

of one common terminology list, and creates a ranked list of these terms. It allows us to compare such a list with another list obtained using the same method from a different corpus. For common terms, the program indicates for which corpora they are more representative.

In our experiments, we used a standard built-in grammar for candidate selection. It applies a simple shallow grammar describing most typical Polish noun phrases, i.e. nouns, nouns modified with adjectives placed before or after a noun (it respects case, gender and number) and nominal phrases post-modified with nominal phrases in the genitive. The ordering is performed using the slightly modified C-value coefficient. This coefficient is computed on the basis of the number of times a phrase occurs within the text, its length, and the number of different contexts this phrase occurs within the text. The definition of the C-value coefficient is given in (1).

$$C\text{-}value(p) = \begin{cases} l(p) * (freq(p) - \frac{1}{r(LP)} \sum_{lp \in LP} freq(lp)), & if\ r(LP) > 0, \\ l(p) * freq(p), & if\ r(LP) = 0 \end{cases} \tag{1}$$

p is a phrase under consideration,
LP is a set of phrases containing p,
$r(LP)$ is the number of different phrases in LP,
$l(p) = log_2(length(p))$.

In this paper, we focus on the further stage of processing the term list, i.e. its filtering, independently of the extraction method used to obtain it.

3 Domain corpora

In our work, we analyzed six different sets of texts. The first five are domain corpora, while the last one is more general:

- *ChH* – a set of patients records from a children hospital,
- *Music* – a part of the ART Corpus[1] related to music and its history,
- *HS* – books and articles on the history of art, a part of the ART Corpus,
- *Lit* – literature papers from the ART Corpus,
- *wikiE* – a part of Polish Wikipedia with articles related to economy (`http://zil.ipipan.waw.pl/plWikiEcono`),
- *KS* – journalistic books from the Polish National Corpus (NKJP) (`http://clip.ipipan.waw.pl/NationalCorpusOfPolish`).

The details about the size of each corpus and the number of recognized terms are given in Table 1. We observed that although the total number of multi-word terms constitute about one third of all term occurrences, the number of different phrases is much higher than one half of all of them.

Table 1: Corpora statistics

corpus	tokens	#terms	#mw-terms
ChH	1,966K	26K	21K
Music	1,075K	94K	65K
HS	1,438K	157	126K
Lit	2,410K	220K	185K
wikiE	456K	57K	49K
kS	3,204K	164K	137K

Table 2 presents numbers of common multi-word nominal phrases which occurred in at least three corpora.

4 Term selection based on domain corpora

The lists of terms obtained by any ATR tool contain a large number of valid terminological expressions, but they also contain some out of domain, general and even improperly structured phrases. It had already

---

[1] The data will be soon available.

Table 2: Common multi-word terms

#corpora	6	5	4	3
#shared mwterms	44	353	1441	5113

been proposed to eliminate such terms using corpora-comparing log-likelihood (Rayson and Garside, 2000), Contrastive Selection via Heads (Basili et al., 2001) and Term Frequency Inverse Term Frequency (TFITF) (Bonin et al., 2010), but all these methods perform relatively well only when both corpora – domain and general – are voluminous enough. For specialized domains, we frequently do not have enough data to judge on the basis of one comparison. To make the decisions more reliable, we compare several (not necessary very big) corpora to gain the necessary information out of many comparisons. We analyze three different solutions to this problem and compare them on the same set of corpora.

I. Co-occurrence in multiple corpora   The simplest approach for detecting general (or out-of-domain) terms could be identification of terms which occur in more than one terminology list. Although multi-word terms do not occur very frequently, general phrases should occur in many different contexts i.e. their frequencies could be sufficiently high. To test this hypothesis we check multi-word phrases which occur in more than three out of six tested corpora. The problem with this approach is the fact that if we decide to stick to terms which occur in all but one corpora, we may identify a small group of phrases. As for the less frequent terms, we quickly get much less reliable candidates. The second issue is that we treat equally terms that occur very frequently and those which are very rare.

II, IIa C-value standard deviation based weighting   In the second method we utilize information about the strength of a particular term within each corpora, i.e. its C-value. We normalize the C-value to have the same overall sum in all corpora and assign each term a weight depending on whether it is not present in a corpus (-1), has a C-value near 0 (0.5), below 1 (1), below a selected threshold equal to 8 (2) and above it (3). Then, we count the standard deviation between all weights and order terms according to their ascending value. The top terms are equally important (or unimportant) in all corpora. Terms which only have a high C-value on some of the term lists are moved towards the end of the final ranking. This method promotes terms which are important and their relative position from the top of the list is similar. In the modified version of the method, named IIa, we used $\log_{10}$ of the C-values instead of the rigid weights (still -1 was assigned to non-present terms).

$$C_{IIa}(t) = \frac{\Sigma_{all\_corpora}\ \sigma_{\log_{10}(C\text{-}value\text{-}norm(t))}}{number\text{-}of\text{-}corpora}$$

III   Another method is based on the observation made in (Lopes et al., 2016) where it is suggested that terms that appear in the contrasting corpora should have been penalized proportionally to the number of their occurrences. Thus, the absolute frequency of the term in the domain corpus is divided by a geometric composition of its absolute frequency in each of the contrasting corpora. We adapted this idea to calculate a list of general terms ordered by a geometric composition of their C-values in all the corpora examined. The higher the coefficient C_{III}, the lower the probability that the term is domain related.

$$C_{III}(t) = \prod_{\forall corpora C} (1 + \log_{10}(C\text{-}value^C(t))$$

II+III, IIa+III Second order methods.   When analyzing the results obtained by all the above methods, we observed that the number of common terms on top of the lists computed by the **II** (**IIa**) and the **III** method are the smallest. Thus, we combined these two methods in one by means of linear combination of their normalized values. As the coefficients obtained by the methods are ordered in the opposite way, the equation looks as below, where α is a number between 0 and 1.

$$C_{IIa+III}(t) = \alpha(1 - C_{IIa\text{-}norm}(t)) + (1 - \alpha) * C_{III\text{-}norm}(t)$$

5 Term selection based on term contexts in a general corpus

We decided to compare the results obtained with the methods described in Section 4 to a method which judges the term generality on data obtained from a single (many domain or general) corpus. This method is based on the observation that domain terms usually occur together with other terms from the same domain so their contexts mainly consist of in-domain expressions/words together with the general ones. On the contrary, general terms and functional expressions can accompany expressions from many unrelated domains and, thus, they tend to have much more diverse contexts. To measure this diversity, we apply a clustering coefficient described in (Hamilton et al., 2016) to measure a word's contextual diversity and, thus, polysemy. In method IV, we ordered all terms according to the increasing diversity coefficient $d(w)$. This coefficient measures the percentage of related context pairs within the set of pairs of contexts which are highly related to the analyzed term. A related pair of words is defined as a pair which has a non-zero Positive Pointwise Mutual Information (PPMI) value. A pair consists of two context words in the first case, and of a term and a context word in the latter.

$$d(w) = \frac{\Sigma_{c_i, c_j \in N_{PPMI}(w)} C_{N\_PPMI}(c_i, c_j)}{|N_{PPMI}(w)|(|N_{PPMI}(w)| - 1)}$$

$C_w = \{w_i \ : \ w_i \ is \ in \ a \ context \ of \ w\}, N_{PPMI}(w) = \{w_j \in C_w \ : \ PPMI(w, w_j) > 0\}$ and $C_{N\_PPMI}(c_i, c_j) = \{1 \ if \ PPMI(c_i, c_j) > 0 \ and \ 0, otherwise\}$. The PPMI value represents the strength of correlation between two words. The larger is the number of common occurrences in a relation to all possible two word pairs, the stronger correlation.

$$PPMI(w, z) = max\{log(p(w, z)/(p(w) * p(z)), 0\}$$

The tested hypothesis was whether the increasing order of this coefficient, which is aimed at reflecting the decreasing polysemy factor, represents satisfactorily the difference between the general terms that can be used in very different contexts, thus gaining different meaning, and domain related terms which are less polysemous. As in principle, a general term could not have any highly related contexts, we suggest modifying the $d(w)$ coefficient by replacing the nominator by the number of all possible context pairs (limiting the context only by the number of occurrences not by a non-zero PPMI). The modified d_M coefficient is defined as follows:

$$d_M(w) = \frac{\Sigma_{c_i, c_j \in N_{PPMI}(w)} C_{N\_PPMI}(c_i, c_j)}{|C_w|(|C_w| - 1)}$$

To deal with small corpora, for which the original method is unable to judge many terms as they do not have any contexts classified as related, a variant of method IV is introduced. For such a case, we propose an additional step for selecting terms which are similar to the analyzed one. Similarity is defined here as the cosine similarity of the vectors from the word2vec model (Mikolov et al., 2013) trained on the corpus in which multi-word term occurrences were replaced by the concatenation of the term elements and thus were treated as singular model features. We trained the standard continuous bag-of-words model with the 5 word window and 200 features. Next, we combined all the contexts of a term with the contexts of all terms for which the similarity was greater than 0.44. We observed that, for multi-word terms, the similarity coefficient is generally lower than for one-word terms and that, in small corpus, the higher threshold provides very few similar terms. In Tables 3–5, we gave examples of similar multi-word terms calculated on the basis of the domain corpora described in Section 3. For the first two expressions, the method found helpful similar terms, while Table 5 rather contains terms unrelated to the considered one, i.e., *dzieło stworzenia* 'act of creation'.

In the next step, we used the same procedure as before, that is we counted the $d(w)$ diversity coefficient for all contexts of similar terms clustered together.

Table 3: Similar multi-word terms for *duże wrażenie* 'big impression'

term	similarity	translation
ogromne wrażenie	0.755	'huge impression'
wielkie wrażenie	0.740	'great impression'
dobre wrażenie	0.514	'good impression'
wielki wpływ	0.463	'great influence'

Table 4: Similar multi-word terms for *dziwiętnasty wiek* 'nineteenth century'

term	similarity	translation
XVII wiek	0.506	'17th century'
XIX wiek	0.503	'19th century'
XVIII wiek	0.497	'18th century'
XX wiek	0.489	'20th century'
wiek XVIII	0.487	'18th century'
dwudziesty wiek	0.483	'twentieth century'
początek xx wiek	0.448	'beginning of the twentieth century'
XIX stulecie	0.448	'19th century'
wiek dziewiętnasty	0.438	'nineteenth century'
początek wieku	0.438	'beginning of the century'
minione stulecie	0.434	'past century'

6 Evaluation

To evaluate our method we prepared two manually annotated lists. The first one, called *COM*, consists of 7151 terms which occur in at least three of the six selected corpora. Annotation was done by two annotators and then the third one resolved the conflicts to obtain the gold standard annotation (GS). The annotators introduced five labels representing *non-terms, general-terms, domain-terms-used-generally, domain-terms, improper-phrases*. At the evaluation stage as *general-terms* we treated the first three classes together. Table 6 includes the number of annotations of each type. The difficulty of the task and the lack of the strict guidelines is reflected in a relatively low Cohen's kappa-coefficient which is equal to 0.45. As the first test set contained a lot of phrases located very low on the ranked terminological lists, we also prepared the second test set (*MFQ*) to verify our context based method. This test set is based on the first 1000 terms from the terminological lists obtained separately for all corpora except the medical one.[2] The resulting 3250 terms were annotated by the same two annotators. To reduce the influence of the subjectivity of judgments (the kappa coefficient was 0.5), the final test set contains only 2341 terms which were annotated identically by both annotators. 964 terms are included in both test sets.

As our results are ranked lists, we had to introduce a threshold indicating which part of the lists should be treated as general terms. For the first method, we selected terms which occur in at least 4 corpora; for the others, we treated 70% of the lists as general terms. This is roughly the most desirable partition as the *COM* test set contains a little more than 73% of general terms.

Table 7 gives the number of common annotations made using the above methods and the threshold.

For the evaluation of the IV method we performed the experiments in which we used two data sets and two lists of terms. The first (*art*) corpus consisted of four of the corpora described in section 3 (all except the hospital data set – ChH). It consists of about 845K tokens. The second data set ((*nkjp+art*) is much larger, with 1.3G words from the complete NKJP — National Corpus of Polish Language (Przepiórkowski et al., 2012) added to the (*art*) corpus. The term list is the same list of 7151 terms described above. While counting the diversity coefficient $d(w)$ we only selected contexts which were

---

[2]Most terms from this set of data occur very frequently in the NKJP corpus.

Table 5: Similar multi-word terms for *dzieło stworzenia* 'act of creation'

term	similarity	translation
kłos zboża	0.459	'ear of grain'
postać ludzka	0.439	'human figure'
świat widzialny	0.438	'visible world'
wspólne dzieło	0.431	'joined act'

Table 6: Manual annotation

	COM test set			*MFQ* test set		
	An1	An2	GS	An1	An2	GS
general-term	6228	5228	5273	1493	1296	999
non-general-term	799	1641	1741	1571	1893	1342
error	124	282	237	175	51	–

strings containing only lower case letters. We excluded named entities from this set. We also disregarded the most common words (e.g. prepositions and pronouns). For this purpose, we used the list of stop words from the Wikipedia page. As the PPMI value is biased towards low frequency phenomena, we took into account only pairs which occur in NKJP more than 5 times.

Table 7: Common annotations for *COM* test set

method	I	II	IIa	III	IIa+III	IV_{art}	$IV_{nkjp+art}$
GS	2970	3720	3717	3726	3187	4020	4762
I	-	3818	3752	5229	4167	2791	2983
II	-	-	6100	5722	6252	2285	3411
IIa	-	-	-	1888	6696	2364	3387
III	-	-	-	-	2301	3646	3394
IIa+III	-	-	-	-	-	2532	3413
IV_{art}	-	-	-	-	-	-	3772

For all methods we counted how many terms annotated as general in the GS file were found in each part of the ranked lists. The results for every 500 element segments are shown in Figure 1, while Figure 2 shows the overall precision by steps of 500 terms.

Figures 1 and 2 show that the most methods do not differ much. The most stable results were achieved for IIa and the combination IIa+III. For the latter method we tested several values of α from 0.2 to 0.8 and the best results were obtained with α 0.4. The methods I and III are shown to be the least consistent. The method IV showed the quickest decrease of the percentage of the general terms for each five hundred positions, thus proving to be the most selective one.

In the second experiment, in which we check the contexts of the phrases, the results obtained for a small corpus containing four sets described in Section 3 (IV_{art}) turned out to be rather poor. The list of terms with non-zero related contexts was very short — it contained only 301 elements. The resulting precision was only 0.33. For this data set, the addition of similar terms ($IV_{art^{add}}$) improved the results. In this approach we found relevant contexts for 948 terms with a precision equal to 0.64 for the first 500 elements and 0.5 for the entire set. For the big corpus, the results achieved by adding similar terms ($IV_{nkjp+art^{add}}$) were slightly worse, as was expected. Table 8 summarizes the results and presents the precision obtained by all our methods for the first 500 elements and for the entire set (* indicates that the method did not process the entire *COM* list).

In the next set of experiments we tested more extensively different variants of the IV method which is based on contextual information. On two term test sets described above, apart form the basic version of the method, we tested the newly introduced d_M coefficient and the non-uniform treatment of the context words. In a weighted d^w schema we assigned smaller weights to context words which are more distant from the given term (in a 5 word window, the farthest word has weight equal to 0.2 while the closest neighbour has the weight of 1). We performed tests on the big *nkjp+art* corpus. The results shown in

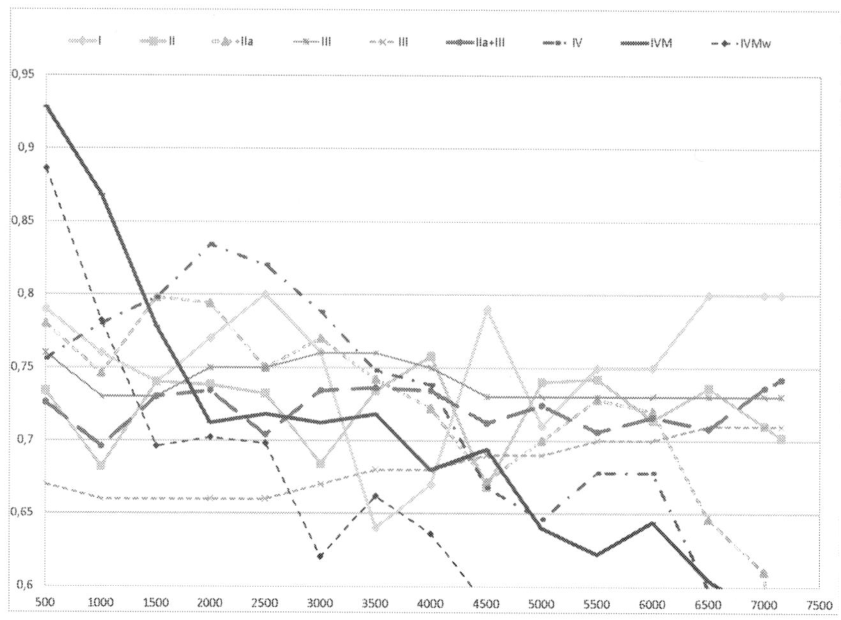

Figure 1: Percentage of general terms for every 500 terms individually for all methods – *COM* test set

Table 8: Precision of all the methods – *COM* test set

	I	II	IIa	III	IIa+III	IV_{art}	$IV_{art^{add}}$	$IV_{nkjp+art}$	$IV_{nkjp+art^{add}}$
first 500 terms	0.79	0.73	0.78	0.73	0.73	0.33	0.64	0.74	0.66
entire list	0.47	0.58	0.62	0.58	0.58	*0.33	*0.50	0.58	0.69

Table 9 confirm improvement in cases where the d_M coefficient was used. The number of the general terms at the beginning of the list is higher and this proportion constantly decreases, which was not the case for the other methods. The non-uniform weighting of context words caused deterioration of results.

Table 10 shows how many terms were filtered out from the top part of terms in the 5 domain corpora. We tested lists of, at most 1800, top general terms obtained by 9 methods separately. We tested only the top parts of all domain term lists consisting of 10K terms. It shows that method III is more efficient in eliminating phrases from the top of the term list than the other methods. Unfortunately, it concerns both types of terms: out-of-domain terms and false positive out-of-domain terms.

7 Conclusions

Differentiation between general terms and domain specific terms is a hard task. The methods proposed in this paper allows for preselecting sets of phrases containing more than seventy percent of general terms.

For the methods based on domain corpora, the most efficient and, at the same time, simple method relies on standard deviation for C-value coefficient. Such a set can help when preparing lists of concepts shared by several domains. However, its usage for the task of eliminating general terms from the terminological list obtained automatically is limited, as many of these candidates are located low on these

Table 9: Precision of different variants of IV method, *nkjp+art* corpus

	COM test set					*FRQ* test set		
	IV	IV^M	IV^{Mw}			IV	IV^M	IV^{Mw}
first 500 terms	0.74	0.93	0.89	first 250 terms		0.72	0.83	0.77
second 500 terms	0.72	0.90	0.78	second 250 terms		0.53	0.61	0.55
entire list	0.58	0.64	0.62	entire list		0.55	0.62	0.62

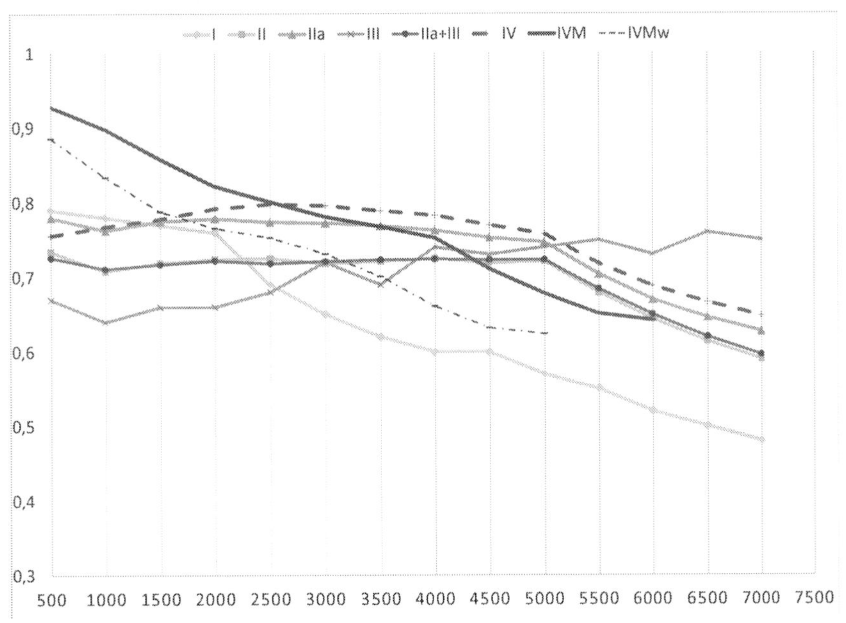

Figure 2: Precision of all methods at every 500 terms – *COM* test set

Table 10: Filtered out out-of-domain terms in 10K top terms

corpus	I	II	IIa	III	IIa+III	IV_{art}	$IV_{nkjp+art}$	$IV^{M}_{nkjp+art}$	$IV^{Mw}_{nkjp+art}$
ChH	**89**	41	43	83	52	3	61	66	77
HS	359	27	50	**482**	124	64	290	345	368
Music	387	27	71	469	145	46	**484**	449	450
Lit	640	37	86	**819**	179	79	334	740	747
wikiE	262	27	71	**301**	138	30	222	260	286

lists. The method **III** seems to be the best for selecting highly located general terms but it needs further research.

The method based on term contexts requires a large corpus for context recognition. The experiments performed on the small corpus gave rather poor results, but they were improved if contexts of similar terms were added. On lager corpus, this method gave much better results – the percentage of the general terms at the top of the ranked list was larger than average and larger than for all the other methods. The best variant of the method is based on the newly introduced d_M coefficient which measures the relative number of highly inter-related contexts.

Using vector similarities to expand the number of contexts did not improve results on a large corpus. For future research, we plan to use word2vec model for extending the list of general terms by phrases close to those recognized in the data as we observed many similar general terms to be relatively well clustered by cosine similarity within a model using 200 vector dimensions.

8 Acknowledgements

The paper is partially supported by the National Science Centre project *Compositional distributional semantic models for identification, discrimination and disambiguation of senses in Polish texts* number 2014/15/B/ST6/05186.

References

Roberto Basili, Alessandro Moschitti, Maria Teresa Pazienza, and Fabio Massimo Zanzotto. 2001. A contrastive approach to term extraction. *Terminologie et intelligence artificielle. Rencontres*, pages 119—128.

Francesca Bonin, Felice Dell'Orletta, Giulia Venturi, and Simonetta Montemagni. 2010. A contrastive approach to multi-word term extraction from domain corpora. In *Proceedings of the 7th International Conference on Language Resources and Evaluation, Malta*, pages 19—21.

Katerina Frantzi, Sophia Ananiadou, and Hideki Mima. 2000. Automatic Recognition of Multi-Word Terms: the C-value/NC-value Method. *Int. Journal on Digital Libraries*, 3:115–130.

William L. Hamilton, Jure Leskovec, and Dan Jurafsky. 2016. Diachronic word embeddings reveal statistical laws of semantic change. In *Proceedings of the 54th Annual Meeting of the Association for Computational Linguistics, ACL 2016, August 7-12, 2016, Berlin, Germany, Volume 1: Long Papers*. The Association for Computer Linguistics.

Lucene Lopes, Paulo Fernandes, and Renata Vieira. 2016. Estimating term domain relevance through term frequency, disjoint corpora frequency - tf-dcf. *Knowledge-Based Systems*, 97:237–249.

Małgorzata Marciniak, Agnieszka Mykowiecka, and Piotr Rychlik. 2016. TermoPL — a flexible tool for terminology extraction. In *Proceedings of 10th edition of the Language Resources and Evaluation Conference*.

Tomas Mikolov, Wen-tau Yih, and Geoffrey Zweig. 2013. Linguistic regularities in continuous space word representations. In *Human Language Technologies: Conference of the North American Chapter of the Association of Computational Linguistics, Proceedings, June 9-14, 2013, Westin Peachtree Plaza Hotel, Atlanta, Georgia, USA*, pages 746–751.

Roberto Navigli and Paola Velardi. 2004. Learning domain ontologies from document warehouses and dedicated web sites. *Computational Linguistics*, 30(2):151–179.

Adam Przepiórkowski, Mirosław Bańko, R. L. Górski, and Barbara Lewandowska-Tomaszczyk, editors. 2012. *Narodowy Korpus Języka Polskiego*. Wydawnictwo Naukowe PWN, Warszawa.

Paul Rayson and Roger Garside. 2000. Comparing corpora using frequency profiling. In *Proceedings of the Workshop on Comparing Corpora - Volume 9, WCC '00*, pages 1—-6.

Johannes Schäfer, Ina Rösiger, Ulrich Heid, and Michael Dorna. 2015. Evaluating noise reduction strategies for terminology extraction. In Thierry Poibeau and Pamela Faber, editors, *Proceedings of the 11th International Conference on Terminology and Artificial Intelligence, Universidad de Granada, Granada, Spain, November 4-6, 2015.*, volume 1495 of *CEUR Workshop Proceedings*, pages 123–131. CEUR-WS.org.

Contextual term equivalent search using domain-driven disambiguation

Caroline Barrière
Centre de Recherche
Informatique de Montréal
Montréal, QC, Canada
barrieca@crim.ca

Pierre André Ménard
Centre de Recherche
Informatique de Montréal
Montréal, QC, Canada
menardpa@crim.ca

Daphnée Azoulay
Laboratoire OLST
Université de Montréal
Montréal, QC, Canada
daphnee.azoulay@umontreal.ca

Abstract

This article presents a domain-driven algorithm for the task of term sense disambiguation (TSD). TSD aims at automatically choosing which term record from a term bank best represents the meaning of a term occurring in a particular context. In a translation environment, finding the contextually appropriate term record is necessary to access the proper equivalent to be used in the target language text. The term bank TERMIUM Plus®, recently published as an open access repository, is chosen as a domain-rich resource for testing our TSD algorithm, using English and French as source and target languages. We devise an experiment using over 1300 English terms found in scientific articles, and show that our domain-driven TSD algorithm is able to bring the best term record, and therefore the best French equivalent, at the average rank of 1.69 compared to a baseline random rank of 3.51.

1 Introduction

We will start this article by introducing, in Section 2, a terminological database called TERMIUM Plus® (referred to as TERMIUM for the rest of the article), which was manually constructed over many years by expert terminologists at the Translation Bureau of Canada. TERMIUM full terminological database has recently been released in an open-data format allowing its use for various research experiments in computational terminology, such as database-wide statistical measures. One particular measure of interest is the notion of similarity between domains, which we present in Section 3.

Section 4 describes our main research contribution, a domain-driven term sense disambiguation (TSD) algorithm. TSD aims at automatically determining which term record from a term bank best represents the meaning of a term given its context. This is a task that translators must perform on a regular basis when translating specialized texts containing specialized terminology. Finding the contextually appropriate term record leads the translator to the proper equivalent to use in his or her translation. Making the algorithm *domain-driven* means that the information that will be used to perform the disambiguation task is the domain information provided in each term record of the term bank. For example, according to TERMIUM, the French equivalent *promontoire* would be proper for the word *head* found in a text segment about the TOPONYMY domain, but the equivalent *tête* would be more appropriate in other domains such as STRING INSTRUMENT, or GOLF.

In Section 5, we present an experiment to evaluate the performances of our algorithm. We will describe the dataset composed of 1500 terms found in abstracts of scientific publications, the human annotation performed to build a gold standard, the algorithm parameter optimisation using a subset of 200 terms, and the final results on the remaining 1300 terms.

Domain-driven TSD is definitely an underexplored task within the Natural Language Processing literature, and Section 6 will give some pointers to only a few related works which rather use domain information as complementing other information for disambiguation. Term disambiguation in general, domain-driven or not, is rarely explored perhaps due to a misconception that terms are monosemous and that disambiguation is not necessary in specialized domains. Although that statement is true of most

Proceedings of the 5th International Workshop on Computational Terminology,
pages 21–29, Osaka, Japan, December 12 2016.

multi-word terms, it is certainly not true of the many single-word terms found in specialized texts which tend to lead to multiple term records.

Finally, in Section 7, we conclude and give an outlook to future work.

2   TERMIUM as an open-data terminological resource

TERMIUM has been in constant expansion for over 20 years, and is the result of much labour from terminologists at the Translation Bureau of Canada. But only since 2014 has TERMIUM been openly and freely available as part of Canada's Open Government initiative[1].

The 2015 open-data version of TERMIUM, used in the current research, contains 1,348,065 records, organized within 2203 domains. Each record corresponds to a particular concept within particular domains, with its multilingual term equivalents. For example, a record for the concept defined as *Irregularity or loss of rhythm, especially of the heartbeat* within the MEDICAL domain, would provide three term equivalents: *arrhythmia* (English), *arythmie* (French), and *arritmia* (Spanish). Even though some terms are quite specific to a single domain, such as *arrhythmia*, some other terms, such as *head*, do belong to 55 domains, including TOPONYMY, SHIP AND BOAT PARTS, STRING INSTRUMENT, METAL FORMING, GOLF, and STOCK EXCHANGE.

Table 1 shows a few single-word terms, in general more polysemous than multi-word terms, chosen to illustrate the variability in the number of records associated to each term (column 2), the number and variety of possible French equivalents (column 3 and 4), and the number and variety of possible domains (column 5 and 6). There is no one-to-one relation between term equivalents and domains. For example the term *resistance* leads to 14 domains and only 2 French equivalents, whereas *quenching* leads to 7 domains and 5 equivalents. Although TERMIUM covers three languages (English, French, Spanish), we will focus on the English/French language pair in this article.

Table 1: Examples of terms in TERMIUM

English term	Nb records	Nb Equiv	Examples of French equivalents	Nb domains	Examples of domains
resistance	14	2	résistance, défense	14	CROP PROTECTION, TEXTILE INDUSTRIES, HORSE HUSBANDRY, PADDLE SPORTS
nucleus	10	3	noyau, nucléus, germe	19	CYTOLOGY, METALS MINING, BEEKEEPING, ARCHEOLOGY, HAND TOOLS
quenching	5	5	surfusion, refroidissement rapide	7	BIOTECHNOLOGY, ENERGY (PHYSICS), GEOPHYSICS, PLASTIC MATERIALS
evolution	3	1	évolution	4	GENETICS, PALEONTOLOGY, MATHEMATICS

When terminologists create term records, they are required to specify domain information. They are also encouraged to include definitions, contexts of usage, and other observations, but it is not mandatory. We calculated simple statistics for English and French, and found that only 14.2 % of the records contained definitions in English and 14.6 % contained definitions in French. These statistics encourage the development of an algorithm which solely use the domain information and does not rely on the definitional information which would only cover a small percentage of the records. Furthermore, restricting the algorithm to domain information makes the algorithm highly portable to other term banks, like EuroTermBank[2] or IATE [3], that would also be structured using records and domains, as typical term banks are.

3   Measuring domain similarity

In our algorithm of domain-driven disambiguation, presented in the next section, it will be important to assess the similarity between domains. For example, if the algorithm tries to disambiguate a term found in the context of GEOLOGY, TERMIUM might offer only two term records, one within the domain of EARTH SCIENCE and the other one within the domain of ANIMAL BEHAVIOUR. In such case, the algorithm

---

[1]TERMIUM Plus®, Government of Canada, `http://open.canada.ca/data/en/dataset/`.

[2]EuroTermBank can be found at `http://www.eurotermbank.com`

[3]InterActive Terminology for Europe (IATE) can be found at `http://http://iate.europa.eu`

needs some measure of domain similarity to decide between the term records, since neither one refers to the exact same domain as the text.

TERMIUM does provide a simple domain hierarchy with coarse-grained and fine-grained domains, intrinsically showing some similarity between domains. For example, the domain AGRICULTURE would include sub-domains such as CROP PROTECTION, CULTURE OF FRUIT TREES, and GRAIN GROWING, whereas the domain HEALTH AND MEDICINE would include sub-domains such as RESPIRATORY TRACT, ACUPUNCTURE and RADIOTHERAPY. Unfortunately, such hierarchy is not sufficient to measure similarities among the sister domains (e.g., RESPIRATORY TRACT, ACUPUNCTURE) which will be required for our algorithm.

We rather opt for similarity measures commonly used for measuring word collocation strengths, such as Overlap or Point-Wise Mutual Information (PMI), which we will adapt to measure domain similarity. Most measures of collocation strength between two words, W_1 and W_2, rely on three counts: the number of segments (e.g., documents, sentences or fixed-sized text windows) in which W_1 and W_2 occur together, the number of segments in which W_1 occurs, and the number of segments in which W_2 occurs.

We transpose this idea to the terminological database, considering each term record as a possible segment. The similarity between two domains, D_1 and D_2, then refers to their collocation strength, meaning how likely they are to co-occur on a term record.

For example, the domain of GENETICS is present on 4664 records, of which 203 are also assigned to BIOCHEMISTRY. On the other hand, the same domain GENETICS has zero record in common with the domain of REPROGRAPHY. Using these counts, the domain similarity measures will be able to express that GENETICS is more similar to BIOCHEMISTRY than it is to REPROGRAPHY.

The two measures we have tested to compare two domains, D_1 and D_2, are provided below, with $NbRecords$ representing a number of term records.

$$PMI(D_1, D_2) = \frac{NbRecords(D_1, D2)}{NbRecords(D_1) * NbRecords(D_2)} \tag{1}$$

$$OVERLAP(D_1, D_2) = \frac{NbRecords(D_1, D2)}{MIN(NbRecords(D_1), NbRecords(D_2))} \tag{2}$$

In Table 2, we see the results with both the PMI measure (Equation 1) and the Overlap measure (Equation 2) as to the top 10 closest domains to REPROGRAPHY and CYCLING. The lists are slightly different (domains in common between the two measures are highlighted in bold), but it is very hard to provide a real evaluation of these lists until they are actually used in different tasks requiring them. In general, intrinsic evaluation of similarity measures is quite difficult out of context, leading to much subjectivity and therefore low inter-annotator agreement. As our goal is term disambiguation, we will instead perform an extrinsic evaluation, by determining which similarity is best for our task, as we describe in Section 5.3.

Table 2: Examples of closest domains (PMI and Overlap)

Domain	Measure	Closest domains
Reprography	PMI	**NON-IMPACT PRINTING** / **INTAGLIO PRINTING** / **POWER TRANSMISSION TECHNIQUES** / **LITHOGRAPHY, OFFSET PRINTING AND COLLOTYPE** / **PHOTOGRAPHY** / **PRINTING PROCESSES - VARIOUS** / INKS AND COLOUR REPRODUCTION (GRAPHIC ARTS) / **OFFICE EQUIPMENT AND SUPPLIES** / BIOMETRICS / OFFICE MACHINERY
	Overlap	**NON-IMPACT PRINTING** / **PHOTOGRAPHY** / **OFFICE EQUIPMENT AND SUPPLIES** / **INTAGLIO PRINTING** / AUDIOVISUAL TECHNIQUES AND EQUIPMENT / **POWER TRANSMISSION TECHNIQUES** / **LITHOGRAPHY, OFFSET PRINTING AND COLLOTYPE** / **PRINTING PROCESSES - VARIOUS** / GRAPHIC ARTS AND PRINTING / OFFICE AUTOMATION
Cycling	PMI	**MOTORCYCLES AND SNOWMOBILES** / **MINING TOPOGRAPHY** / **MOTORIZED SPORTS** / **SPORTS EQUIPMENT AND ACCESSORIES** / **CONSTRUCTION WORKS (RAILROADS)** / **SHELTERS (HORTICULTURE)** / **ROADS** / **TRACK AND FIELD** / **WHEELS AND TIRES (MOTOR VEHICLES AND BICYCLES)** / SPORTS FACILITIES AND VENUES
	Overlap	**MOTORCYCLES AND SNOWMOBILES** / **MINING TOPOGRAPHY** / **MOTORIZED SPORTS** / **SPORTS EQUIPMENT AND ACCESSORIES** / **CONSTRUCTION WORKS (RAILROADS)** / **SHELTERS (HORTICULTURE)** / **TRACK AND FIELD** / HORSE RACING AND EQUESTRIAN SPORTS / **ROADS** / **WHEELS AND TIRES (MOTOR VEHICLES AND BICYCLES)**

4 Domain-driven disambiguation algorithm

Assume a textual context C, such as the small paragraph below, and a term T, such as *virus* or *nucleus*, to be disambiguated in order to find its proper French equivalent.

Transforming infection of Go/G1-arrested primary mouse kidney cell cultures with simian virus 40 (SV40) induces cells to re-enter the S-phase of the cell cycle. In Go-arrested cells, no p53 is detected, whereas in cells induced to proliferate by infection, a gradual accumulation of p53 complexed to SV40 large T-antigen is observed in the nucleus. Heat treatment of actively proliferating SV40-infected cells leads to inhibition of DNA synthesis and growth arrest. To determine the fate of p53 after heat treatment, proliferating infected cells were exposed to mild heat (42.5C) for increasing lengths of time.

We present a domain-driven disambiguation algorithm which aims at disambiguating T given context C. There are three important steps to this algorithm which we present in details.

4.1 Extracting profiling terms

Profiling terms are terms found in context C which are representative of its content. For our particular purpose, these profiling terms must be present in TERMIUM as they will serve to further determine the domains conveyed in the text.

The context C is pre-processed through tokenization, lemmatization and POS-tagging[4]. Once the text is lemmatized, we choose the longest sequences of lemmas found as terms in TERMIUM leaving out overlapping shorter terms. For example, the segment *primary mouse kidney cell cultures with simian virus 40 (SV40) induces cells* contains two multi-word TERMIUM terms, *kidney cell culture* and *simian virus 40*, as well as four single-word terms, *primary*, *mouse*, *induce* and *cell*.

The initial set of profiling terms can then be reduced through syntactic and semantic filtering. Section 5.3 will measure the impact of such filtering on the disambiguation task. The syntactic filtering makes use of the POS tagging, allowing to restrict the list of terms to only verbs and nouns (removing the adjective *primary* in the example above), or even to only nouns (further removing the verb *induce* in the example above).

The semantic filtering is based on the degree of polysemy allowed for the profiling terms. The first line of Table 3 shows that 13 profiling terms would be kept if the maximum polysemy allowed was of 10 term records, following a syntactic filter for keeping nouns only. The following lines of Table 3 show how the number of profiling terms reduces significantly as the semantic filter further limits the degree of polysemy. Only two terms are left, *cell cycle* and *kidney cell culture*, when restricting to monosemous terms only. The hypothesis to be later confirmed is that perhaps profiling a text using only its monosemous terms, or slightly polysemous terms, would lead to a better disambiguation overall.

Table 3: Impact on profiling terms when filtering with a threshold on polysemy

Max polysemy	Profiling terms retained
10 records	synthesis, heat, infection, fate, arrest, cell cycle, length, nucleus, inhibition, heat treatment, virus, mouse, kidney cell culture
5 records	synthesis, infection, fate, cell cycle, virus, mouse, kidney cell culture
3 records	synthesis, infection, fate, cell cycle, virus, kidney cell culture
2 records	cell cycle, virus, kidney cell culture
1 record	cell cycle, kidney cell culture

4.2 Building a domain profile

Once a set of profiling terms has been extracted, we can automatically search in TERMIUM for their associated domains. For example, if we take the subset of profiling terms having a maximum number of three term records (see Table 3), we can see their associated domains in Table 4. This information is used to build the actual domain profile, a subset of which is shown in Table 5.

The weight of each domain within the domain profile is based on a simple $tf * idf$ style of weighting, where tf is the number of times a profile term occurs in context C, and where idf is calculated as $\frac{1}{N}$

---

[4]Stanford Core NLP tagger was used, available at http://nlp.stanford.edu/software/tagger.shtml.

Table 4: Domains found on the term records of the profiling terms

Term	Nb Records	Domains
synthesis	3	[BIOTECHNOLOGY, BIOLOGICAL SCIENCES, ARTIFICIAL INTELLIGENCE]
infection	3	[HUMAN DISEASES, EPIDEMIOLOGY, BREWING AND MALTING, IT SECURITY]
fate	3	[AGRICULTURAL CHEMICALS, MENTAL DISORDERS, BANKING, ENVIRONMENTAL STUDIES AND ANALYSES]
cell cycle	1	[BIOTECHNOLOGY, CYTOLOGY]
virus	2	[MICROBIOLOGY AND PARASITOLOGY, COMPUTER PROGRAMS AND PROGRAMMING, IT SECURITY]
kidney cell culture	1	[CYTOLOGY]

where N is the number of domains associated with the profile term within TERMIUM. For example, the *idf* for *fate* is 0.25 since it occurs in four domains. A domain's total weight (column 3) is the sum of the profile term weights contributing to it. The contributing terms to each domain are shown in column 4.

Table 5: Domain Profile

Domain Profile (DP_i)	Domain name	weight (W_{DP_i})	Contributing term
DP_1	CYTOLOGY	1.5	kidney cell culture (1.0), cell cycle (0.5)
DP_2	BIOTECHNOLOGY	0.83	synthesis (0.33), cell cycle (0.5)
DP_3	IT SECURITY	0.58	infection (0.33), virus (0.25)
DP_4	ARTIFICIAL INTELLIGENCE	0.33	synthesis (0.33)
DP_5	BIOLOGICAL SCIENCES	0.33	synthesis (0.33)
...	...	...	...
DP_{13}	HUMAN DISEASES	0.25	infection (0.25)
DP_{14}	MENTAL DISORDERS	0.25	fate (0.25)

As we previously discussed in Section 4.1, both syntactic and semantic filters will affect the set of profile terms, which consequently will affect the domain profile. Table 6 shows different domain profiles associated with different combinations of syntactic and semantic filters on the profiling terms. It is quite difficult and somewhat subjective to assess the domain profiles directly, and the impact of the various parameters will rather be measured on the disambiguation task.

Table 6: Examples of corresponding domain profiles

Syntactic Filter	Semantic Filter	Top 5 Domains
None	Max 10 records	GENERAL VOCABULARY (2.78) CYTOLOGY (1.55), TRANSLATION (GENERAL) (1.07), BIOTECHNOLOGY (1.05), DENTISTRY (1.0)
Nouns	Max 20 records	CYTOLOGY (1.55), BIOTECHNOLOGY (0.89), IT SECURITY (0.65), BIOLOGICAL SCIENCES (0.42), COMPUTER PROGRAMS AND PROGRAMMING (0.39)
Nouns	Max 3 records	CYTOLOGY (1.5), BIOTECHNOLOGY (0.83), IT SECURITY (0.58), ARTIFICIAL INTELLIGENCE (0.33), BIOLOGICAL SCIENCES (0.33)
Nouns-Verbs	Max 1 records	CYTOLOGY (1.5), DENTISTRY (1.0), BIOTECHNOLOGY (0.5)

4.3 Establishing the most likely domain for term T

The last step in our algorithm requires a domain-to-domain similarity matrix, M, providing a similarity measure for each domain pair found in TERMIUM. Such matrix M will show, for example, that BIOLOGY is similar to ZOOLOGY, but unrelated to FINANCIAL MARKET. Section 3 discussed how to measure domain similarity.

Having pre calculated M for all domain pairs in TERMIUM, we use M to establish the most likely domain for T. Let's refer to a possible domain of T as D_i, among N possible domains $D_1..D_N$. For each D_i, we calculate its domain strength by summing its similarity to each of the X domains $DP_1..DP_X$ making up the domain profile of context C. Each similarity, $M(D_i, DP_j)$, is further weighted by the score of each domain in the profile (see for example column 3 of Table 5). Equation 3 shows the calculation.

$$DomainStrength(D_i) = \sum_{j=1}^{X} M(D_i, DP_j) * W_{DP_j} \qquad (3)$$

As an example, we show in Table 7 the top 5 term records obtained for the term *nucleus*, after performing the calculation above for each of its possible domains. Note that a term record is often associated to more than one domain. In such cases, the score of the term record is set to the average domain strength of its domains.

If the algorithm performs well, the highest score (rank 1) should be the correct term record. The experiment described in the next section presents a proper evaluation of the performances of the algorithm.

Table 7: Examples of ranking term records for the term *nucleus*

Record Rank	Domains	Score	French
1	[BIOTECHNOLOGY, CYTOLOGY]	1.378	noyau
2	[MOLECULAR BIOLOGY, ATOMIC PHYSICS]	0.118	noyau
3	[METALLOGRAPHY]	0.036	germe
4	[COMPUTER PROGRAMS AND PROGRAMMING]	0.032	noyau
5	[AQUACULTURE, MARINE BIOLOGY, JEWELLERY, MOLLUSKS, ECHINODERMS AND PROCHORDATES]	0.008	nucleus

5 Experiment: term disambiguation from scientific abstracts

This section describes a term sense disambiguation experiment applied on a large dataset of 1500 terms. We first describe the dataset and the human domain annotation performed to obtain our gold standard. Then, we describe the various parameter adjustments performed on a subset of 200 annotated terms which we used as our development set. Finally, we describe the results of the fine-tuned algorithm on the remaining set of 1300 terms.

5.1 Dataset

For our experiment, we use a dataset described in (Carpuat et al., 2012) of scientific abstracts from various journals published by the Research Press of National Research Council of Canada[5]. In total, the dataset contains 3347 abstracts from eleven journals covering topics of biology, earth science, chemistry, and more.

The short example text used in Section 4 for describing the algorithm was taken from an abstract of an article in a biology journal. The abstracts are usually followed by three to five author-provided specialized keywords (terms). We earlier discussed how *nucleus* could be such a possible term from this abstract.

For a term to be included in our dataset, we require that it be present in TERMIUM and be polysemous. Given these constraints, we gathered 1500 terms for testing from which 200 terms were used for development. The degree of polysemy varies largely among the dataset. To provide a few statistics, we measured that 38.3% of the terms led to only 2 records, 22.8% led to 3 and 4 records, but there are also 20.7% of the terms leading to more than 10 records, providing quite a challenge for automatic disambiguation.

5.2 Annotation effort

The human effort required to choose the proper term record corresponds to what a translator needs to do when searching for the proper equivalent in a term bank to best convey the meaning of a term occurring in a particular context. To simulate this effort and provide a gold standard for our task, a master's student in terminology annotated 1500 terms chosen randomly from the various scientific abstracts. For each term, the annotator had to indicate the most contextually appropriate TERMIUM term record. Disambiguation of the 1500 terms represented a 40 hour effort. The annotator reported that for the majority of terms, finding the appropriate record was done easily by using the domain information.

Through the annotation, some interesting cases came about. First, the annotator noticed duplications within TERMIUM as some records corresponded to similar domains, had similar definitions, and usually

---

[5]The list of journals can be seen at http://nrcresearchpress.com/, and the dataset can be found at http://www.umiacs.umd.edu/~hal/damt/ as part of JHU Summer Workshop in Domain Adaptation in Machine Translation.

also shared the same French equivalent, indicating that they could have been grouped into a single record. In such cases, both records were indicated as correct in the gold standard.

Second, the annotator found cases when no term record contained a domain which exactly matched the context of occurrence of the term. The followed annotation guideline was that if a term record contained a domain that was somewhat related to the expected domain and that it also contained an appropriate French equivalent, then it should be chosen as the correct term record. For example, if the term *sugar* was expected in the BIOCHEMISTRY domain, but TERMIUM contained FOOD INDUSTRY as the closest domain on a term record, that term record was chosen as correct. This guideline made sense for our particular gold standard since the domain-driven algorithm used in our experiment only has access to the domains provided in TERMIUM and chooses the best one among them.

Finally, the annotator found cases when no term record contained domains close enough to the context, nor did any term record contained any contextually suitable definition or proper equivalent. For example, if the term *hedgehog* was expected in the GENETICS domain, but TERMIUM only contained term records within the NAVAL DOCKYARDS and FIELD ENGINEERING domains, neither seemed close enough to be appropriate. The guideline for such cases was to annotate the term as "no record". The terms corresponding to this annotation were discarded from the current experiment, although they could be used in future work toward the evaluation of an extended algorithm further able to determine when no record is appropriate.

A more extensive annotation effort would involve multiple annotators and a measure of inter-annotator agreement. For the current experiment, given resource limitations, a single annotator was asked to perform the task. Although limited, it was deemed nonetheless appropriate as we performed an intra-annotator test, with the same annotator waiting two weeks between two annotation efforts of a same sample of 50 terms. Such test showed that the annotator's decisions were reliable enough to be used as a gold standard.

5.3   Parameter tuning

The original development dataset of 200 terms had to be reduced to 178 terms for two reasons. The first one is that some of the terms led to the annotation "no record" by the annotator (as mentioned in the previous section). The second one is that we found out too late that the on-line version of TERMIUM used for the human annotation was not exactly the same as the open-data one used for the experimentation, leading to some choices of domains made by the annotator which were actually not among the ones present in the open-data version.

We have seen in Section 4, as we described the three steps of the algorithm, that multiple parameters could influence the final results. First, for the domain similarity matrix (Section 3), we tested two possible similarity measures, PMI and Overlap. Second, for the profiling terms (Section 4.1), we suggested imposing syntactic restrictions, keeping only words tagged with specific parts of speech, as well as imposing semantic restrictions, keeping only terms leading to a maximum number of records within TERMIUM. As for syntactic restrictions, we tried without filter, with noun and verb filter and with noun-only filter. As for the semantic restrictions, we tried with maximum number of records of 1, 2, 5 and 10 records.

Our development set is sufficiently small, and our disambiguation process sufficiently fast, that we could vary all the different parameters in combination. Such experiment showed that all parameters were influential in the quality of the results: (1) the domain similarity measure (PMI largely outperforming Overlap), (2) the degree of polysemy of the profile terms (lower, even complete monosemy, was best) and (3) the syntactic constraint put on the profile terms (keeping only nouns outperformed the other options). The variation in results was quite significant. For 178 terms, with the best combination of parameters (PMI, monosemic terms, keeping only nouns), we have an average rank of 1.62, and with the worst combination (Overlap, polysemy up to 10 records, keeping nouns and verbs) we have an average rank of 2.30. The rank of a random baseline would be of 3.84, given the average number of records being 7.68. The best combination of parameters will be used for the evaluation in the next section.

5.4 Evaluation

In the same way that our development set was reduced from 200 terms to 178 terms given the various cases encountered during the annotation effort, the evaluation dataset also ended up being reduced from 1300 terms to 1175 terms.

On these 1175 terms, the random rank was evaluated at 3.51 and the domain-driven disambiguation algorithm, using the best combination of parameters (PMI, monosemic terms, keeping only nouns), reduced that rank to 1.69, showing a significant improvement.

In Table 8, we further show the proportion of terms leading to the various ranks. It is interesting to see that for almost 75% of the terms, the algorithm succeeds in bringing the best record to the top (rank 1).

Table 8: Percentage of terms per rank obtained for the correct answer

Rank 1	Rank 2	Rank 3	Rank 4	Rank 5	> Rank 5
74.5 %	13.8 %	4.0 %	2.0 %	1.9 %	3.2 %

From an application point of view, the most interesting result lies in the disambiguation capability of the algorithm for largely polysemous terms, since those would be time-consuming for translators, requiring them to go through multiple records to find the appropriate record given the context. For example, the term *disturbance* has 12 term records, *roughness* has 13, *binding* has 25 and *cluster* has 40, and for all those terms, the algorithm was able to bring the contextually appropriate term record to the top rank.

6 Related work

Given that a term bank does not always contain definitions of terms, we have restricted our algorithm to the use of domain information, and opted for a domain-driven disambiguation approach. This is quite different from many unsupervised word sense disambiguation approaches, which make use of the definitions of the senses for comparing them with the context of use of the ambiguous word. Such definition-based approach is often called Lesk-like, given its root in (Lesk, 1986), and later modified into multiple variations (Vasilescu et al., 2004).

Some work has focused on subject fields in Wordnet. Integration of subject field codes (Magnini and Cavaglia, 2000) in WordNet, also called WordNet domains[6], has led to some domain-driven algorithms for word sense disambiguation (Magnini et al., 2002). In (Gliozzo et al., 2004), a domain relevance estimation is performed to assign domains to text. Their domain relevance estimation is similar in intent to our context profiling, but performed with a supervised machine learning approach.

The present research builds on our previous work (Barrière, 2010) which developed a domain-driven disambiguation algorithm using the Grand Dictionnaire Terminologique (GDT)[7] as term bank. Unfortunately, our previous results were unreproducible for other researchers in the community since the GDT is not published in an open-data format. The recent release of TERMIUM in an open-data format allowed us to implement, test, and further refine our earlier algorithm. Our evaluation in (Barrière, 2010) was also not too convincing, since we measured success based on the finding of the proper equivalent and not the proper term record. Given that multiple records could lead to the same term equivalent, such evaluation was quite optimistic. Our current annotation effort at the record level allows us to provide a more realistic evaluation. Yet, given the refinements we introduced in the current algorithm, our realistic results at 1.69 average rank is better than the earlier optimistic result at 2.0 average rank.

We are not aware of other work addressing the term sense disambiguation problem as such, using domain-driven methods to counter the lacking presence of definitions in term banks.

---

[6]WordNet domains are available at `http://wndomains.fbk.eu/`.

[7]The Grand Dictionnaire Terminologique is published by the Office québécois de la langue française and can be consulted online at `http://gdt.oqlf.gouv.qc.ca/`.

7 Conclusion and future work

We presented TERMIUM Plus®, a resource from the Translation Bureau of Canada. TERMIUM is intended for translators as end users, but its recently released open-data version could make it a resource of much interest to the computational terminology research community. We showed its usefulness in a term equivalent search experiment. We presented a domain-driven disambiguation algorithm, relying on domain similarity estimations on the overall resource, and on context profiling. Our algorithm significantly reduced the average rank of the appropriate equivalent from 3.51 (baseline of random assignment) to 1.69, on an unseen dataset of 1175 terms.

From an application point of view, our domain-driven term sense disambiguation algorithm could be used for automatic pre-translation of specialized terms in text. Or perhaps, the algorithm could point out to possible translation errors, in cases of a discrepancy between the translator's choice and what seems to be the best equivalent according to automatic disambiguation. To support this idea, let us point out that we noticed a few examples in our dataset where the actual term equivalent found on the appropriate record was not the one chosen by the translator.

Even though TERMIUM was the chosen term bank for our experiment, it would be very interesting to put our domain-driven disambiguation algorithm to the test using other term banks, such as EuroTermBank or IATE, which would be structured given their own set of domains. Wikipedia categories, although much more loosely defined than the domains in TERMIUM, and in a collaborative manner rather than a curated one, are also worth investigating for implementing a category-driven disambiguation approach. We can also explore the approach described by (Pang and Biuk-Aghai, 2010) to determine category similarity. More recently, (Gella et al., 2014) have suggested a method for mapping WordNet domains with Wikipedia Categories, which would perhaps allow us to explore the combination of both resources within a text profiling and domain-driven disambiguation approach.

References

Caroline Barrière. 2010. Recherche contextuelle d'équivalents en banque de terminologie. *Traitement Automatique des Langues Naturelles (TALN'2010)*.

Marine Carpuat, Hal Daumé III, Alexander Fraser, Chris Quirk, Fabienne Braune, Ann Clifton, Ann Irvine, Jagadeesh Jagarlamudi, John Morgan, Majid Razmara, Ales Tamchyna, Katharine Henry, and Rachel Rudinger. 2012. Domain Adaptation in Machine Translation: Final Report. In *2012 Johns Hopkins Summer Workshop Final Report*.

Spandana Gella, Carlo Strapparava, and Vivi Nastase. 2014. Mapping WordNet Domains , WordNet Topics and Wikipedia Categories to Generate Multilingual Domain Specific Resources. pages 1117–1121.

Alfio Gliozzo, Bernardo Magnini, and Carlo Strapparava. 2004. Unsupervised Domain Relevance Estimation for Word Sense Disambiguation. *Proc. of the 2004 Conference on EMNLP*, pages 380–387.

Michael Lesk. 1986. Automatic Sense Disambiguation Using Machine Readable Dictionaries: How to Tell a Pine Cone from an Ice Cream Cone. In *SIGDOC'86: Proceedings of the 5th annual international conference on Systems documentation*, pages 24–26, New York, NY, USA.

Bernardo Magnini and G Cavaglia. 2000. Integrating Subject Field Codes into WordNet. *In Proceedings of LREC 2000*, pages 1413–1418.

Bernardo Magnini, Carlo Strapparava, Giovanni Pezzulo, and Alfio Gliozzo. 2002. The role of domain information in Word Sense Disambiguation. *Natural Language Engineering*, 8(4):359–373.

Cheong-Iao Pang and Robert P Biuk-Aghai. 2010. A Method for Category Similarity Calculation in Wikis. In *WikiSym'10*, Gdansk, Poland.

Florentina Vasilescu, Philippe Langlais, and Guy Lapalme. 2004. Evaluating Variants of the Lesk Approach for Disambiguating Words. In *Language Resources and Evaluation (LREC)*, pages 633–636.

A Method of Augmenting Bilingual Terminology by Taking Advantage of the Conceptual Systematicity of Terminologies

Miki Iwai
Graduate School of
Interdisciplinary
Information Studies,
The University of Tokyo
mikii
@g.ecc.u-tokyo.ac.jp

Koichi Takeuchi Kazuya Ishibashi
Graduate School of
Natural Science and
Technology,
Okayama University
{koichi, ploi5t2g}
@cl.cs.okayama-u.ac.jp

Kyo Kageura
Graduate School of
Education,
The University of Tokyo
kyo@p.u-tokyo.ac.jp

Abstract

In this paper, we propose a method of augmenting existing bilingual terminologies. Our method belongs to a "generate and validate" framework rather than extraction from corpora. Although many studies have proposed methods to find term translations or to augment terminology within a "generate and validate" framework, few has taken full advantage of the systematic nature of terminologies. A terminology of a domain represents the conceptual system of the domain fairly systematically, and we contend that making use of the systematicity fully will greatly contribute to the effective augmentation of terminologies. This paper proposes and evaluates a novel method to generate bilingual term candidates by using existing terminologies and delving into their systematicity. Experiments have shown that our method can generate much better term candidate pairs than the existing method and give improved performance for terminology augmentation.

1 Introduction

In this paper, we propose a new way of generating new bilingual multi-word term pairs for augmenting existing bilingual terminologies.

There is growing demand for properly managed terminologies in many areas of society, e.g. in document authoring and management, in technical translation, in knowledge transfer and education, and in IR/NLP (Sager, 1990; Wright and Wright, 1997; Budin, 2008; Kockaert and Steurs, 2015). With the constant introduction of new terms in many domains, timely augmentation and update of terminologies is critical for proper terminology management, and automatic assistance for this process is greatly needed (Kockaert and Steurs, 2015). Many researchers have proposed various methods to augment terminologies automatically. As we will see in Section 2, these can be divided into two broad approaches, i.e. "extraction from corpora" approach and "generate and validate" approach. We focus on the latter approach, which fits better for augmenting or expanding *existing* terminologies, the task which is in strong demand in language industries but has not been much addressed from the NLP point of view.

A term in a terminology of a domain represents a concept of that domain. Majority of terms are complex in most domains in most languages. These complex terms represent concepts analytically, with each constituent element representing an important feature of the concept. A terminology, i.e. the set of terms of a domain, represents the structure of concepts of that domain more or less systematically. Although the extent of systematicity differ from language to language and from domain to domain, new terms are generally formed systematically within the conceptual system of the domain. If we can take into account this aspect of term formation for generating term candidates in the task of augmenting terminologies, we would be able to develop an effective way of help augmenting existing terminologies.

Against this backdrop, this paper proposes a new method of generating bilingual term candidates by taking advantage of the structural feature of terminology. The basic idea is as follows: define terminological network that reflects conceptual systematicity; identify "motivated" subnetworks within which term formation is supposed to be activated, and generate term candidates for each subnetwork.

Proceedings of the 5th International Workshop on Computational Terminology,
pages 30–40, Osaka, Japan, December 12 2016.

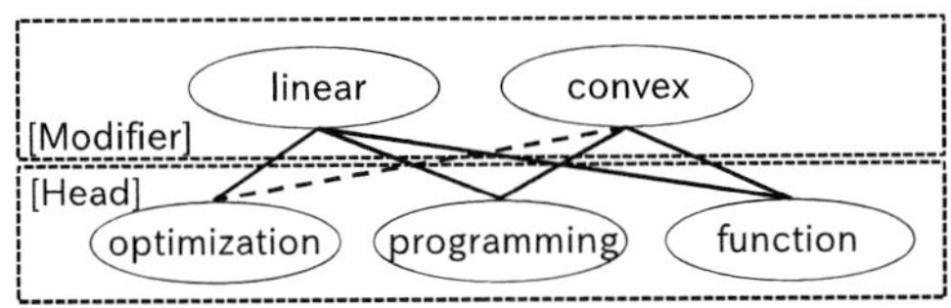

Figure 1: Example of generating a term candidate

The rest of this paper is organised as follows. Section 2 looks at related work and places the present work in context. Section 3 explains our proposed method. Sections 4 and 5 introduce the experimental setup and the results, respectively. Section 6 summarises the results and discusses remaining issues.

2 Related work

2.1 Automatic extraction/augmentation of bilingual terms/terminology

Bilingual term extraction from parallel or comparable corpora has been actively pursued since the 1990s (Dagan and Church, 1997; Fung and Mckeown, 1997; Gaussier, 1998; Chiao and Zweigenbaum, 2002; Kwong et al., 2004; Bernhard, 2006; Robitaille et al., 2006; Daille and Morin, 2008; Lefever et al., 2009; Laroche and Langlais, 2010), most of which use contextual information such as co-occurrence within aligned segments or contextual similarity. Research into the improvement of quality of corpora is also pursued (Morin et al., 2010; Li and Gaussier, 2010). The European project TTC (Terminology extracting Translation Tools and Comparable Corpora) is the culmination of this trend of research (Blancafort et al., 2010).

Some use the correspondence at the level of constituent elements of terms in finding term translations (Grefenstette, 1999; Tonoike et al., 2005; Tonoike et al., 2006; Daille and Morin, 2008), i.e. they generate term candidates in target language by translating constituent elements and validate their existence. These studies partly adopt the "generate and validate" framework. Sato et al. (2013) generated multi-word term pairs as bilingual term candidates by considering all possible pairs of constituent elements of terms in a terminology. The generated pairs are then validated by using web documents.

Our method adopts this "generate and validate" framework. More specifically, we take Sato et al. (2013) as a point of departure as the aim of this work is the same as the present work, i.e. extending existing bilingual terminologies. The method proposed by Sato et al. (2013) takes advantage of a general tendency that if one term is a compound, a part of the term is a term and a part of the term can be changed. For example, if a terminological lexicon contains, "linear programming", "linear optimization", "linear function", "convex programming" and "convex function", they can expect that the term "convex optimization" exists, even if this term is not listed in the lexicon. They generate term candidates consisting of two constituents by defining head-modifier bipartite graph and interpolate missing edges. Figure 1 shows this idea graphically.

The problems we identify with their method are (a) if applied straightforwardly, a huge number of bilingual term candidates are generated, and (b) the Kernighan-Lin algorithm they adopted (Kernighan and Lin, 1970) to partition head-modifier bipartite graph in order to reduce term candidates does not reflect systematic structure of terminologies. Following theoretical research in terminology (Sager, 1990; Kageura, 2002), we understand that new terms are formed within the conceptual terminological subsystem surrounding the new concepts. So our main task is concerned with consolidating these subsystems consisting of tightly-related or "motivated" terms/concepts within which new terms are formed.

2.2 Structural nature of terminology

Terminologies in most languages contain a substantial number of complex terms (Cerbah, 2000; Nomura and Ishii, 1989). Research has shown that complex terms tend to show conceptual relationships systematically, with each constituent element representing an important feature of concepts represented by terms (Felber, 1984; Sager, 1990; Kageura, 2002).

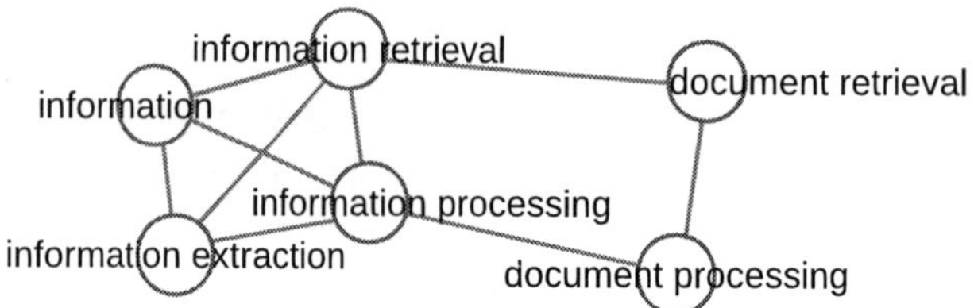

Figure 2: Terminology network of a putative terminology

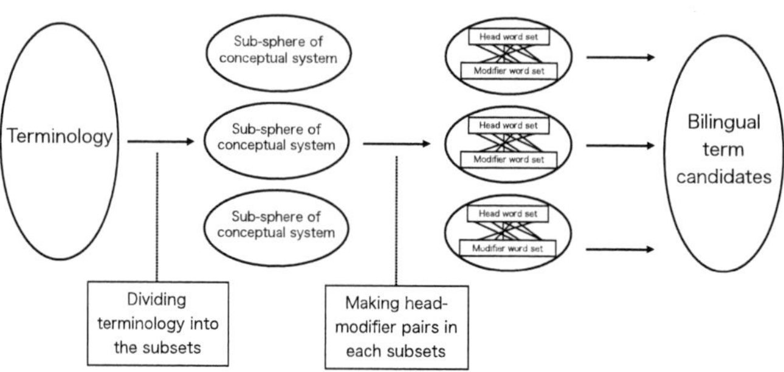

Figure 3: Proposed method

Kageura (2012) examined the systematic nature of terminologies by introducing terminological network, the vertices of which are terms and the edges of which consist of common constituent elements between terms. For instance, a putative terminology consisting of six terms, "information", "information retrieval", "information extraction", "document retrieval", "document processing", and "information processing" makes a network as shown in Figure 2.

Kageura and Abekawa (2007) applied partitive clustering over the terminological network to obtain sub-groups of terminologies. Asaishi and Kageura (2011) comparatively analysed the formal nature of terminological structure by defining terminological networks of English and Japanese bilingual terminologies of several domains. Iwai et al. (2016) have shown that there is a reasonable amount of cross-lingual correspondence between sub-groups of English and Japanese terms identified by using community detection algorithms over the terminological network. As stated above, to identify conceptual subsystems consisting of closely-related concepts in terminology constitutes an essential part of our method. Iwai et al. (2016) showed that meaningful conceptual subsystems can be identified and extracted by applying relevant network partition algorithms to terminological networks.

3 Method of term candidate generation

Starting from a given terminology, the method of term candidate generation we propose consists of two steps:

1. Dividing a terminology into subgroups each of which consists of terms representing closely related concepts; and

2. Generating bilingual term candidates by generating possible combinations of constituent elements of terms included in each subgroup.

Figure 3 shows an outline of the method.

While Sato et al. (2013) firstly considered all possible head-modifier pairs for all terms in terminology and then reduced the number of term candidates by applying Kernighan-Lin algorithm to the head-modifier bipartite graph, our method first consolidate subgroups of terms and generate term candidates for each subgroup separately. Note that this is not just a methodological alternative, but reflects theoretical understanding of how new terms are formed, as stated above.

3.1 Identifying "motivated" sub-groups of terms

We first construct terminological networks (Kageura, 2012), and then apply partitive clustering or community detection algorithm to the network. This manipulation identifies motivated sub-groups of terms within a given terminology. As terms are formed within subsystems of concepts, this serves for reducing the number of generated term candidates while at the same time increasing the plausibility of candidates. After dividing terminological networks into sub-groups or clusters, we generated a head-modifier set for each cluster.

The steps for this process are as follows:

1. Decompose each term into its constituent elements;

2. Generate terminological network with terms as vertices and common constituent elements as edges;

3. Divide the generated terminological network into clusters using a community detection algorithm.

For step 1, we used MeCab[1] with UniDic[2] to decompose Japanese terms into constituent elements. For English terms, we decompose terms using spaces and other punctuations and then apply stemming and lemmatisation of constituent words using a lemmatiser[3]. Although POS taggers, such as Stanford POS Tagger[4], are widely used for pre-processing English sentences or phrases, we used here the lemmatiser because (a) our aim is to extract semantically identical units by removing inflectional (and sometimes derivational) variations and (b) we do not need POS-information. Previous work has shown that approximately matching units can be extracted for English and Japanese terminologies by applying these pre-processing steps (Asaishi and Kageura, 2011).

For step 2, we used python igraph library[5] to generate terminology networks for English and Japanese. We removed functional words (symbols, numbers, prepositions and articles for English; symbols, numbers, particles and auxiliary verbs for Japanese) as they do not represent conceptual characteristics.

For step 3, we adopted Potts spin glass algorithm to divide the terminology networks into clusters. Many community detection algorithms have been proposed (Clauset et al., 2004; Rosvall and Bergstrom, 2008; Raghavan et al., 2007; Blondel et al., 2008; Pons and Latapy, 2006; Newman, 2006). After examining several commonly used methods, we decided to adopt Potts spinglass-based method (Reichardt and Bornholdt, 2006), which works by solving the global optimization problem (Kirkpatrick, 1984). Not only is this method reported to work well in several experiments, the underlying concept reflects nicely the task of extracting motivated sub-groups of terminologies (Kageura and Abekawa, 2007).

3.2 Generating bilingual term candidates

After obtaining clusters on sub-groups of terms, we generated bilingual term candidates as follows:

1. Identify corresponding English and Japanese terms contained in each cluster. As English and Japanese clusters do not match completely (Iwai et al., 2016), we generated term candidate pairs in three different ways in step 1: (a) based on Japanese clusters (Japanese), (b) based on English clusters (English), and (c) based on the intersections of Japanese and English clusters (mix).

2. Generate bilingual pairs of constituent elements (henceforth constituent pairs). This is carried out first by identifying single-word term pairs and then subtracting them from multi-word terms and making remaining elements as pairs recursively.

3. Generate head-modifier pairs for constituent elements of source language terms, as shown in Figure 4. We identify head-modifier relations by identifying constituents on the left as modifiers and on the right as heads, as English (and Japanese, for that matter) complex terms are head final. We also assumed that if a term constitutes more than three words, two constituent elements can replace as one semantics unit. For example, we can consider that "data" is the modifier and "processing

---

[1] http://code.google.com/p/mecab/
[2] http://pj.ninjal.ac.jp/corpus_center/unidic
[3] http://www.nltk.org/api/nltk.stem.html
[4] http://nlp.stanford.edu/software/tagger.shtml
[5] http://igraph.org

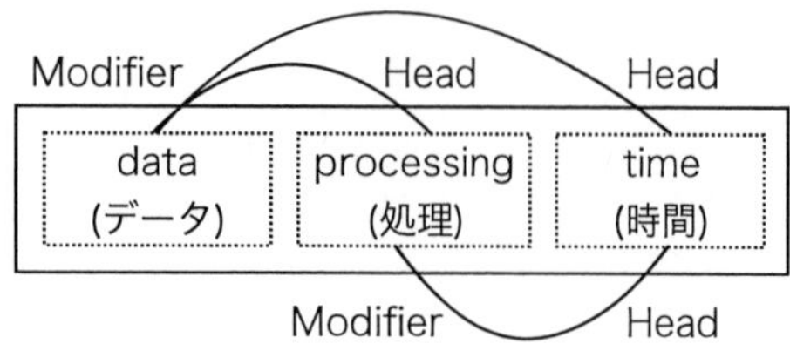

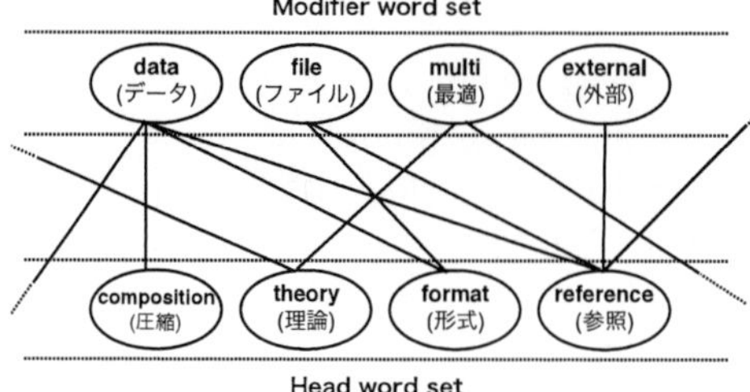

Figure 4: Extracting head-modifier pairs   Figure 5: Example of bipartite graph

Dom.	Lang.	T	1	2	3	4+
Com.	En	16259	2634 (16.20%)	9044 (55.62%)	3645 (22.42%)	936 (5.76%)
	Ja	16259	2002 (12.31%)	7141 (43.92%)	4782 (29.41%)	2334 (14.36%)
Ecn.	En	9120	1219 (13.37%)	4858 (53.27%)	1659 (18.19%)	1384 (15.17%)
	Ja	9120	947 (10.38%)	3753 (41.15%)	2814 (30.86%)	1606 (17.61%)

Table 1: The distribution of terms in each terminology

time" is the head in Figure 4. However, we considered only head-modifier pairs by minimum unit in this time. We set English as source language for convenience of processing; there is no inherent technical reason for us to make the process directional in terms of languages.

4. Generate a bipartite graph based on the head-modifier pairs of the source language, as shown in Figure 5.

5. Take the direct product of the head and modifier vertices to generate extended head-modifier pairs from that bipartite graph.

6. Create new bilingual term pairs by taking translations for each constituent elements of the head-modifier pairs using constituent pairs.

The candidate term pairs generated through this process are then validated using web documents.

4 Experimental setup

4.1 Seed terminologies

For evaluation, we used two terminological dictionaries, i.e. one in the field of computer science (Aiso, 1993) and the other in the field of economics (Yuhikaku, 1986). These are two of the five terminological dictionaries used in Sato et al. (2013). Table 1 shows the number and ratio of terms by length in each terminology, i.e. single terms, terms with two constituents, terms with three constituents and terms with four or more constituents. "Dom." stands for domain, "Lang." stands for language, and "T" indicates the number of terms. From Table 1, we can observe that these terminologies contain many complex terms.

4.2 Terminological network and candidate generation

We constructed terminological networks for English and for Japanese separately for these two datasets. Table 2 shows the quantitative nature of the terminological networks, in which N stands for the number of constituent elements, V the number of vertices, E the numbers of edges, and S the number of isolated terms. We can observe that each network consists of a single giant component (max subgraph) and several small components (others) including isolated vertices.

We then extracted max subgraph and divided it into clusters. The number of clusters was set in two ways, i.e. 25 and 10. These numbers were decided heuristically, referring to the number of subdomains listed in handbooks and in academic societies. The number of candidates generated from these clusters is given in Table 3, which also provides the number of candidates generated from the method by Sato et al. (2013). Note that our method produces smaller number of term candidates.

Dom.	Lang.	T	V	E	S	max subgraph	
						V	E
Com.	En	16259	14186	992319	1100	13046	992293
	Ja	16259	15062	998245	1468	13380	997034
Ecn.	En	9120	8922	278836	749	8127	278812
	Ja	9120	4647	267603	863	8096	26784

Table 2: Basic quantities of terminologies and terminological networks

Dom.	10clusters			25clusters			Sato et al. (2013)
	En	Ja	mix	En	Ja	mix	
Com.	106,422	37,741	27,252	93,175	27,342	20,891	202,446
Ecn.	33,348	12,478	10,009	29,075	9,112	7,885	82,806

Table 3: The number of generated term candidates

4.3 Collecting web documents for validation

Web documents are collected separately for two languages and stored in a database. To avoid collecting irrelevant web pages, we used domain keywords (the name of the domain such as "computer science") together with individual terms for collecting documents.

Web documents for computer science were collected in October and November 2014, by using terms and the domain keywords "computer science" (English) and "情報科学" ("information science" for Japanese) (see 3.1). Web documents for economics were collected at the end of December 2014, with domain keywords "economics" (English) and "経済学" ("economics" for Japanese). Table 4 shows the basic quantities of the collected documents. We extracted 200 pages randomly from the English data and manually checked the number of technical documents. The result is shown in Table 5. Approximately 60 % of the documents were technical in both domains.

5 Evaluation

We evaluated our method in two ways. First, we compared our result with Sato et al. (2013) in terms of the number of retained candidates after validation. Second, to evaluate precision, we extracted top 100 candidates ranked according to (a) the sum of English and Japanese occurrences and (b) the Jaccard coefficient. Note that we do not make comparison between our approach and the approach of extracting terms from corpora, because their experimental setups are very different to each other.

5.1 Comparison of the number of retained candidates after validation

The candidate term pairs generated in six different ways (two cluster sizes of 10 and 25 by based on Japanese clusters, based on English clusters, and based on the intersections of Japanese and English clusters) were validated by 2 steps using the web documents (see 4.3).

1. Searching bilingual term candidates from collected web documents and retaining candidate pairs of which both English part and Japanese part occur at least once in the documents.

2. Calculating a Jaccard coefficient by using retained candidate pairs.

In step 1, instead of using the web search directly, we first pool the web documents relevant to the two domain. It is to avoid repeatedly searching the web for every candidate pairs. In step 1, we validate English and Japanese terms separately, as we can assume that the candidates are aligned. However, it is still useful to validate the bilingual co-occurrences in the web documents. In order to observe that, we used Jaccard coefficient.

Dom.	English	Japanese	total
Com.	121,740	43,868	165,608
Ecn.	98,630	58,411	157,040

Table 4: The number of collected web documents

Dom.	Technical documents	percentage
Com.	126	63.0%
Ecn.	130	65.0%

Table 5: Percentage of technical documents

Dom.	10clusters			25clusters			Sato et al. (2013)
	En	Ja	mix	En	Ja	mix	
Com.	39,198 (36.83%)	17,239 (45.68%)	13,583 (49.84%)	34,683 (37.22%)	14,123 (51.65%)	11,628 (55.67%)	9,849 (4.87%)
Ecn.	12,105 (36.30%)	6,718 (52.70%)	5,957 (59.52%)	10,862 (37.36%)	5,707 (62.63%)	5,227 (66.29%)	6,523 (7.88%)

Table 6: The result of validation (filtering)

5.1.1 Filtering by using collected web documents

We first did the filtering by using collected web documents to reduce the number of generated bilingual term candidates. Candidate pairs of which both English part and Japanese part occur at least once in the corpus were retained as validated terms. Table 6 shows the result. The first line in each domain shows the number of validated candidates. The second line shows their percentage against the number of candidate pairs given in Table 3. It shows that the number of terms retained after validation is generally larger in our methods than Sato et al. (2013), with exceptions ("mix" for 10 clusters, and "Ja" and "mix" for 25 clusters in economics). In all cases, the ratio of retained candidates is much higher in our method than Sato et al. (2013). These results indicate that our proposed method:

- performs both more effectively in terms of computational cost and in terms of recall, assuming that the validated terms have roughly the same level of pairing precision and termhood precision; and

- enables us to control the balance between recall and precision, by changing the number of clusters as well as the pairing methods.

The first point indicates that our method successfully captures the conceptual subsystems/terminological subgroups within the dynamics of which new terms are formed. The second point shows that our method gives us applicational flexibility.

5.1.2 Calculating Jaccard coefficient

After filtering by collected web documents, we searched retained bilingual term candidates with search engine and calculated Jaccard coefficient by using the number of hit. In order to keep the comparison with Sato et al. (2013) sensible, we chose the validated candidates generated from "mix" for 25 clusters, as the number of validated terms in the two domains is close to that by Sato et al. (2013) (although "Ja" pairing for 10 clusters is the closest in economics, we chose the same setting for the two domains). Jacard coefficient is defined as:

$$Jaccard(L1, L2) = \frac{H(L1) \wedge H(L2)}{H(L1) \vee H(L2)} = \frac{H(L1) \wedge H(L2)}{H(L1) + H(L2) - H(L1 \wedge L2)},$$

where $L1$ and $L2$ indicate English and Japanese parts (or vice versa) of a candidate pair in our case, and $H(x)$ is the number of documents in which they occur. If the number of hits is zero, the Jaccard coefficient is defined to be zero. In filtering by using collected web documents, the process retained candidate pairs that either English part or Japanese part occur. Therefore, it is considered that non-parallel candidate pairs are retained. By calculating Jaccard coefficient with the number of hit in search engine and retaining candidate pairs that Jaccard coefficient is positive, we finally extract candidate pairs that is validated parallel. We used Bing search API as search engine. Table 7 shows the result of the total

Dom.	"mix" for 25 clusters	Sato et al. (2013)
Com.	9,471 (81.45%)	2,261 (23.00%)
Ecn.	4,707 (90.05%)	2,286 (35.05%)

Table 7: The result of total number of positive Jaccard coefficients

	Occurrences			Jaccard		
Dom.	pairing	term	partial	pairing	term	partial
Com.	82 (61)	56 (28)	16 (17)	86 (89)	72 (51)	13 (15)
Ecn.	87 (56)	69 (37)	24 (16)	95 (91)	86 (60)	8 (18)

Table 8: Precision of top 100 candidates

number of candidate term pairs that take positive values of Jaccard coefficients. The result indicates that our method generates many more potentially valid candidate pairs than the method by Sato et al. (2013).

5.2 Precision of top 100 candidates

The top 100 candidates generated by "mix" for 25 clusters, ranked according to the sum of English and Japanese occurrences and to the Jaccard coefficient, were manually evaluated for each domain. The evaluation was carried out from two points of view, i.e. (a)whether the Japanese and English matches or not (pairing), and (b)whether the Japanese candidates can be regarded as a term in the domain in question (term). For (b), we also counted partial-terms (partial). The evaluation was carried out by one of the authors. Table 8 shows the result, together with the corresponding results given in Sato et al. (2013) (in bracket). Table 8 shows that except for "pairing" by Jaccard in computer science, our method is consistently better than Sato et al. (2013) in terms of precision as well.

6　Conclusion and future work

In this paper we proposed a method of augmenting existing bilingual terminological lexicon. We introduced a way of generating candidate term pairs which reflect the conceptual system/terminological group within which new terms are formed, by taking advantage of the "motivated" structure of terminologies. Compared with the method proposed so far, our method consistently shows higher performance, which indicates that our method succeeded in identifying, to a reasonable extent, the conceptual subsystem/terminological subgroups within which terms are formed. The method also has more applicational flexibility.

We are currently addressing the following issues:

- Extending our method so that it can generate and validate terms with more than three constituent elements. For example, if a term consists of more than three words, it is natural to decompose it into 2 words as one unit and the other one word from the point of semantic structure. In this way, we try to apply generating bilingual term candidates that consists of more than three words.

- Improving the pairing module. As of now, we examined English as source language and Japanese as target language. However, we can consider reverse pattern in our proposed method. Directional property of language and correspondence of translation words are one of the points of that we need to address in the future.

- Analysing non-validated candidates (error analysis). Now that it was shown that the proposed method can capture, to a reasonable extent, conceptual subsystem within which new terms are generated, it is important to analyse non-validated candidates to obtain further insights into candidate generation process.

- Finding a way of suggesting reasonable number of clusters. As can be inferred from Tables 4 and 7, the best number of clusters may differ from domain to domain.

In addition, we are planning to extend our research into the following directions:

- Applying our method to different language pairs. We are planning to apply our method to Chinese-English and Korean-English pairs.

- Clarifying the difference between the "generate and validate" framework and extraction from parallel or comparable corpora. Although the comparison of these two approaches are difficult, because not only the theoretical assumption and the range of relevant applications but also the range of data which can be used differ greatly (the "generate and validate" approach in general can use wider variety of data as they are used for validation rather than sources from which terms are extracted), it would still be interesting to examine the relationship between these two approaches on the empirical basis.

Acknowledgements

This work is partly supported by JSPS Grant-in-Aid (A) 25240051 "Archiving and using translation knowledge to construct collaborative translation training aid system."

References

Hideo Aiso. 1993. *Dictionary of information processing*. Tokyo: Ohm.

Takuma Asaishi and Kyo Kageura. 2011. Comparative analysis of the motivatedness structure of Japanese and English terminologies. In *Proceedings of the 9th International Conference on Terminology and Artificial Intelligence (TAI)*, pages 38–44.

Delphine Bernhard. 2006. Multilingual term extraction from domain-specific corpora using morphological structure. In *Proceedings of the 11th Conference of the European Chapter of the Association for Computational Linguistics (EACL)*, pages 171–174.

Helena Blancafort, Béatrice Daille, Tatiana Gornostay, Ulrich Heid, Claude Méchoulam, and Serge Sharoff. 2010. TTC: Terminology extraction, translation tools and comparable corpora. In *Proceedings of the 14th European Association for Lexicography (EURALEX) International Congress*, pages 263–268.

Vincent D. Blondel, Jean-Loup Guillaume, Renaud Lambiotte, and Etienne Lefebvre. 2008. Fast unfolding of communities in large networks. *Journal of Statistical Mechanics: Theory and Experiment*, 2008.

Gerhard Budin. 2008. Global content management. *Topics in Language Resources for Translation and Localisation*, pages 121–134.

Farid Cerbah. 2000. Exogeneous and endogeneous approaches to semantic categorization of unknown technical terms. In *Proceedings of the 18th International Conference on Computational Linguistics (COLING)*, pages 145–151.

Yun-Chuang Chiao and Pierre Zweigenbaum. 2002. Looking for candidate translational equivalents in specialized, comparable corpora. In *Proceedings of the 19th International Conference on Computational Linguistics (COLING)*, volume 2, pages 1–5.

Aaron Clauset, Mark E. J. Newman, and Cristopher Moore. 2004. Finding community structure in very large networks. *Physical Review*, 70:66–111.

Ido Dagan and Ken Church. 1997. Termight: Cordinating humans and machines in bilingual terminology acquisition. *Machine Translation*, 12:89–107.

Béatrice Daille and Emmanuel Morin. 2008. Effective compositional model for lexical alignment. *In Proceedings of the 3rd International Joint Conference on Natural Language Processing (IJCNLP)*, pages 95–102.

Helmut Felber. 1984. *Terminology manual*. UNESCO, Paris.

Pascale Fung and Kathleen Mckeown. 1997. Finding terminology translations from non-parallel corpora. In *Proceedings of 5th International Workshop of Very Large Corpora (WVLC-5)*, pages 192–202.

Éric Gaussier. 1998. Flow network models for word alignment and terminology. In *Proceedings of the 17th International Conference on Computational Linguistics (COLING)*, pages 444–450.

Gregory Grefenstette. 1999. The world wide web as a resource for example-based machine translation tasks. In *Proceedings of the ASLIB Conference on Translating and the Computer*, volume 21.

Miki Iwai, Koichi Takeuchi, and Kyo Kageura. 2016. Cross-lingual structural correspondence between terminoogies: The case of English and Japanese. In *Proceedings of the 12th International conference on Terminology and Knowledge Engineering (TKE)*, pages 14–23.

Kyo Kageura and Takeshi Abekawa. 2007. Modelling and exploring the network structure of terminology using the Potts spin glass model. *In Proceedings of the 10th Conference of the Pacific Association for the Computational Linguistics (PACLING)*, pages 236–245.

Kyo Kageura. 2002. *The dynamics of terminology: A descriptive theory of term formation and terminological growth*. John Benjamins, Amsterdam.

Kyo Kageura. 2012. *The quantitative analysis of the structure and dynamics of terminologies*. Amsterdam: John Benjamins.

Brian W. Kernighan and Shunjiang Lin. 1970. An efficient heuristic procedure for partitioning graphs. *Bell Systems Technical Journal*, 49(2):291–307.

Scott Kirkpatrick. 1984. Optimization by simulated annealing: Quantitative studies. *Journal of Statistical Physics*, pages 975–986.

Hendrik J. Kockaert and Frieda Steurs, editors. 2015. *Handbook of terminology*, volume 1. John Benjamins, Amsterdam.

Oi Yee Kwong, Benjamin K. Tsou, and Tom B. Y. Lai. 2004. Alignment and extraction of bilingual legal terminology from context profiles. *Terminology*, 10(1):81–99.

Audrey Laroche and Philippe Langlais. 2010. Revisiting context-based projection methods for term-translation spotting in comparable corpora. In *Proceedings of the 23rd International Conference on Computational Linguistics (COLING)*, pages 617–625.

Els Lefever, Lieve Macken, and Veronique Hoste. 2009. Language-independent bilingual terminology extraction from a multilingual parallel corpus. In *Proceedings of the 12th Conference of the European Chapter of the Association for Computational Linguistics (EACL)*, pages 496–504.

Bo Li and Eric Gaussier. 2010. Improving corpus comparability for bilingual lexicon extraction from comparable corpora. *In Proceedings of the 23rd International Conference on Computational Linguistics (COLING)*, pages 644–652.

Emmanuel Morin, Béatrice Daille, Koichi Takeuchi, and Kyo Kageura. 2010. Brains, not brawn: The use of "smart" comparable corpora in bilingual terminology mining. *ACM Transactions on Speech and Language Processing (TSLP)*, 7(1).

Mark E. J. Newman. 2006. Finding community structure in networks using the eigenvectors of matrices. *Physical Review E*, 74(3):36–104.

Masaaki Nomura and Masahiko Ishii. 1989. *List of stems in Japanese technical terms*. Technical report, National Institute for Japanese Language and Linguistics, Tokyo.

Pascal Pons and Matthieu Latapy. 2006. Computing communities in large networks using random walks. *Journal of Graph Algorithms and Applications*, 10(2):191–218.

Usha Nandini Raghavan, Réka Albert, and Soundar Kumara. 2007. Near linear time algorithm to detect community structures in large-scale networks. *Physical Review E*, 76(3):36–106.

Joerg Reichardt and Stefan Bornholdt. 2006. Statistical mechanics of community detection. *Physical Review E*, 74(1):16–110.

Xavier Robitaille, Yasuhiro Sasaki, Masatsugu Tonoike, Satoshi Sato, and Takehito Utsuro. 2006. Compiling French-Japanese terminologies from the web. In *Proceedings of the 11th Conference of the European Chapter of the Association for Computational Linguistics (EACL)*, pages 225–232.

Martin Rosvall and Carl T. Bergstrom. 2008. Maps of random walks on complex networks reveal community structure. *Proceedings of the National Academy of Sciences of the United States of America (PNAS)*, 105(4):1118–1123.

Juan C. Sager. 1990. *A practical course in terminology processing*. Amsterdam: John Benjamins.

Koichi Sato, Koichi Takeuchi, and Kyo Kageura. 2013. Terminology-driven augmentation of bilingual terminologies. *In Proceedings of the XIV Machine Translation Summit (MT Summit)*, pages 3–10, 9.

Masatsugu Tonoike, Mitsuhiro Kida, Toshihiro Takagi, Yasuhiro Sasaki, Takehito Utsuro, and Satoshi Sato. 2005. Effect of domain-specific corpus in compositional translation estimation for technical terms. *Proceedings of the 2nd International Joint Conference on Natural Language Processing (IJCNLP)*, pages 116–121.

Masatsugu Tonoike, Mitsuhiro Kida, Toshihiro Takagi, Yasuhiro Sasaki, Takehito Utsuro, and Satoshi Sato. 2006. A comparative study on compositional translation estimation using a domain/topic-specific corpus collected from the web. In *Proceedings of the 2nd Web as Corpus Workshop*, pages 11–18.

Sue Ellen Wright and Leland D. Wright Jr.. 1997. Terminology management for technical translation. *Handbook of Terminology Management*, 1:147–159.

Yuhikaku. 1986. *Dictionary of economy terms*. Yuhikaku, Tokyo.

Acquisition of semantic relations between terms:
how far can we get with standard NLP tools?

Ina Rösiger[1], Julia Bettinger[1], Johannes Schäfer[1], Michael Dorna[2] and Ulrich Heid[3]
[1]Institute for Natural Language Processing, University of Stuttgart, Germany
[2]Robert Bosch GmbH, Germany, [3]University of Hildesheim, Germany
{roesigia|bettinja|schaefjs}@ims.uni-stuttgart.de
michael.dorna@de.bosch.com, heid@uni-hildesheim.de

Abstract

The extraction of data exemplifying relations between terms can make use, at least to a large extent, of techniques that are similar to those used in standard hybrid term candidate extraction, namely basic corpus analysis tools (e.g. tagging, lemmatization, parsing), as well as morphological analysis of complex words (compounds and derived items). In this article, we discuss the use of such techniques for the extraction of raw material for a description of relations between terms, and we provide internal evaluation data for the devices developed.

We claim that user-generated content is a rich source of term variation through paraphrasing and reformulation, and that these provide relational data at the same time as term variants. Germanic languages with their rich word formation morphology may be particularly good candidates for the approach advocated here.

1 Introduction

While term candidate extraction from texts typically targets domain objects, a fuller domain model, as needed for terminological, lexicographic or text classification purposes, requires in addition the provision of data on hyponymy relations between domain objects (taxonomic relations), on properties of domain objects and on events that involve these domain objects.

The objective of this paper is to provide an assessment of the applicability of standard state-of-the-art computational linguistic tools for the task of extracting evidence from which taxonomic relations between domain objects, as well as events involving the domain objects can be derived. We work with German data, but we expect most of our results to be generalizable to other Germanic languages. The tools in question are (i) basic corpus preprocessing tools (tokenizing, pos-tagging, lemmatization, parsing) as well as coreference resolution, (ii) query tools applicable to the preprocessed corpora and (iii) word formation analyzers. We use these tools, because we also carry out term candidate extraction on the basis of this same infrastructure and intend to explore to which degree one and the same standard hybrid approach can be used both to extract term candidates and to extract evidence for relations between them. In this paper, we do not address actual ontology construction.

The remainder of this paper is structured as follows: Section 2 presents the background of our experiments: the text collection used, as well as the tools for pre-processing, data extraction and ranking of term candidates. In Section 3, we discuss the extraction of evidence for relations between domain objects, in terms of relevant linguistic phenomena, different extraction techniques and, for each one, first evaluation results. Section 4 is structured in parallel to Section 3 and deals with raw material for verb-derived events involving domain objects. A comparison with the state of the art follows in Section 5 and we conclude in Section 6.

2 Background and objectives

2.1 Text basis

We use a corpus of German forum posts collected from several online forums in the domain of do-it-yourself (DIY) projects, e.g. work with wood or stone. The posts have been contributed in part by

Proceedings of the 5th International Workshop on Computational Terminology,
pages 41–51, Osaka, Japan, December 12 2016.

domain experts (giving e.g. advice on techniques, tools, etc.) and in part by end users describing their own projects[1]. Alongside, we use texts from a few professional sources, such as an online encyclopedia and a wiki for DIY work, tools and techniques. The corpus used for the work described here totals ca. 11 M words, with 20% expert text vs. 80% end-user data.

Forum data, as most user-generated content, presents properties of orality (in the sense of Koch and Oesterreicher (1985)): greeting forms (*hallo, tschüss*), contracted forms (verb+pronoun: *hamse* for *haben sie* etc.), orthographic, morphological and syntactic deviance. We also find elements typical of computer-mediated communication, such as addressing (@Peter: ...) or emoticons. The texts contain deviant orthography, spelling errors, compounds written in two chunks instead of one (*Bohrer Spitze* for *Bohrerspitze*, drill bit) etc., covered partly by normalization at tokenizing time. We cannot yet quantify the loss in recall due to these deviances, as far as e.g. parsing-based data extraction is concerned (cf. however Section 4.2.1 and 4.2.2 for precision figures). Terminology in these texts is characterized (i) by term variation ((morpho-) syntactic, in Daille (2007)'s terms) and (ii) by considerable amounts of specialized terms also retrievable from conceptually oral texts[2].

2.2   A standard hybrid term candidate extractor and its computational linguistic components

The extraction of relations between terms presupposes a preceding step of term candidate extraction. Our system uses a standard hybrid approach (cf. Schäfer et al. (2015)): on the basis of either tagged and lemmatized or of parsed text ("preprocessing" in Figure 1), it first applies symbolic patterns (pos-patterns or (morpho-)syntactic patterns) to extract all candidates that follow a given pattern ("pattern search" in Figure 1), before computing termhood measures (such as Ahmad et al. (1992)'s weirdness ratio) to rank candidates by comparison with a general-language corpus (SdeWaC (Faaß and Eckart, 2013)). In the standard term candidate extraction mode, domain experts are then asked to verify the term candidates. Variant recognition is an optional part of the same architecture.

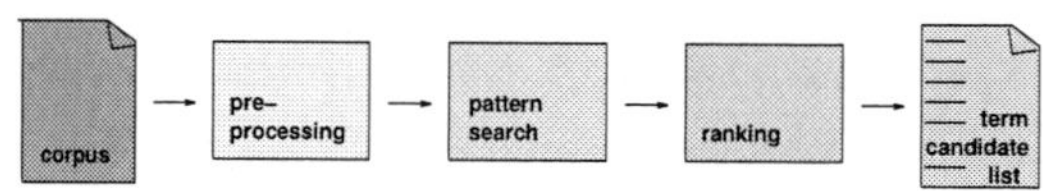

Figure 1: Steps in term candidate extraction: overview

The texts are tokenized and normalized (homogeneous orthography of e.g. numeric indications, cf. *60x40 cm*), tagged and lemmatized using RFTagger (Schmid and Laws, 2008), and dependency parsed using the mate parser (Bohnet, 2010). An automatic correction step is applied for lemmatization. Dependency parses are in addition annotated with phrase boundaries and heads, such that information corresponding to both techniques, constituent and dependency parsing, is available: the full verb of each sentence, its subject and complements, as well as adjuncts and negation are annotated and thus retrievable as context parameters.

An additional step of linguistic annotation is coreference resolution and discourse processing. We use IMS HotCoref DE (Rösiger and Kuhn, 2016), a state-of-the-art coreference resolver for German. In a post-processing step, we annotate personal, possessive, demonstrative and relative pronouns with the closest non-pronominal antecedent identified by the resolver. Experiments on the use of coreference resolution to enhance recall in the extraction of verbs and their arguments can be found in Section 4.2.3.

For compound splitting we use CompoST (Cap, 2014), a compound splitter which combines the use of a rule-based morphology system (SMOR (Schmid et al., 2004)) with morpheme verification in corpus data, thereby extending and improving on the approach proposed by Koehn and Knight (2003) for statistical machine translation. For all components of a compound, including those which are complex themselves, the tool verifies the presence and number of occurrences in a (set of) texts. In our application, the do-it-yourself corpus is used as a knowledge source for this check, in addition to a (newspaper-based) general language corpus. Splits that involve implausible or rare components are dispreferred.

---

[1] A typical forum of this type is "1-2-do.com"

[2] Work on quantifying the terminological richness of more vs. less oral/CMC texts is under way.

Pattern-based search on all levels, with the exception of coreference resolution, is performed by use of the Corpus Workbench (CWB) system (Evert and Hardie, 2011).

2.3 Objective: Assessment of applicability for the extraction of evidence for relations

The architecture and tools described above may be combined to support the search and retrieval of evidence for relations between objects and for events. The objective for the present article is to provide an assessment of the precision of the standard tools when applied to relation extraction. An assessment of recall requires the availability of gold standard data; while work on manual annotation of relations is ongoing, this resource is not yet complete.

Figure 2 shows the collection of semantic relations for the exemplary term *Bohrer (drill)*. The different arrows represent the source of the semantic relation as well as its type. The remainder of the paper will present the techniques used and evaluations of these techniques.

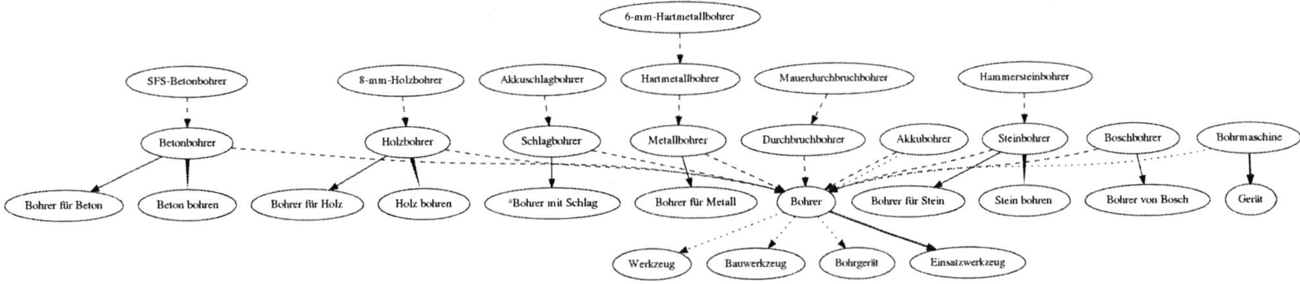

Figure 2: An exemplary subset of relations found for the term *Bohrer*. Bold lines = Hearst patterns (hyponymy relation), normal lines= compounds and their nominal paraphrases (synonymy), dashed lines= compound analysis (hyponymy), broad lines= compounds and their verbal paraphrases (associated events), dotted lines= GermaNet (hyponymy). Not included due to space restrictions are verbs and their arguments.

3 Identifying relations between domain objects

3.1 Relevant phenomena

Taxonomic relations between domain objects: Taxonomic (= hyponymy) relations can be extracted from definition-like sentences ("an X is a Y which ...") and from list-like enumerations ("Xs, such as Y1, Y2 ..."), as first discussed for English by Hearst (1992). Such relations may also be extracted from parsed text by use of verbal predicates which denote class membership (e.g. *gehören zu* ("belong to"), *zählen zu* ("be part of") etc.).

Similarly, determinative compounds can be interpreted as hyponyms of their morphological heads (*Band|säge → Säge, "band|saw"→ "saw"*).

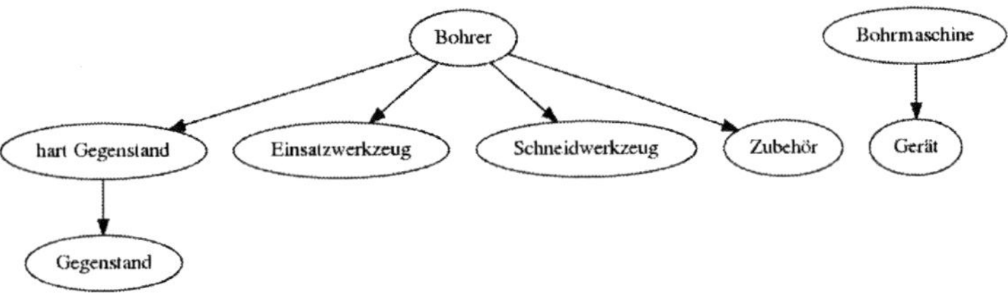

Figure 3: A subset of relations found for *Bohrer* using Hearst patterns; arrows indicate a relation of hyponymy, e.g. "*Bohrer* is-a *Schneidewerkzeug*".

Figures 3 and 4 show an exemplary subset of taxonomic relations for the term *Bohrer* (drill). The figures show partial hierarchies derived from result data of each procedure. As Figure 4 shows, no

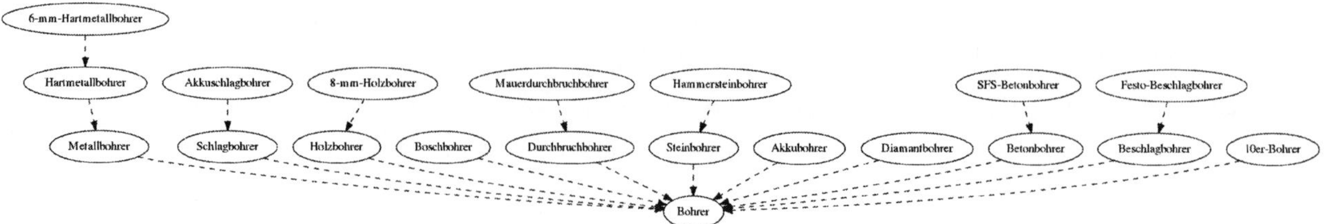

Figure 4: A subset of relations found for *Bohrer* by compound analysis; arrows indicate a relation of hyponymy, e.g. *"Holzbohrer* is-a *Bohrer"*.

inferencing or synonym search has yet been applied (we consider such techniques to be part of the actual ontology construction work), so that e.g. *10er-Bohrer* and *10-mm-Bohrer* are not identified as synonymous, and *Akkubohrer* is not related with *Akkuschlagbohrer*.

Non-taxonomic relations between domain objects: In our texts, many compound terms are paraphrased by means of NP+PP constructions where the preposition makes the relation explicit which exists between the compound head and its modifier. Obviously, prepositions themselves may be ambiguous, in unrestricted contexts, with respect to the relation they indicate; this problem is however less acute within the discourse domain of DIY projects ("one sense per discourse"): the most frequent paraphrase tends to be the adequate one.

Thus, we get, for example, corpus occurrences for both, compounds and their paraphrases:

- *Kupferschraube* ↔ *Schraube aus Kupfer* (material: "copper screw")
- *Befestigungsschraube* ↔ *Schraube zur Befestigung* (purpose: "fixation screw")
- *Senkkopfschraube* ↔ *Schraube mit Senkkopf* (property (or: part/whole): "countersunk screw")

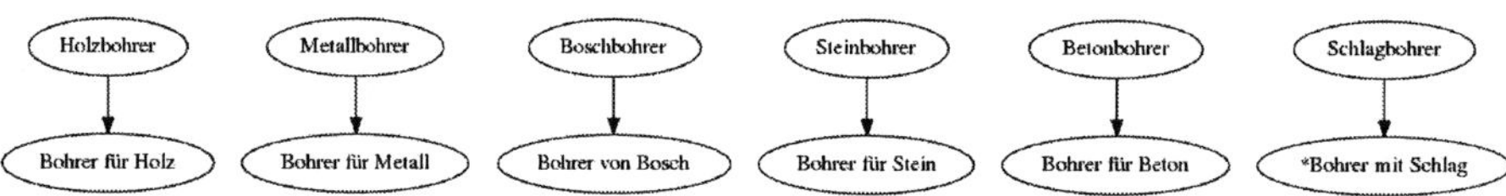

Figure 5: A subset of relations found by assigning compounds NP+PP paraphrases; arrows indicate quasi-synonymy, e.g. *"Holzbohrer* equals *Bohrer für Holz.*

Alongside the isa-relation (*"copper screw"* → *"screw"*), we can thus also extract further meaningful relations from paraphrases of compounds, cf. Figure 5. The same holds for complex NPs (*Holz der Fichte* ↔ *Holz aus Fichte* (↔ *Fichtenholz*), "spruce wood"). Obviously, some ambiguity remains: *Holzfarbe* may be paraphrased by *Farbe von Holz* ("color of wood"), as well as by *Farbe für Holz* ("color applicable to wood(en surfaces)").

3.2 Extraction and evaluation

3.2.1 Hearst-type sentences

To verify the applicability of Hearst (1992)'s approach, we implemented a German version of the classical hypernym patterns. We reproduce abstract queries (shown here in a simplified regular expression notation) in the following (where N_{sup} is the superordinate, N_{sub} the subordinate term[3]):

– N_{sub1} , N_{sub2} (und|oder) (ander.*|vergleichbar.*|sonstig.*|weiter.*) (Adj)? N_{sup}
– (Adj)? N_{sup} (,)? insbesondere (Adj)? N_{sub}

---

[3]The German conjunctions, adjectives and adverbs are, in sequential order "and|or", "other","comparable", "further"; "in particular"; "including"; "such as", "and|or|as well as".

– (Adj)? N_{sup} (,)? einschließlich (Adj)? N_{sub}

– (Adi) N_{sup} wie N_{sub1} (,)? N_{sub2} (('und|oder|sowie') (Adj) N_{sub3}))*

The patterns are not mere translations of the original English patterns, but have been carefully adapted to German, including many additional constraints on the part-of-speech and lemma level to filter out wrong candidates. For example, while the EN version of pattern four (N_{sup} such as N_{sub}) is highly effective, the German adaptation results in many wrong pairs, as in *Hubzahl wie für Baustahl* ("stroke frequency as (used) for structural steel"). Thus, we excluded e.g. results where "wie" was followed by a preposition.

Parsing is not required to identify these patterns; they can equally well be extracted from POS-tagged and lemmatized data. However, for the extraction of verbal predicates which denote class membership we have also implemented an extraction from parsed text. There, we search for the two predicates *zählen* ("be part of") and *gehören* ("belong to") and extract the head of their p-object as the hypernym while the head of the subject is considered to be the hyponym. We also extract predicate constructions in the form of (X_{sub} is a Y_{sup}).

In a first evaluation, we only evaluated the POS-based nominal patterns described above. We are currently planning an evaluation of the verbal patterns[4].

We evaluated the top 200 search result pairs sorted by frequency regarding the question whether the hyponymy relation holds. This is true for 163 out of the 200 pairs, i.e. the accuracy of this technique is about 82%. Errors typically occur in pairs extracted by the fourth pattern, e.g. as in *Unterschied wie Tag und Nacht* ("difference as night and day").

In a second version, we filtered out pairs in which none of the two nouns is a term (i.e. not in the gold standard list), sorted by frequency. We then performed a two-fold evaluation. In the first step, we looked at the validity of the hyponymy relation: do the pairs establish plausible hyponym-hypernym pairs. Out of 200 pairs, 164 were considered valid (82% accuracy). Regarding the question whether the pairs are also domain relevant, 151 out of the 164 valid pairs turned out to be domain relevant (92%).

Overall, the impression in our data is that the quality of the extracted pairs is acceptable, and many of the pairs are relevant for our domain[5].

3.2.2 Compounds

Compound analysis for taxonomic relations We split compounds using the compound splitting tool CompoST (Cap, 2014), see above. We consider the head as the superordinate, and the compounds as subtypes of their heads: *Säge (saw)* has subordinates such as *Kreissäge (buzz saw), Bandsäge (bandsaw)*. The implementation is aware of complex non-heads, i.e. we check for attested morpheme combinations in our specialized corpus as well as in a large general language corpus to exclude wrong splits. For example, for *Eigenbaubandsäge* ("self-constructed bandsaw"), we first split into morphemes (Eigen| bau | band | säge) and then check for attested combinations: *Bandsäge* (valid, found), *Baubandsäge* (not found), *Eigenbau-X* (valid, found), resulting in the correct split *Eigenbau| Bandsäge*.

A script sorts all heads together with their compounds and builds a partial hierarchical structure for every head. An example hierarchy is given in Figure 4.

While these hierarchies have not yet been evaluated, their accuracy is solely dependent on the performance of the compound splitting tool. We are currently planning a comparative evaluation of several compound splitting tools to assess the quality of the compound splits. Overall, the impression when looking at a small set of these hierarchies is that they very rarely contain wrong hyponyms.

Compound analysis and paraphrases for non-taxonomic relations We acquire paraphrases for compounds of the form $Noun_1+Noun_2$ with nominal heads by querying $Noun_2+preposition+Noun_1$ or $Noun_2+determiner+Noun_1$ (in genitive case) in the 11M corpus. Finding nominal paraphrases for heads and non-heads of compounds helps us determine the relation between the parts of the compound. It can also help us disambiguate between possibly ambiguous relations, e.g. to decide whether a drill is

---

[4]The results will be available by end-November 2016.

[5]An error analysis is ongoing and will become available by end-November 2016.

Compound	Paraphrase	Relation
Steinbohrer (stone drill)	Bohrer für Stein (for)	purpose
Metallbohrer (metal drill)	Bohrer für Metall (for)	purpose
Diamantbohrer (diamond drill)	Bohrer aus Diamant (made of)	material
Heizkörperverkleidung (radiator cover)	Verkleidung vor Heizung (in front of)	location
Kellerraum (basement room)	Raum im Keller (in)	location
Schutzfolie (protection film)	Folie zum Schutz (for)	purpose
Aluprofil (aluminium profile)	Profil aus Alu (made of)	material
Pendelhubstichsäge (scroll jigsaw)	*Stichsäge ohne Pendelhub (without)	–
Wasserhaus (water house)	*Haus unter Wasser (under)	–

Table 1: Some exemplary paraphrases found in our data and the relations they indicate

(partially) made of a certain material (*Diamantbohrer – Bohrer aus Diamant*, diamond drill- drill made of diamond) or used to drill a specific material (*Steinbohrer – Bohrer für Stein*, stone drill - drill made for drilling stone). Further examples are given in Table 1. We indicate the compound, the paraphrase found in the corpus and the relation inferred by rule from the preposition. Certain prepositions, like for example *ohne* (without), are excluded as they almost never lead to relevant paraphrases.

In a precision-based evaluation, we manually evaluated the top 200 paraphrase-compound pairs, sorted by compound frequency. 157 out of 200 candidate paraphrases were valid paraphrases, resulting in 79% type accuracy. Errors are mainly due to implausible prepositions, such as *Rest im Holz* (rest in the wood) for *Holzrest* (scrap wood). Taking into account the frequencies of the paraphrases for every compound, 814 paraphrases out of 959 total paraphrase occurrences turned out to be valid paraphrases, resulting in a token accuracy of 85%.

4   Identifying events involving domain objects

4.1   Relevant phenomena

Predicate+argument-structures   To find events involving the domain objects, we extract predicates and their subjects and complements as well as context information in the form of negation and adverbs.

Based on dependency output as produced by mate (Bohnet, 2010), we can extract the following categories:

- Verb object pairs:
  Holz bohren (to drill wood), einen Kreis bohren (to drill a circle), ...

- Subject verb pairs:
  Holz verzieht sich (wood warps), eine Absaugeeinrichtung spart Zeit (a suction device saves time)

- Verb-dependent and adjunct PPs:
  auf Gehrung sägen (to miter), für Stabilität sorgen (to ensure stability),
  mit der Stichsäge ausschneiden (to cut with a jigsaw)

- Negation:
  die Sicherheitskappe nicht abziehen (do not remove the safety cap)

- Adverbs:
  heiß verleimen (to hot glue), trocken reiben (to rub dry), dünn beschichten (to coat thinly)

- Predicative constructions: X is Y (Y can be adjectival or nominal):
  Bohrer ist ein Elektrowerkzeug (drill is a power tool)
  Spitze ist besonders dünn (tip is very thin)

We can also combine these extractors to search for longer patterns, including negation or adverbs.
Subj V Obj: *Holzspiralbohrer haben eine lange Zentrierspitze (wood drills have long lathe centers)*;
Subj V PP: *Beton besteht aus Zement und Wasser (concrete is made of cement and water)* ;
Subj V Obj +Negation:*Kupfer benötigt keinen schützenden Anstrich (copper requires no protective coat)*.

Verb-derived items as a source of relational data Many morphologically complex words are derived from verbal (or adjectival) predicates. German is rich in noun compounds whose heads are nominalizations of verbs or adjectives (e.g. *Holzoberflächengestaltung* "design of wooden surface(s)", *Anwendbarkeit der Magnetfarbe* "applicability of magnetic colour"). Compound participles are equally productive and allow for an analysis of the underlying verbal element in terms of its predicate-argument structure (cf. *alumimiumbeschichtete Oberfläche*, "aluminium-coated surface").

Also here, the combination of compound splitting and search in syntactically annotated data provides pairs of terms and their paraphrases, where the latter make the relations explicit that exist between the items involved (see Figure 6). Alongside the above mentioned complex NPs, we also find verb+complement constructions, such as *Holzoberfläche*$_{Obj}$+ *gestalten* (to design a wooden surface), *Magnetfarbe*$_{Obj}$+*anwenden* (apply magnetic color) or *Oberfläche*$_{Obj}$+ *mit Aluminium beschichten* (coat surface with aluminium). We exploit not only verb+object pairs, but also verb+PP groups, subject+verb groups and predicative constructions. In all cases, we start from morphologically complex items and search their paraphrases. In addition, paraphrase patterns can also be exploited, in the sense of "knowledge-rich contexts" (Meyer, 2001) as models or types of events with instances which do not correspond, in the available data, to morphologically complex items: compound participles of the type *aluminiumbeschichtet* correspond to a pattern such as *X[agent] beschichtet Y[target] mit Z[coating]*, where the expressions in brackets are taken to be informally noted participant roles similar to Frame Elements of FrameNet (cf. Ruppenhofer et al. (2013)) . This pattern provides a large number of pairs of domain objects related by the ad-hoc relation "coated with", most of which are relevant for the domain and correctly recognized[6].

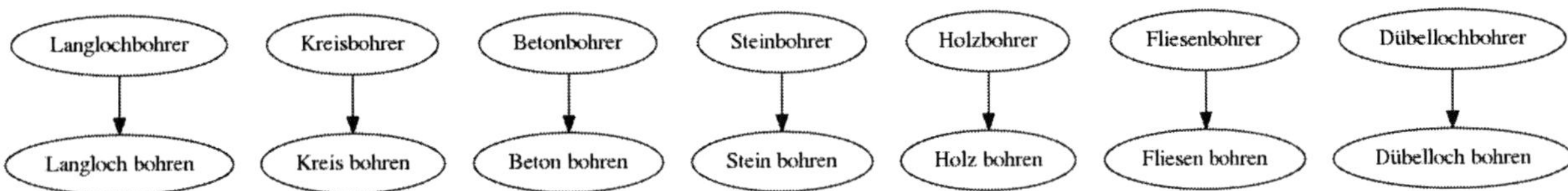

Figure 6: A subset of events found for *Bohrer* by matching compounds and their verbal paraphrases; arrows indicate a corresponding event.

4.2   Extraction and evaluation

4.2.1   Verb and object

This section describes the evaluation of verb object pairs, such as *Dübelloch bohren (drill dowel hole)*, *Sägeblatt verwenden (use saw blade)*, or *Fliesen verlegen (lay tiles)*.

We first evaluated whether the extracted verb object pairs are syntactically valid. Thus, we manually checked the top 250 pairs ranked according to their termhood measure (in this case: domain specificity value (Ahmad et al., 1992)), only looking at pairs with a frequency > 5. The decision is made given an example sentence. Out of the 250 top pairs, 15 are syntactically invalid due to pre-processing and parsing errors. This means that 94% of the extracted pairs are syntactically plausible. Therefore, the parsing quality, although not trained on data from the DIY domain, seems well-suited as a basis to extract data.

A second evaluation looks at the question of domain relevance. Again, we analyze the 250 top ranking pairs V-O candidate pairs sorted by the ranking measure, excluding the verbs *haben, sein* and *geben* (have, be, give). The decision in this case was made between the categories "term", "no term" and "preprocessing error". 27 errors occurred (10%) due to preprocessing or parsing errors. 150 out of the 250 candidates are good terms (60%), whereas 73 bad terms (30%) are not relevant for our domain. Bad terms very often occur only because part of the subcategorization of the verb has not been covered by the extraction pattern, such as in

Werfen Sie Elektrowerkzeuge nicht in den Hausmüll $\Rightarrow$ *Elektrowerkzeuge*$_{OBJ}$+*werfen* $_V$

---

[6]An evaluation is ongoing. Results will be available by December.

(Do not throw power tools into the trash $\Rightarrow$ throw$_V$+ power tools$_{OBJ}$)

These cases can be excluded by using longer patterns involving PPs and negation. Sometimes, the area between terms and non-terms is blurred, e.g. in *Alurohr umdrehen (turn aluminium tubes), Fliesenkleber benötigen (require tile cement), Kochfeld einbauen (assemble hob)*. While these may not be top terms, they definitely are not general terms, either.

4.2.2 Verb and p-object

We performed a top 200 precision-based evaluation, assessing the verb PP pairs according to the question whether the pairs are syntactically valid. We found that 191 of 200 are syntactically plausible, resulting in an accuracy of 96%.

Most of the extracted pairs are very relevant to the domain, such as

für festen Halt sorgen (ensure stability), zum Lieferumfang gehören (belong to delivered items), auf Gehrung sägen (to miter), mit Kies beschweren (weigh down with gravel), auf Rechtwinkligkeit achten (ensure perpendicularity).

Almost all bad pairs are PP attachment problems, such as in *Ich suche ein Gerät mit Akkubetrieb (I'm looking for a device with battery operation) – [suchen mit Akkubetrieb]*. The user generated content is also clearly visible in the extracted pairs, for example in *um einen Hammer abwerten – Ich werte um einen Hammer ab wegen der schlechten Bedienung (Giving this one hammer less due to bad usability)* or in *an die Schraube glauben – Ich glaube an die Schraube (I believe in this screw).*

4.2.3 The role of coreference resolution
for the enhancement of recall in the extraction of predicate argument structures

Many times, arguments of verbs are pronominalized. In order to make use of them for relation extraction, we need to resolve them using a coreference resolver. Thus, we performed some experiments on the use of a state-of-the-coreference resolver (IMS HotCoref (Rösiger and Kuhn, 2016)) for verb object extraction. Coreference resolution in user-generated texts is considered difficult, as there is a decrease in performance of the pre-processing tools when they are used on non-standard data. We only evaluate the quality of coreference resolution indirectly, by looking at the verb object pairs extracted.

We found that, in our data, about 40% of the verb object pairs contained pronominalized objects. One assumption about using coreference resolution therefore was that we can get more candidate pairs. This is true, as the number of verb object pairs rose from 3996 to 4189 candidates (+5%). We further checked whether the newly found candidates are good candidates. We found 82% of the 193 new candidates relevant to the domain, e.g. *120er-Schleifpapier verwenden (use 120-grit sandpaper), 6-mm-Loch bohren (drill 6-mm hole)*. We also found more evidence for pairs already retrieved from the version without coreference resolution, in the form of higher frequencies. We expect the assumptions proven to be true for verb object pairs to be true for other arguments as well, such as subjects or p-objects.

4.2.4 Compound analysis and verbal paraphrases

For compounds with nominalized verbs as heads, we can search for verbs and their respective object as the non-head of the compound. If we find a match, this is evidence that the compound describes an event corresponding to the verb and its object.

Compound	Paraphrase
Abflussreiniger (drain cleaner)	Abfluss reinigen (clear drain)
Bodendämmung (floor insulation)	Boden dämmen (insulate floors)
Fensterisolierung (window insulation)	Fenster isolieren (insulate windows)
Betonbohrung (concrete drilling)	Beton bohren (drill concrete)
Leimverteilung (paste distribution)	Leim verteilen (distribute paste)

We evaluated the 125 most frequent and the 125 least frequent compounds for which a verb+object paraphrase was found with respect to the question whether the verb object-paraphrase was valid for the given compound. The analysis of the top 125 resulted in an accuracy of 74%, for the bottom 125 the accuracy was 82%.

5 Related work

Our work applies a set of strategies that have been introduced in the literature on German user-generated and expert text. Corpus-driven ontology creation has been proposed in many papers, e.g. in Barrière (2004), Auger and Barrière (2008) or Manser (2012), to name only a few. However, to the best of our knowledge, we are not aware of any papers that test and extend these strategies on German texts.

Similar to our strategy is the approach by Gillam et al. (2005) which is also based on hybrid terminology extraction; cf. also Drouin (2003)'s approach. They apply a number of collocation and linguistic patterns to extract relations between terms from specialized English texts. Arnold and Rahm (2014) extract semantic concept relations for German terms from Wikipedia definitions. However, this approach is dependent on Wikipedia sites (i.e. expert text) and not easily applicable to user-generated text. Joslyn et al. (2008) present a distributional semantics approach, where they apply the lattice theoretical technology of Formal Concept Analysis to relations of predicates extracted from a corpus. Even though 11M words is a comparatively "large" amount of material for specialized texts, it may not necessarily be enough for a distributional approach. We also intend to be able to work on smaller corpora.

There are many papers building on the patterns described by Hearst (1992). In the approach by Snow et al. (2005), hypernym-hyponym-pairs are collected firstly by using WordNet. Then a corpus is used to find sentences in which both nouns of the pair occur. The dependency paths of the matched sentences are extracted and used as features for a classifier to determine if an unseen pair of nouns describes a taxonomic relation. Fundel et al. (2007) focus on the extraction of biomedical relations, e.g. the interaction between proteins. Dependency paths connecting the proteins of a given pair are extracted before a set of rules for filtering information is applied. This, of course, extracts relations beyond standard taxonomic ones, such as "A regulates B", but the dependency parse based approach is also applicable on the hypernym-hyponym pair detection. Maynard et al. (2009) differentiate between instance-class and subclass-superclass relations. Only persons, organizations and locations are considered as instances whereas other noun phrases are classes, extracted by patterns including "classification verbs" like *fall into, group into* or *contain* (cf. *zählen, gehören zu*, above). Zouaq et al. (2012) claim that the extraction of relations with lexico-syntactic patterns is an important basic step in structuring data that requires post-processing steps of filtering operations. Their patterns are classified into hierarchical relation patterns (also reusing Hearst Patterns) and patterns for conceptual relationships. e.g. verb (subject, object)-relations. Evaluations showed that the hierarchical patterns achieved the highest precision without post-processing of the results.

The approach described in Ritter et al. (2009) also starts with the extraction of relations using Hearst Patterns. They then filter the matches by using different methods. As applying a frequency based classifier is not sufficient, a SVM classifier is implemented to rate every extracted pair in terms of correctness. As features, a variety of frequencies is used. Finally, they develop an HMM language model to make an evaluation possible even if a certain noun does not have a match with any of the Hearst Patterns.

6 Conclusions and future work

We presented a set of techniques to acquire semantic relations between terms and showed that overall, one can achieve acceptable precision when applying standard tools to relation extraction. Future work will include more morpho-syntactic patterns to extract such relations, as well as external knowledge sources such as e.g. BabelNet. While our work focused on precision-based evaluations of highly frequent cases for the single techniques, more detailed evaluations are planned on the combination of the approaches presented here, as well as the creation of a gold standard, to also be able to assess recall.

Acknowledgments

The work reported in this paper has been carried out in the framework of the collaborative research project "Textanalyse und Ontologieaufbau" financed by the corporate research department of Robert Bosch GmbH. We gratefully acknowledge this support.

References

Khurshid Ahmad, Andrea Davies, Heather Fulford, and Margaret Rogers. 1992. What is a term? - the semi-automatic extraction of terms from text. In *Translation Studies - An Interdiscipline*, pages 267 – 278. Selected papers from the Translation Studies Congress, Vienna.

Patrick Arnold and Erhard Rahm. 2014. Extracting semantic concept relations from wikipedia. In *Proceedings of the 4th International Conference on Web Intelligence, Mining and Semantics (WIMS14)*, WIMS '14, pages 26:1–26:11, New York, NY, USA. ACM.

Alain Auger and Caroline Barrière. 2008. Pattern-based approaches to semantic relation extraction: A state-of-the-art. *Terminology: international journal of theoretical and applied issues in specialized communication*, 14(1):1–19.

Caroline Barrière. 2004. Building a concept hierarchy. *Terminology*, 10(2):241–263.

Bernd Bohnet. 2010. Very high accuracy and fast dependency parsing is not a contradiction. In *Proceedings of the 23rd International Conference on Computational Linguistics (COLING 2010), Beijing, China*, pages 89–97. Association for Computational Linguistics.

Fabienne Cap. 2014. Morphological processing of compounds for statistical machine translation. Dissertation, Institute for Natural Language Processing (IMS), University of Stuttgart.

Béatrice Daille. 2007. Variations and application-oriented terminology engineering. pages 163 – 177.

Patrick Drouin. 2003. Term extraction using non-technical corpora as a point of leverage. *Terminology*, 9(1):99–115.

Stefan Evert and Andrew Hardie. 2011. Twenty-first century corpus workbench: Updating a query architecture for the new millennium.

Gertrud Faaß and Kerstin Eckart. 2013. Sdewac a corpus of parsable sentences from the web. In *Language Processing and Knowledge in the Web: 25th International Conference, GSCL 2013, Darmstadt, Germany, September 25-27, Proceedings*, pages 61 – 68.

Katrin Fundel, Robert Küffner, and Ralf Zimmer. 2007. Relex – relation extraction using dependency parse trees. *Bioinformatics*, 23(3):365–371.

Lee Gillam, Mariam Tariq, and Khurshid Ahmad. 2005. Terminology and the construction of ontology. *Terminology*, 11:55–82.

Marti A. Hearst. 1992. Automatic acquisition of hyponyms from large text corpora. In *Proceedings of the 14th Conference on Computational Linguistics - Volume 2*, COLING '92, pages 539–545, Stroudsburg, PA, USA. Association for Computational Linguistics.

Cliff Joslyn, Patrick Paulson, and Karin Verspoor. 2008. Exploiting term relations for semantic hierarchy construction. In *Semantic Computing, 2008 IEEE International Conference on*, pages 42–49. IEEE.

Peter Koch and Wulf Oesterreicher. 1985. Sprache der nähe–sprache der distanz. *Romanistisches Jahrbuch*, 36(85):15–43.

Phillip Koehn and Kevin Knight. 2003. Feature-rich statistical translation of noun phrases. In *Proceedings of ACL 2003*.

Mounira Manser. 2012. État de l'art sur l'acquisition de relations sémantiques entre termes: contextualisation des relations de synonymie. In *Actes de la conférence JEP-RECITAL*, pages 163–175.

Diana Maynard, Adam Funk, and Wim Peters. 2009. Sprat: a tool for automatic semantic pattern-based ontology population. In *International conference for digital libraries and the semantic web, Trento, Italy*.

Ingrid Meyer. 2001. Extracting knowledge-rich contexts for terminography. *Recent advances in computational terminology*, 2:279.

Alan Ritter, Stephen Soderland, and Oren Etzioni. 2009. What is this, anyway: Automatic hypernym discovery. In *AAAI Spring Symposium: Learning by Reading and Learning to Read*, pages 88–93.

Ina Rösiger and Jonas Kuhn. 2016. IMS HotCoref DE: A Data-driven Co-reference Resolver for German. In *Proceedings of LREC 2016*.

Josef Ruppenhofer, Hans C. Boas, and Collin F. Baker. 2013. The framenet approach to relating syntax and semantics. In Rufus H. Gouws, Ulrich Heid, Wolfgang Schweickard, and Herbert Ernst Wiegand, editors, *Dictionaries. An international encyclopedia of lexicography*, volume Supplementary volume: Recent developments with special focus on computational lexicography, pages 1320–1329. De Gruyter.

Johannes Schäfer, Ina Rösiger, Ulrich Heid, and Michael Dorna. 2015. Evaluating noise reduction strategies for terminology extraction. In *Proceedings of TIA 2015*, Granada, Spain, November.

Helmut Schmid and Florian Laws. 2008. Estimation of conditional probabilities with decision trees and an application to fine-grained pos tagging. In *Proceedings of the 22nd International Conference on Computational Linguistics - Volume 1*, pages 777 – 784.

Helmut Schmid, Arne Fitschen, and Ulrich Heid. 2004. Smor: A german computational morphology covering derivation, composition, and inflection. In *Proceedings of the IVth International Conference on Language Resources and Evaluation (LREC 2004)*, pages 1263 – 1266, Lisbon, Portugal.

Rion Snow, Daniel Jurafsky, and Andrew Y. Ng. 2005. Learning syntactic patterns for automatic hypernym discovery. In L. K. Saul, Y. Weiss, and L. Bottou, editors, *Advances in Neural Information Processing Systems 17*, pages 1297–1304. MIT Press.

Amal Zouaq, Dragan Gasevic, and Marek Hatala. 2012. Linguistic patterns for information extraction in ontocmaps. In *Proceedings of the 3rd International Conference on Ontology Patterns-Volume 929*, pages 61–72. CEUR-WS. org.

Evaluation of distributional semantic models: a holistic approach

Gabriel Bernier-Colborne   **Patrick Drouin**
Observatoire de linguistique Sens-Texte (OLST), Université de Montréal
C.P. 6128, succ. Centre-Ville, Montréal (QC) Canada, H3C 3J7
`{gabriel.bernier-colborne|patrick.drouin}`@umontreal.ca

Abstract

We investigate how both model-related factors and application-related factors affect the accuracy of distributional semantic models (DSMs) in the context of specialized lexicography, and how these factors interact. This holistic approach to the evaluation of DSMs provides valuable guidelines for the use of these models and insight into the kind of semantic information they capture.

1   Introduction

Distributional semantic models (DSMs) can be very useful tools for specialized lexicography, as they can help identify semantic or conceptual relations between terms based on corpus data, among other uses. The quality of the results produced by these models depends on two types of factors: model-related factors and application-related factors. First, they depend on the type of model and the settings used for each of the model's (hyper)parameters. Second, they depend on various aspects of the target application. In the case of specialized lexicography, these factors include the kinds of terms that will be included in the lexical resource and the kinds of relations that will be described therein. The target relations can include typical paradigmatic relations such as (near-)synonymy (e.g. *preserve→protect*), but also others such as syntactic derivation (e.g. *preserve→preservation*). There may also be interactions between the various factors: for instance, the optimal parameter settings may depend on the target relations.

We investigated how these two types of factors affect the quality of the results produced by DSMs, and how they interact, i.e. how various aspects of specialized lexicography must be accounted for when choosing and tuning a model. The aspects considered in this paper are the the the part-of-speech (POS) of the terms included in the resource, the descriptive framework, and the target relations. To this end, we carried out an experiment in which DSMs were built on domain-specific corpora and evaluated on gold standard data we extracted from specialized dictionaries.

2   Related work

Numerous studies have addressed the evaluation and optimization of DSMs. These studies tend to focus on model-related factors, by comparing different models or analyzing the influence of their (hyper)parameters, although some studies use several different tasks or datasets for evaluation purposes (Bullinaria and Levy, 2007; Bullinaria and Levy, 2012; Kiela and Clark, 2014; Baroni et al., 2014), thereby taking the target application into account to some extent. Studies that systematically assess the influence of both model-related and application-related factors are relatively rare. In the case of the DSM which we refer to as the bag-of-words (BOW) model, research conducted as early as the 1960s showed that its parameters, such as the size of the context window, affected the kinds of semantic relations that were captured (Moskowich and Caplan, 1978). Systematic evaluations of DSMs have recently been carried out, some of which take into account the target relations (Sahlgren, 2006; Lapesa et al., 2014) or the POS (Hill et al., 2014; Tanguy et al., 2015). These studies tend to show that the accuracy of DSMs depends on such application-related factors, as do their optimal (hyper)parameter settings. Our work is

Proceedings of the 5th International Workshop on Computational Terminology,
pages 52–61, Osaka, Japan, December 12 2016.

related to these studies, but takes into account a wider range application-related factors, including the descriptive framework, and systematically evaluates how they affect accuracy and how they interact with model-related factors. Furthermore, the target relations considered include not only typical paradigmatic relations, but also syntactic derivation (see Section 3). This relation has not been studied in the context of DSM evaluation as far as we know, and it is not represented in the datasets that are commonly used to evaluate DSMs. The analogy dataset used by Mikolov et al. (2013a) does include adjective-adverb morphological derivatives, but we do not know of any commonly used datasets that cover morphological derivation more extensively, nor any that represent syntactic derivation specifically.

This study contains a comparative evaluation of two differents DSMs, namely the BOW model and the neural word embeddings produced by `word2vec` (Mikolov et al., 2013a; Mikolov et al., 2013b). Several such evaluations have been carried out recently. Baroni et al. (2014) compared the BOW model and `word2vec`[1] on several datasets and found that `word2vec` systematically provided better results. However, the word representations they made available were evaluated by Ferret (2015) on a different dataset, and the BOW model performed better. Levy et al. (2015) showed that when the models' (hyper)parameters are tuned correctly, the BOW model and `word2vec`[2] provide similar accuracy, and the best model depends on the task used for evaluation purposes. To our knowledge, the ability of these two types of DSM to detect various semantic relations has not been evaluated systematically. This is one of the contributions of this study. Moreover, we investigate how various application-related factors come into play when tuning `word2vec`'s hyperparameters. Another original aspect of this work is that we compare the two DSMs on domain-specific data.

3 Data

The corpus used to build the models is a specialized corpus on the environment which is freely available to researchers, called the PANACEA Environment English monolingual corpus[3] (ELRA-W0063). The corpus was compiled automatically using a focused web crawler (Prokopidis et al., 2012). Basic preprocessing was applied, which included extracting the text from the XML files that comprise the corpus[4], replacing non-ASCII characters with ASCII equivalents[5], lemmatizing[6] and converting to lower case.

Models were evaluated using two types of evaluation data[7] (or gold standards), that represent two descriptive frameworks, namely a lexico-semantic approach to terminology (L'Homme, 2004) and frame semantics (Fillmore, 1982). These datasets, which were extracted from specialized dictionaries on the environment domain, are comprised of pairs of semantically related terms or sets of terms that evoke the same semantic frame (e.g. the frame Change_of_temperature is evoked by terms such as *cool, cooling, warm,* and *warming.*) respectively. We created 7 different datasets of semantic relations and one dataset for frame-evoking terms. These datasets, which are described in Table 1, are comprised of query terms mapped to a set of related terms. Models are evaluated by computing the nearest neighbours of each query and looking up the query's related terms in this sorted list of neighbours.

The semantic relations were extracted from DiCoEnviro[8]. We extracted four kinds of semantic relations, namely (near-)synonyms, antonyms, hypernyms/hyponyms and syntactic derivatives. The first three types of relations are typical paradigmatic relations that involve two terms of the same POS. Syntactic derivatives (Mel'čuk et al., 1995, p. 133) are terms that have the same meaning, but belong to different POS, and thus have different syntactic behaviours – they may be morphologically related, but this need not be the case (e.g. *city* and *urban*). A dataset was created for each of these four relations. We also created three datasets for the three POS we took into account, namely nouns, verbs, and adjectives.

---

[1]More specifically, the CBOW architecture.

[2]Here, the skip-gram architecture was used rather than the CBOW architecture.

[3]`http://catalog.elra.info/product_info.php?products_id=1184`

[4]Documents containing less than 50 words were excluded.

[5]We use the Unidecode Python library (`https://pypi.python.org/pypi/Unidecode`).

[6]TreeTagger (Schmid, 1994) was used for lemmatization.

[7]We have made these datasets available, as well as the code we developed for this study. See `https://github.com/gbcolborne/exp_phd`.

[8]`http://olst.ling.umontreal.ca/cgi-bin/dicoenviro/search-enviro.cgi?ui=en`

These contain all the relations between two terms of a given POS (so they do not contain any syntactic derivatives). As for the sets of frame-evoking terms, these were extracted from the Framed DiCoEnviro[9].

Name	Queries	Relations	Description
QSYN	282	517	Synonyms, near-synonyms, co-hyponyms or term variations, e.g. *green*: {*alternative, clean, pure, smart*}.
ANTI	77	109	Antonyms, e.g. *absorb*: {*emit, radiate, reflect*}.
HYP	61	87	Hyponyms and hypernyms, e.g. *precipitation*: {*rain, snow, hail*}.
DRV	174	175	Syntactic derivatives, e.g. *adaptive*: {*adapt, adaptation*}.
NN	190	404	Nouns are mapped to all related nouns (QSYN, ANTI or HYP).
VV	84	187	Verbs are mapped to all related verbs (QSYN or ANTI).
JJ	67	122	Adjectives are mapped to all related adjectives (QSYN or ANTI).
SETS	168	480	Frame-evoking terms are mapped to terms that evoke the same frame, e.g. *warming*: {*warm, cool, cooling*}.

Table 1: Datasets used for evaluation.

It is important to note that only single-word terms were included in these datsets. For various reasons, we decided not to include any multi-word terms in the target words that were evaluated (see Section 4), and only terms that were among these target words were included in the gold standard datasets. Multi-word terms could be included among the target words if required by the target application. Compositionality-based methods (Mitchell and Lapata, 2008; Baroni and Zamparelli, 2010; Mikolov et al., 2013b; Weeds et al., 2014) could also be used to account for multi-word terms.

4 Methodology

The experiment we carried out involves a comparative evaluation of two DSMs and a systematic exploration of their (hyper)parameters. Both of these models produce vector representations of words based on the contexts in which they appear in a corpus, the underlying hypothesis being that words that appear in similar contexts have similar meanings (Harris, 1954; Firth, 1957). Words that appear in similar contexts will thus have similar vector representations, and the semantic similarity of any two words can then be estimated by computing the similarity of their vectors.

The contexts of a word can be defined in various ways. In both of the DSMs we evaluated, the contexts of a word are the words that co-occur with it. Since the contexts are also words, we will sometimes call them *context words*. In this work, we use a sliding context window to determine which words co-occur. The context window spans a certain number of words on either side of a given word token.

The first DSM we evaluated is a simple vector space model which has been studied extensively in the past few decades (Schütze, 1992; Lund et al., 1995; Sahlgren, 2006; Lapesa et al., 2014, inter alia), but whose origins can be traced back to the 1960s (Harper, 1965; Moskowich and Caplan, 1978). We will call this the bag-of-words (BOW) model. To build a BOW model, we compute a matrix M in which value M_{ij} is the weighted cooccurrence frequency of word w_i and context c_j. Various weighting schemes can be used, one popular choice being positive pointwise mutual information (PPMI). Each word w_i is represented by a vector $M_{i:}$ in which each value represents the association strength of w_i and a specific context word. The matrix M can be transformed in other ways once the cooccurrence frequencies have been counted and weighted, e.g. by applying some form of dimensionality reduction, but in this work, we use the basic BOW model, in which words are represented by sparse, high-dimensional vectors.

The second DSM we evaluated is built using the neural probabilistic language model known as `word2vec`. This model learns distributed word representations (often called *embeddings*) which can be used in the same way as BOW vectors to estimate the semantic similarity of words. These representations are learned by training a neural network that aims to predict each word token based on its contexts

---

[9]`http://olst.ling.umontreal.ca/dicoenviro/framed/index.php`

(co-occurring words). An alternative approach aims to predict the contexts of each word token. These two architectures are known as *continuous bag-of-words* (CBOW) and skip-gram respectively.

As with all DSMs, the BOW model and `word2vec` have several (hyper)parameters that must be set in order to build or train a model. We have already mentioned three such parameters: the size of the context window, the weighting scheme (for the BOW model), and the architecture (for `word2vec`). These parameters have an effect on the word representations that are produced, and on the accuracy of the word similarity scores we obtain by comparing the word representations.

In order to assess the influence of the (hyper)parameters of both DSMs, we tried several settings for each parameter and evaluated every possible combination of these parameter settings.

For the BOW model, we examined three parameters related to the context window. The context window has not only a size, but a shape, which is a function that determines the increment that is added to the cooccurrence frequency of a given (word, context) pair, based on the distance between word and context. In a rectangular window, this increment is always 1, regardless of distance. In a triangular window, the increment is inversely proportional to the distance between the word and the context: 1 if the distance is 1 word, $\frac{1}{2}$ if the distance is 2, and so forth. The window also has a direction: we can look left, right, or in both directions. In the latter case, we can sum the frequencies observed left and right of a given word, or encode these frequencies separately, in which case the matrix M contains two dimensions for each context word, one for each direction. These two types of windows are sometimes called left+right (L+R) and left&right (L&R).

We also assessed the influence of the weighting scheme. This is usually an association measure such as mutual information. We tested the 6 simple association measures defined in Evert's (2007, ch. 4) work on collocations. These measures compare the observed cooccurrence frequency (O) of two words to their expected cooccurrence frequency (E). For instance, (pointwise) mutual information is defined as $\text{MI} = \log_2\left(\frac{O}{E}\right)$. If O is much greater than E, this suggests a strong association between the two words. We use Evert's definitions for all these measures, but calculate E somewhat differently:

$$E(w_i, c_j) = \frac{\sum_{j'} M_{ij'} \sum_{i'} M_{i'j}}{\sum_{i'} \sum_{j'} M_{i'j'}}$$

where M is the unweighted cooccurrence frequency matrix. Negative association scores were always set to 0 (so MI becomes PPMI). A transformation (log or sqrt, where $\log(x) = \ln(x + 1)$ and $\text{sqrt}(x) = \sqrt{x}$) was applied to some of the association measures, following Lapesa et al. (2014), and based on our own preliminary experiments. We also tried applying a simple log transformation to the cooccurrence frequencies, without applying an association measure beforehand.

The settings we tested for each of the four parameters are:

- Type of context window: L+R or L&R.

- Size of context window: 1-10 words.

- Shape of context window: rectangular or triangular.

- Weighting scheme: log, MI, MI^2, MI^3, log(local-MI), log(simple-LL), sqrt(t-score), sqrt(z-score).

In the case of `word2vec`, we examined the five hyperparameters that have an important effect on performance according to the documentation of `word2vec`[10]. The architecture used to learn the word embeddings is one of these hyperparameters. We must also select a training algorithm: whatever the architecture, the model can be trained using a hierarchical softmax function, or by sampling negative examples (or classes), in which case we also have to choose the number of negative samples. `word2vec` also provides a function that subsamples frequent words, i.e. words whose relative frequency in the corpus is greater than some threshold. This function randomly deletes occurrences of these frequent words before the model is trained, each occurrence having a certain probability of being deleted, which depends on the word's frequency. The last two hyperparameters are the dimensionality of the word embeddings and the size of the context window. The settings we tested for each hyperparameter are:

---

[10]`https://code.google.com/p/word2vec/`

- Architecture: CBOW or skip-gram.

- Negative samples: 5, 10 or none (hierarchical softmax is used instead).

- Subsampling threshold: low (10^{-5}), high (10^{-3}) or none (no subsampling).

- Size of context window: 1-10 words.

- Dimensionality of word embeddings: 100 or 300.

A few more details regarding the training and evaluation of the two DSMs may be worth mentioning. In the case of the BOW model, the set of context words contained all the target words that were used for evaluation purposes. These target words (for both models) were the 10K most frequent words in the (lemmatized) corpus, excluding stop words and words that contained any character other than a letter, a digit or a hyphen. In the case of the BOW model, out-of-vocabulary words were not deleted, simply ignored, and the context window was allowed to span sentence boundaries. For word2vec, we used the word2vec software as is, using the default settings for all hyperparameters except those whose influence we investigated. It is also worth noting that the context window implemented in word2vec has a shape that gives more weight to contexts that are closer to a given word (similar to a triangular window) – this is implemented by drawing the effective window size for a given token uniformly between 1 and the size specified by the user (Levy et al., 2015).

The measure we used to evaluate the models is mean average precision[11] (MAP). This measure tells us how accurate the sorted list of neighbours we get for a given query is, based on the rank of its related terms according to the gold standard. The nearer the related terms are to the top of this list on average for each of the queries, the higher the MAP. The sorted list of neighbours is obtained by computing the similarity (or distance) between the query's vector and the vectors of all other target words. We use the cosine similarity (Salton and Lesk, 1968), which is the most commonly used measure for distributional similarity (Turney and Pantel, 2010). The sorted list of neighbours is then evaluated on the various datasets.

5   Results

First, we compare the BOW model and word2vec (W2V), by observing the MAP of each model on each of the datasets. The maximum MAP achieved by each model is shown in Table 2. These results show that the BOW model achieves a higher MAP than W2V on the three paradigmatic relations (QSYN, ANTI, and HYP) if its parameters are tuned correctly, but W2V achieves a much higher MAP on DRVs. In other words, the BOW model is better at estimating the semantic similarity of terms that have similar syntactic behaviours, whereas W2V is better at estimating the similarity of terms that have different syntactic behaviours, but the same meaning[12]. Furthermore, the BOW model produces a higher MAP than W2V on all three parts-of-speech (when only paradigmatic relations are considered) on average, though the best W2V model on verbs has a slightly higher MAP than the best BOW model. As for the sets of frame-evoking terms (SETS), W2V achieves a higher accuracy, but the BOW model performs slightly better on average.

Dataset	BOW	W2V
QSYN	**0.418** (0.321 ± 0.056)	0.396 (0.298 ± 0.042)
ANTI	**0.383** (0.247 ± 0.056)	0.321 (0.228 ± 0.039)
HYP	**0.252** (0.211 ± 0.017)	0.199 (0.153 ± 0.019)
DRV	0.458 (0.328 ± 0.080)	**0.544** (0.347 ± 0.118)
NN	**0.398** (0.329 ± 0.045)	0.373 (0.299 ± 0.034)
VV	0.326 (0.255 ± 0.048)	**0.329** (0.239 ± 0.046)
JJ	**0.501** (0.317 ± 0.086)	0.454 (0.274 ± 0.050)
SETS	0.326 (0.282 ± 0.026)	**0.348** (0.275 ± 0.031)

Table 2: Maximum MAP (with average and std. dev. in brackets) of BOW and W2V models on each dataset.

---

[11]See http://goo.gl/qdlQ7n.

[12]This may be due to the dimensionality reduction that occurs in the word2vec model.

If we compare the maximum MAP obtained on each of the datasets (by either BOW or W2V), we see that DSMs capture syntactic derivatives even more accurately than near-synonyms if the models are tuned for this relation. Antonyms are captured almost as accurately as synonyms, but the MAP obtained on hypernyms/hyponyms is quite a bit lower. As for the POS, DSMs model adjectives most accurately, followed by nouns, then verbs. The MAP achieved on the SETS is lower than on all the semantic relations except for hypernyms/hyponyms. This is due to at least two factors. First, the SETS contain a relatively high number of verbs, and as we have seen, verbs are the most challenging POS for these two DSMs. Second, the sets of frame-evoking terms represent a mixture of syntactic derivation and typical paradigmatic relations, especially synonymy, and although we achieve a high MAP on both of these relations, the (hyper)parameter settings that work best for each are very different, as we will show below.

Now that we have assessed the quality of the results with respect to various aspects of the target application (the descriptive framework, the target relations, the POS) and compared the two DSMs, we turn our attention to the influence of their (hyper)parameters. For each such parameter, we will observe the average MAP for each setting of that parameter. We use the average MAP instead of the maximum in order to determine which settings produce consistently good results, regardless of the settings used for the other parameters. Interactions between the parameters are not accounted for in the analysis presented in this paper.

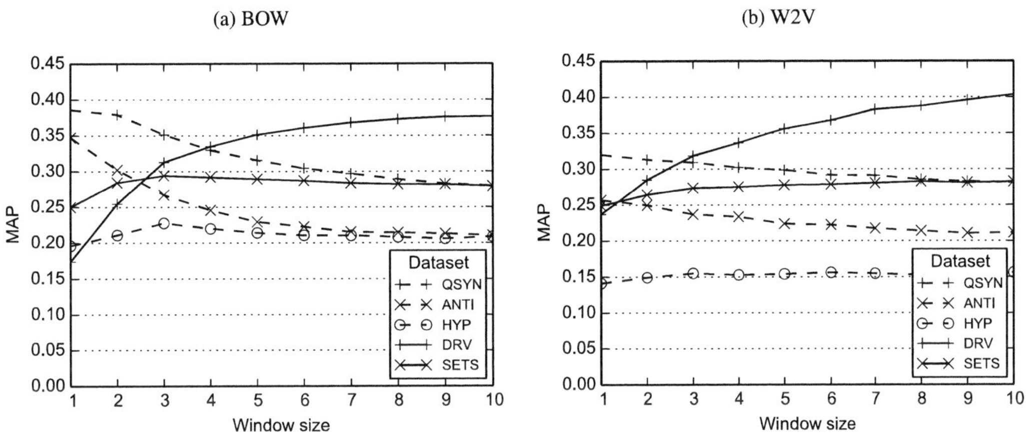

Figure 1: Average MAP of (a) BOW and (b) W2V models wrt window size.

The influence of the window size on the accuracy of both DSMs is illustrated in Figure 1. This figure shows that for the three paradigmatic relations (QSYN, ANTI, and HYP), the optimal window size is small, i.e. 1-3 words. Though the figure does not show the results for each POS separately, this is true for every POS. The optimal size is 1 for adjectives, and accuracy quickly drops off as window size increases. The optimal size is 1 for verbs also, and 1 or 3 for nouns (BOW and W2V respectively). On the other hand, the optimal window size for DRVs is quite large. The average MAP does not seem to have peaked even with a window size of 10, however the maximum MAP we observed was achieved with a window of 9 words (with both models). Thus, narrow windows capture paradigmatic relations most accurately, but wider windows are better for syntactic derivatives. This may be due to a tendency of syntactic derivatives to co-occur, as wider windows lead to co-occurring words having more similar distributional representations. For instance, if we observe the sequence of words a x y b, then a is a context of both x and y (if the window size is at least 2), and so is b. Every time x and y appear next to each other (or close enough, depending on the size of the window), they share contexts, which increases the similarity of their representations.

As for sets of frame-evoking terms, the window size should be at least 3, but the average MAP does not vary much with respect to window size beyond this point. As the window size increases, accuracy improves on DRVs, but worsens on paradigmatic relations, such that accuracy on the SETS, which represent a mixture of these relations, remains relatively stable.

The figure also shows that the influence of the window size is very similar in the BOW and W2V models. We could investigate whether this is the case for other (hyper)parameters that are applicable to both models (e.g. the window shape) or can be adapted from one model to the other (e.g. context distribution smoothing for the negative sampling function (Levy et al., 2015)). Instead of comparing the influence of the same parameters in both models, we chose to investigate the influence of a set of parameters that are typical of each model. Our observations on the influence of the window size suggest that the influence of parameters that are common to both DSMs would be very similar.

Parameter	Setting	QSYN	ANTI	HYP	DRV	NN	VV	JJ	SETS
Window	L&R	**0.332**	**0.257**	**0.213**	0.288	**0.336**	**0.266**	**0.334**	0.274
type	L+R	0.311	0.237	0.209	**0.368**	0.323	0.244	0.301	**0.291**
Window	Rectangular	0.297	0.223	0.209	**0.337**	0.310	0.233	0.282	0.273
shape	Triangular	**0.346**	**0.270**	**0.213**	0.320	**0.348**	**0.276**	**0.352**	**0.292**
	None	0.172	0.196	0.070	0.205	0.168	0.160	0.180	0.182
	log	0.266	0.211	0.201	0.304	0.272	0.206	0.277	0.258
	MI	0.321	0.239	0.212	**0.353**	0.338	0.254	0.303	0.283
	MI^2	0.308	0.238	**0.224**	0.292	0.315	0.243	0.309	0.264
Weighting	MI^3	0.300	0.232	0.215	0.302	0.304	0.235	0.306	0.271
scheme	log(local-MI)	0.348	0.258	0.210	0.343	0.353	0.277	0.337	0.294
	log(simple-LL)	**0.349**	0.261	0.209	0.347	**0.354**	**0.281**	0.339	**0.301**
	sqrt(t-score)	0.341	0.261	0.220	0.338	0.352	0.272	0.327	0.288
	sqrt(z-score)	0.338	**0.273**	0.198	0.345	0.345	0.270	**0.342**	0.300

Table 3: Average MAP of BOW models wrt to window type, window shape, and weighting scheme.

Table 3 shows the influence of the three other parameters of the BOW model: the type of window, its shape, and the weighting scheme. In the latter case, we added the results we would obtain without weighting the cooccurrence frequencies, in order to show the importance of using some kind of weighting scheme, but it is important to note that the unweighted models were not included in the rest of the analysis presented in this paper. Indeed, using some kind of weighting scheme always improves accuracy, even a simple log transformation, though the association measures almost always provide better results. Interestingly, MI (aka PPMI), which is likely the most common weighting scheme in this kind of DSM, is not among the best-performing schemes, except on one dataset: DRVs. MI is known to have a low-frequency bias (Evert, 2007, p. 19), which appears to be beneficial in the case of syntactic derivatives, whereas near-synonyms and antonyms are detected more accurately using measures which do not have this bias, such as simple-LL.

The shape of the window is another parameter whose optimal setting is different for syntactic derivatives than for other semantic relations. Whereas the triangular window works best for QSYNs and ANTIs, on average, DRVs are detected more accurately using a rectangular window. Since DRVs prefer a wider window, as we have already shown, it intuitively makes sense that they would prefer a rectangular window, as it gives more weight to long-distance contexts than a triangular window.

As for the window type, we again observe a difference between DRVs and other semantic relations. Indeed, the L+R works much better than the L&R window for DRVs, whereas the L&R provides better results for QSYNs and ANTIs, on average. We propose the following explanation. A pair of DRVs are likely to have some collocates in common, but these may appear on opposite sides of the two words (e.g. compare *to emit GHGs* and *GHG emissions*). If the cooccurrence frequencies for the left and right contexts are encoded separately, i.e. if we use a L&R window, the model may not adequately represent the fact that these words have similar collocates. This would explain why the L+R window works better for DRVs.

Hyperparameter	Setting	QSYN	ANTI	HYP	DRV	NN	VV	JJ	SETS
Architecture	skip-gram	0.287	0.226	**0.154**	**0.390**	0.293	0.225	0.266	**0.283**
	CBOW	**0.308**	**0.229**	0.152	0.304	**0.304**	**0.253**	**0.283**	0.266
Negative samples	None	0.284	0.227	0.150	0.333	0.284	0.226	0.274	0.266
	5	0.302	0.227	0.154	0.349	0.305	0.244	0.271	0.276
	10	**0.307**	**0.229**	**0.155**	**0.359**	**0.308**	**0.246**	**0.279**	**0.282**
Subsampling threshold	None	**0.323**	**0.258**	0.152	0.251	**0.316**	**0.267**	**0.307**	0.258
	Low	0.254	0.184	0.149	**0.457**	0.267	0.188	0.225	**0.285**
	High	0.316	0.242	**0.157**	0.334	0.313	0.261	0.291	0.282
Dimensionality	100	0.284	0.228	0.145	0.316	0.285	0.229	0.264	0.255
	300	**0.311**	0.228	**0.160**	**0.379**	**0.312**	**0.248**	**0.285**	**0.294**

Table 4: Average MAP of W2V models wrt the architecture, the number of negative samples for training, the threshold for subsampling and the dimensionality of word embeddings.

Thus, the influence of all four parameters that we have examined in the case of the BOW model is different for DRVs than for near-synonyms and other paradigmatic relations. In the case of W2V, three of the five hyperparameters considered in this study also exhibit such a difference. We have already shown that DRVs prefer wide context windows whereas narrow windows capture paradigmatic relations more accurately. Table 4 shows the influence of the four other hyperparameters. Regarding the neural network's architecture, CBOW works best, on average, for QSYNs, but skip-gram works best for DRVs. As for the subsampling function, it provides little or no gains on the three paradigmatic relations[13], but dramatically increases accuracy on DRVs, especially if the frequency threshold is low, which leads to a more "aggressive" subsampling. Inversely, aggressive subsampling results in quite a large drop in accuracy for QSYNs and ANTIs. Finally, the optimal settings for the dimensionality of the word embeddings and for the training algorithm are the same on all datasets: 300-dimensional embeddings perform better than 100-dimensional ones, and negative sampling works better than a hierarchical softmax, the MAP improving slightly if we use 10 samples rather than 5.

6 Concluding remarks

In this paper, we presented the results of a holistic approach to the evaluation of DSMs in the context of specialized lexicography. We investigated how both model-related and application-related factors affect the quality of the results produced by DSMs, and how they interact. By evaluating models on datasets representing different semantic relations, we showed that DSMs capture syntactic derivatives even better than typical paradigmatic relations such as synonymy, but that the model and (hyper)parameter settings that perform best for these two types of relations are very different. Our results also indicate that verbs are more challenging for DSMs than nouns and adjectives. Furthermore, we showed that the quality of the results depends on the descriptive framework used for the lexical resource being developed. Accuracy was lower on sets of frame-evoking terms than on every semantic relation we considered except hypernymy/hyponymy. This is due to at least two reasons. Sets of frame-evoking terms represent a mixture of syntactic derivation and typical paradigmatic relations such as synonymy, and since the best models for these two types of relations are very different, the ability of a single model to capture terms that evoke the same frame is limited. Furthermore, a high percentage of frame-evoking terms are verbs, which are challenging for DSMs.

Although we only presented the results obtained on English data in this paper, we also conducted this experiment on French data, and the results, a part of which we reported in another paper (Bernier-Colborne and Drouin, 2016b), are very similar.

---

[13]It is worth remembering that we only tested two values for the frequency threshold, these being the limits of the range of recommended values. Other settings might provide better results.

This work provides valuable guidelines for the use of DSMs for lexicographical purposes. It also provides new insights into the kind of semantic information that is captured by these models. Extensions of this work could include testing other DSMs, other (hyper)parameters, or other settings; and evaluating on different tasks or data from different domains. Based on the work presented in this paper, we investigated whether different DSMs could be combined in order to improve accuracy, and showed that combining the best BOW and W2V models increased the MAP on the sets of frame-evoking terms (Bernier-Colborne and Drouin, 2016a).

Acknowledgements

This work was supported by the Social Sciences and Humanities Research Council (SSHRC) of Canada.

References

Marco Baroni and Roberto Zamparelli. 2010. Nouns are vectors, adjectives are matrices: Representing adjective-noun constructions in semantic space. In *Proceedings of the 2010 Conference on Empirical Methods in Natural Language Processing (EMNLP)*, pages 1183–1193. ACL.

Marco Baroni, Georgiana Dinu, and Germán Kruszewski. 2014. Don't count, predict! A systematic comparison of context-counting vs. context-predicting semantic vectors. In *Proceedings of the 52nd Annual Meeting of the Association for Computational Linguistics*, volume 1, pages 238–247, Baltimore. ACL.

Gabriel Bernier-Colborne and Patrick Drouin. 2016a. Combiner des modèles sémantiques distributionnels pour mieux détecter les termes évoquant le même cadre sémantique [in French]. In *Proceedings the 23rd French Conference on Natural Language Processing (TALN)*, pages 381–388.

Gabriel Bernier-Colborne and Patrick Drouin. 2016b. Évaluation des modèles sémantiques distributionnels : le cas de la dérivation syntaxique [in French]. In *Proceedings the 23rd French Conference on Natural Language Processing (TALN)*, pages 125–138, Paris.

John A. Bullinaria and Joseph P. Levy. 2007. Extracting semantic representations from word co-occurrence statistics: A computational study. *Behavior research methods*, 39(3):510–526.

John A. Bullinaria and Joseph P. Levy. 2012. Extracting semantic representations from word co-occurrence statistics: stop-lists, stemming, and SVD. *Behavior research methods*, 44(3):890–907.

Stefan Evert. 2007. Corpora and collocations (extended manuscript). In Anke Lüdeling and Merja Kytö, editors, *Corpus Linguistics. An International Handbook*, volume 2. Walter de Gruyter, Berlin/New York. http://www.stefan-evert.de/PUB/Evert2007HSK_extended_manuscript.pdf.

Olivier Ferret. 2015. Réordonnancer des thésaurus distributionnels en combinant différents critères [in French]. *TAL*, 56(2):21–49.

Charles J. Fillmore. 1982. Frame semantics. In The Linguistic Society of Korea, editor, *Linguistics in the Morning Calm: Selected Papers from SICOL-1981*, pages 111–137. Hanshin Publishing Co., Seoul.

John Rupert Firth. 1957. A synopsis of linguistic theory 1930–1955. In The Philological Society, editor, *Studies in Linguistic Analysis*, pages 1–32. Blackwell, Oxford.

Kenneth E. Harper. 1965. Measurement of similarity between nouns. In *Proceedings of the 1965 Conference on Computational Linguistics (COLING)*, pages 1–23, Bonn. ACL.

Zellig S. Harris. 1954. Distributional structure. *Word*, 10(2–3):146–162.

Felix Hill, Roi Reichart, and Anna Korhonen. 2014. SimLex-999: Evaluating semantic models with (genuine) similarity estimation. *CoRR*, abs/1408.3456.

Douwe Kiela and Stephen Clark. 2014. A systematic study of semantic vector space model parameters. In *Proceedings of the 2nd Workshop on Continuous Vector Space Models and their Compositionality (CVSC) @ EACL 2014*, pages 21–30. ACL.

Gabriella Lapesa, Stefan Evert, and Sabine Schulte im Walde. 2014. Contrasting syntagmatic and paradigmatic relations: Insights from distributional semantic models. In *Proceedings of the Third Joint Conference on Lexical and Computational Semantics (*SEM 2014)*, pages 160–170, Dublin. ACL/DCU.

Omer Levy, Yoav Goldberg, and Ido Dagan. 2015. Improving distributional similarity with lessons learned from word embeddings. *Transactions of the Association for Computational Linguistics*, 3:211–225.

Marie-Claude L'Homme. 2004. A lexico-semantic approach to the structuring of terminology. In *Proceedings the 3rd International Workshop on Computational Terminology (CompuTerm)*, pages 7–14.

Kevin Lund, Curt Burgess, and Ruth Ann Atchley. 1995. Semantic and associative priming in high-dimensional semantic space. In *Proceedings of the 17th Annual Conference of the Cognitive Science Society*, pages 660–665.

Igor' Aleksandrovič Mel'čuk, André Clas, and Alain Polguère. 1995. *Introduction à la lexicologie explicative et combinatoire [in French]*. Duculot, Louvain-la-Neuve.

Tomas Mikolov, Kai Chen, Greg Corrado, and Jeffrey Dean. 2013a. Efficient estimation of word representations in vector space. In *Proceedings of Workshop at the International Conference on Learning Representations (ICLR)*.

Tomas Mikolov, Ilya Sutskever, Kai Chen, Greg Corrado, and Jeffrey Dean. 2013b. Distributed representations of words and phrases and their compositionality. In C.J.C. Burges, L. Bottou, M. Welling, Z. Ghahramani, and K.Q. Weinberger, editors, *Advances in Neural Information Processing Systems 26 (NIPS)*, pages 3111–3119. Curran Associates, Inc.

Jeff Mitchell and Mirella Lapata. 2008. Vector-based models of semantic composition. In *Proceedings of ACL-08: HLT*, pages 236–244.

Wolf Moskowich and Ruth Caplan. 1978. Distributive-statistical text analysis: A new tool for semantic and stylistic research. In G. Altmann, editor, *Glottometrika*, pages 107–153. Studienverlag Dr. N. Brockmeyer, Bochum.

Prokopis Prokopidis, Vassilis Papavassiliou, Antonio Toral, Marc Poch Riera, Francesca Frontini, Francesco Rubino, and Gregor Thurmair. 2012. Final report on the corpus acquisition & annotation subsystem and its components. Technical Report WP-4.5, PANACEA Project.

Magnus Sahlgren. 2006. *The word-space model: Using distributional analysis to represent syntagmatic and paradigmatic relations between words in high-dimensional vector spaces*. Ph.D. thesis, Stockholm University.

Gerard Salton and Michael E. Lesk. 1968. Computer evaluation of indexing and text processing. *Journal of the ACM*, 15(1):8–36.

Helmut Schmid. 1994. Probabilistic part-of-speech tagging using decision trees. In *Proceedings of the International Conference on New Methods in Language Processing*.

Hinrich Schütze. 1992. Dimensions of meaning. In *Proceedings of the 1992 ACM/IEEE Conference on Supercomputing (Supercomputing'92)*, pages 787–796.

Ludovic Tanguy, Franck Sajous, and Nabil Hathout. 2015. Évaluation sur mesure de modèles distributionnels sur un corpus spécialisé : comparaison des approches par contextes syntaxiques et par fenêtres graphiques [in French]. *TAL*, 56(2):103–127.

Peter D. Turney and Patrick Pantel. 2010. From frequency to meaning: Vector space models of semantics. *Journal of Artificial Intelligence Research*, 37(1):141–188.

Julie Weeds, David Weir, and Jeremy Reffin. 2014. Distributional composition using higher-order dependency vectors. In *Proceedings of the 2nd Workshop on Continuous Vector Space Models and their Compositionality (CVSC) @ EACL*, pages 11–20.

A Study on the Interplay Between the Corpus Size and Parameters of a Distributional Model for Term Classification

Behrang Q. Zadeh

Heinrich-Heine-Universität Düsseldorf

`zadeh@phil.hhu.de`

Abstract

We propose and evaluate a method for identifying co-hyponym lexical units in a terminological resource. The principles of term recognition and distributional semantics are combined to extract terms from a similar category of concept. Given a set of candidate terms, random projections are employed to represent them as low-dimensional vectors. These vectors are derived automatically from the frequency of the co-occurrences of the candidate terms and words that appear within windows of text in their proximity (context-windows). In a k-nearest neighbours framework, these vectors are classified using a small set of manually annotated terms which exemplify concept categories. We then investigate the interplay between the size of the corpus that is used for collecting the co-occurrences and a number of factors that play roles in the performance of the proposed method: the configuration of context-windows for collecting co-occurrences, the selection of neighbourhood size (k), and the choice of similarity metric.

1 Introduction

Automatic term recognition (ATR) deals with the extraction of domain-specific lexical units from text. The input of ATR is a large collection of documents, i.e., a *special corpus*,[1] and the output is a vocabulary that is used for communicating specialized knowledge (L'Homme, 2014). This vocabulary comprises a collection of single-token and multi-token lexical units—respectively known as *simple* and *complex* terms—that form a terminological resource. For example, in computational linguistics, *lexicon* and *parsing* are examples of simple terms, while *multilingual corpus* and *information extraction* are complex terms. Similarly, in molecular biology, *collagen* and *cortisol* are examples of simple terms, and *I kappa B* and *plasma prednisolone* are examples of complex terms.

Terms, extracted by an ATR system, represent a broad spectrum of concepts that exist in a domain knowledge. Terms and their corresponding concepts, however, can be further organized in several categories to form a taxonomy; each category characterizes a group of terms from 'similar' concepts in the domain of study (Figure 1). For example, in computational linguistics, the terms *lexicon* and *multilingual corpus* can be categorized under the category of *language resources*, while *parsing* and *information extraction* can be categorized under the concept of *technologies*. Likewise, in molecular biology, instances such as *collagen* and *I kappa B* are categorized as *proteins*, while *cortisol* and *plasma prednisolone* are classified as *lipid substances*.

If the concept categories are not known, a method is used to suggest an organization for terms (e.g., Dupuch et al. (2014); Cederberg and Widdows (2003)). However, concept categories are usually known, or at least, a partial knowledge of them exists. In these scenarios, typically a manually annotated corpus is employed to develop an entity tagger in a supervised fashion, often in the form of a sequence classifier. Bio-entity tagging is an established example of this kind of tasks (Nobata et al., 1999). These methods, however, rely heavily on manually annotated corpora, in which each mention of a term and its concept-

---

[1]Following the terminology proposed by Sinclair (1996), we use the term special corpus; that is, a corpus containing sublanguage material.

Proceedings of the 5th International Workshop on Computational Terminology,
pages 62–72, Osaka, Japan, December 12 2016.

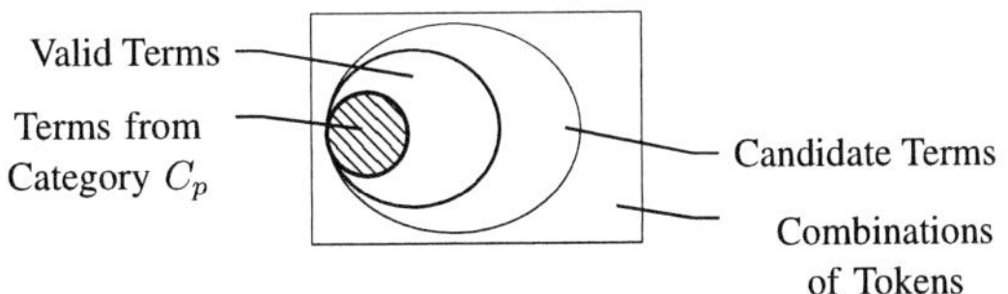

Figure 1: Venn diagram that illustrates the relationship between candidate terms, valid terms, and a particular category of terms C_p. ATR targets the extraction of candidate terms and the identification of valid terms. However, term classification targets the identification of terms that belong to a concepts-category, i.e., a subset of valid terms.

category must be annotated. Provided that enough training data is available, a reasonable performance can be attained in these recognition tasks (Kim et al., 2004).

Yet in several scenarios, the targeted concept categories (similar to entity recognition tasks) are known but no manual annotation is available for the training and development of an entity tagger. This is a familiar problem when a terminological resource with a hierarchical structure must be constructed from scratch, a task with many practical applications (see e.g. Chakraborty et al. (2014)) and renewed interests, e.g., as addressed in *cold-start knowledge base population* (Ellis et al., 2012; Mayfield et al., 2014) and ontology learning. Similarly, this problem surfaces in maintaining terminologies, where constant update and extension is required to accommodate new vocabularies and their usages (Habert et al., 1998).

This paper suggests a method to address this situation: the extraction of terms from a particular class of concepts in the absence of training data for the development of an entity tagger. The proposed method (similar to ATR and in contrast to entity recognition task) works at the corpus level and does not deal with individual term mentions. However, in contrast to ATR (which extracts terms from diverse concept categories in a specific domain knowledge) and similar to entity tagging, the proposed method is designed to extract a subset of terms that belongs to a particular category of concepts in a domain knowledge (i.e., *co-hyponym* terms). Note that each category can be further organised into more refined subcategories to provide abstractions at different levels of granularity. Since co-hyponymy is an inheritable relationship, terms under each category, disregarding the subcategory that they belong to, are still co-hyponym.

Since polysemy is less frequent in specialized vocabularies than in general vocabularies, the proposed approach is effective and useful. We support this claim with a comparison between the proportion of polysemous entries in WordNet (Miller, 1995), i.e., a general vocabulary, and the terminological resource that is induced from the annotated terms in the GENIA corpus (Kim et al., 2003). In WordNet, approximately 17% of entries are polysemous. The GENIA corpus (which is a well-known special corpus in the domain of molecular biology) provides manual concept-category annotations for 92,722 term mentions. These term mentions constitute a vocabulary of 34,077 distinct entries, of which only 1,373 are polysemous (i.e., their individual mentions are annotated with at least two concept categories). Therefore, compared to WordNet, the GENIA terminological resource contains only a small fraction of polysemous entries, i.e., $\frac{1372}{34077} = 4\%$.[2]

The proposed term classification method is realized as an ad hoc term-weighting procedure on top of an ATR system. ATR typically comprises a two-step procedure: candidate term extraction followed by term weighting and ranking (Nakagawa and Mori, 2002). Candidate term extraction deals with term formation and the extraction of candidate terms (Ananiadou, 1994). Following the extraction of candidate terms, as stated byKageura and Umino (1996), an ATR system often combines scores that are known as *unithood* and *termhood* to weight terms. Unithood indicates the degree to which a sequence of tokens can be combined to form a complex term. It characterizes syntagmatic relations between tokens to identify collocations (therefore is only defined for complex terms). Termhood, however, "is the degree that a linguistic unit is related to $\cdots$ some domain-specific concepts" (Kageura and Umino, 1996). Hence, termhood is defined for both simple and complex terms. From a linguistic perspective, termhood char-

---

[2]This comparison can be biased since WordNet has been designed and developed to provide a comprehensive picture of words and their meanings. Therefore, the proportion of polysemous words in a reference corpus (as defined in Sinclair (1996)) can be less than %17. Still, we maintain polysemy is far more frequent in reference corpora than in special corpora.

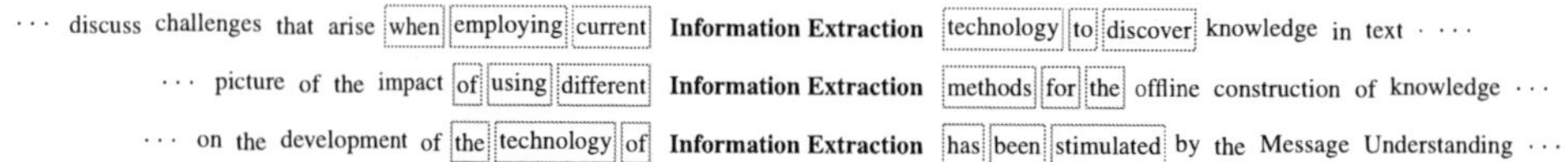

Figure 2: Shown a context-window of size 3 tokens that extend around terms: the occurrences of the candidate term *information extraction* in different sentences of a corpus. For each occurrence of the candidate term in each line, the context-window consists of words that are placed in rectangles. To construct a model, these co-occurrences are collected, counted, and represented by a vector.

acterizes an associative relationship between terms and the communicative context that verbalizes their meaning (in this scenario, the corpus). The major difference between the proposed term classification technique and a general ATR system is, therefore, the way they define termhood.

To actualize the proposed term classification task, a termhood measure that can identify co-hyponym terms must be devised. To achieve this goal, we take a distributional approach. We assume that the association of a term to a concept category is a kind of relation that can be modelled using the syntagmatic relation of the term and its co-occurred words in context-windows extended in the vicinity of the term's mentions in the corpus (Figure 2). We, therefore, hypothesise that co-hyponym terms tend to have similar distributional properties in these context-windows. Note that a similar hypothesis has been employed in many other distributional techniques for terminology extraction. In order to quantify these distributional similarities, vector space models are employed (Turney and Pantel, 2010).

Words that appear in context-windows are represented by the elements of the standard basis of a vector space (i.e., informally each dimension of a vector space) and each candidate term is represented by a vector. In this vector space, the co-occurrence frequency of words and candidate term in context-windows determines the coordinates of the vector that represent the candidate term. Hence, the values assigned to the the vector's coordinates represent the correlation between the candidate term that the vector represents and the words in context-windows. Consequently, we can use the proximity of candidate terms to compare their distributional similarities in this *term-space model*.

In this term-space model, we model a category of terms using a set of *reference terms* (shown by R_s), i.e., a small number of terms that are manually annotated with their corresponding concept category. The averaged distance between vectors that represent candidate terms and the vectors that represent R_s is assumed to determine the association of candidate terms to the concept categories represented by R_s. This association is computed using a k-nearest neighbours (k-nn) method. As explained by Daelemans and Van Den Bosch (2010), the memory-based k-nn technique provides us with a *similarity-based reasoning framework* that can be used to identify term categories without the need for formulating these associations using a meta-language such as rules.

Like other distributional methods, finding a configuration of context-windows (i.e., the way co-occurrence frequencies are collected) that best characterizes co-hyponym terms is a major research concern that must be investigated empirically. Context-windows can be configured differently regarding the position of the candidate terms in them and the direction in which they are stretched. They can be expanded (a) only to the left side of a candidate term to collect the co-occurrences of the candidate term with preceding words in each sentence of the corpus, (b) to the right side to collect co-occurrences with the succeeding words, or (c) around the candidate term, i.e., in both left and right directions. The size of context-windows must also be decided, i.e., the extent of the region on either side of a term for collecting and counting its co-occurrences with neighbouring words. In addition, information about the order of words in context-windows can be ignored or encoded in the constructed distributional model.

Independent of the configuration of context-windows in the proposed method, due to the *Zipfian distribution* of terms and words in context-windows, vectors that represent candidate terms are inevitably high-dimensional and sparse (i.e., most of the elements of vectors are zero). The high-dimensionality of vectors hinders the computation of similarities, and their sparseness is likely to diminish the discriminatory power of the constructed model (i.e., the *curse of dimensionality* problem). To avoid these problems, a dimensionality reduction technique is employed to reduce the dimension of vectors to a certain size.

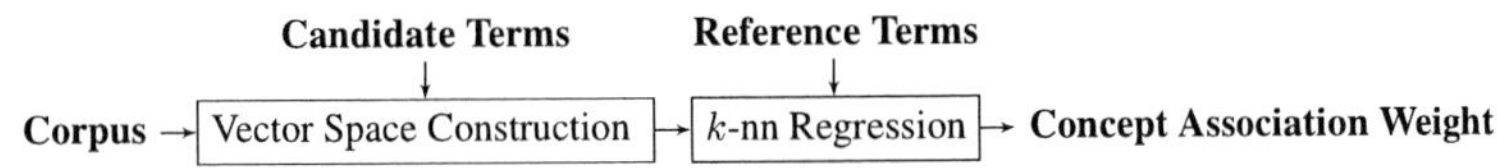

Figure 3: Method of measuring the candidate terms' association to a concept category.

Now that the vectors' dimension is set to a constant size, it is hypothesised that enlarging the size of the corpus reduces the number of zero elements in the vectors, and thus, the performance of the distributional model improves (e.g., as proposed for general language in Bullinaria and Levy (2007), Pantel et al. (2009)and Gorman and Curran (2006)). In this paper, we investigate the interplay between the size of the corpus and choosing the most discriminating configuration for context-windows in the proposed term classification task. We are interested to know (a) whether increasing the size of the corpus that is used for collecting co-occurrence frequencies enhances the performance of the classification task and (b) how doing so influences the choices that are made for configuring context-windows. Section 2 delineates the employed method. Section 3 describes the evaluation materials and framework. Results are reported in Section 4, followed by a conclusion in Section 5.

2 Method

Figure 3 illustrates the method. It is assumed that an ATR system extracts a list of candidate terms and, perhaps, ranks them by its own weighting mechanism. The extracted list of candidate terms is then processed for the construction of a vector space by scanning an input corpus. We assume that a small number of these candidate terms, e.g., 100, are annotated with their concept categories. Vectors that represent these annotated terms form a set of reference vectors R_s. In the constructed vector space, using a k-nn regression algorithm, R_s is employed to assign a concept-association weight c_w to the remaining candidate terms.

Accordingly, for a given candidate term that is represented by the vector $\vec{v}$, c_w is computed using

$$c_w(\vec{v}) = \sum_{i=1}^{k} s(\vec{v}, \vec{r_i})\delta(\vec{r_i}), \tag{1}$$

where $s(\vec{v}, \vec{r})$ denotes similarity between $\vec{v}$ and $\vec{r} \in R_s$, in which R_s is sorted by $s(\vec{v}, \vec{r})$ in descending order. If $\vec{r}$ represents a term from the targeted category of concepts, then $\delta(\vec{r}) = 1$, otherwise $\delta(\vec{r}) = 0$. While s can be defined in a number of ways, we employ three widely used definitions:

- $s(\vec{v}, \vec{r}) = \cos(\vec{v}, \vec{r})$, i.e., the cosine of the angles between $\vec{v}$ and $\vec{r}$;
- $s(\vec{v}, \vec{r}) = \frac{1}{1+\ell_2}$, where ℓ_2 is the Euclidean distance between $\vec{v}$ and $\vec{r}$; and
- $s(\vec{v}, \vec{r}) = \frac{1}{1+\ell_1}$, where ℓ_1 is the City block distance between $\vec{v}$ and $\vec{r}$.

Vector space construction is performed using *sparse stable random projections* (Li, 2007), which is implemented in the form of a sequential algorithm. Each candidate term is assigned to an m-dimensional *term vector $\vec{t}$*. Term vectors are initially empty, i.e., all the elements of $\vec{t}$ are set to zero. The input corpus is then scanned for the occurrences of candidate terms and finding their co-occurring words in context-windows (e.g., see Figure 2). Each of these words is assigned exactly to one *word vector $\vec{w}$*. Similar to term vectors, word vectors are also m-dimensional. However, the elements w_j of each $\vec{w}$ are instantiated with random values with the following distributions:

$$w_j = \begin{cases} \lfloor \frac{-1}{U_1} \rfloor & \text{with probability } \frac{1}{2\alpha} \\ 0 & \text{with probability } 1 - \frac{1}{\alpha} \\ \lfloor \frac{1}{U_2} \rfloor & \text{with probability } \frac{1}{2\alpha} \end{cases} . \tag{2}$$

Once a $\vec{w}$ is generated and assigned to a word, it is stored and kept for later usages.

If the similarity between $\vec{v}$ and $\vec{r}$ is measured using the cosine or Euclidean distance (i.e., in an ℓ_2-normed space), then U_1 and U_2 are set to 1 and $\alpha = O(\sqrt{|\vec{w}|})$, where $|\vec{w}|$ is the number of word vectors.

T_{Mention}	P_{Mention}	T_{Distinct}	P_{Distinct}	T_{Polysemy}	P_{Polysemy}
92,722	34,264	34,077	8,900	1,373	403

Table 1: Statistics of the terminological resource: terms and 'protein terms' are respectively abbreviated by T and P (note $P \subset T$).

In this case, $\vec{w}$ vectors resemble a random projection matrix with asymptotic Gaussian distribution. However, if the similarities are measured using the city block distance (i.e., in an ℓ_1-normed space), then U_1 and U_2 are two independent uniform random variables in $(0, 1)$ and $\alpha = \mathrm{O}(\sqrt{|\vec{w}|}/100)$, where $|\vec{w}|$ is the number of word vectors and the constant factor 0.01 is an approximation of the sparsity of term-word co-occurrences in the corpus. In this case, $\vec{w}$ vectors resemble a random projection matrix with a asymptotic Cauchy distribution. Since $|\vec{w}|$ is very large, α is also relatively large; thus, the generated word vectors are highly sparse, i.e., most elements of $\vec{w}$ are set to zero and only a few have a non-zero value. To capture the co-occurrence of a candidate term and a word, the term vector $\vec{v}$ that represents the candidate term is accumulated by the word vector $\vec{w}$ that represents the word—i.e., $\vec{v} = \vec{v} + \vec{w}$. This procedure is repeated to capture all the co-occurrences of candidate terms and words that appear in context-windows in the input corpus. The result is a vector space that reflects the observed co-occurrences of terms and words at the reduced dimension m.

Subsequent to the construction of a vector space using the method described above, the distances/similarities between vectors are computed. In the ℓ_2-normed constructed vector spaces, for the given two m-dimensional vectors $\vec{v}$ and $\vec{u}$, the cosine between them is calculated using: $cos(\vec{v}, \vec{u}) = \frac{\sum_{i=1}^{m} v_i \times u_i}{\sum_{i=1}^{m} v_i^2 \times \sum_{i=1}^{m} u_i^2}$. Similarly, the Euclidean distance is given by $d_2(\vec{v}, \vec{u}) = \sqrt{\sum_{i=1}^{m} (v_i - u_i)^2}$. In the ℓ_2-normed spaces, therefore, the proposed method is equivalent to the random indexing technique (Sahlgren, 2005; QasemiZadeh and Handschuh, 2015). In the ℓ_1-normed spaces, the city block distance, however, is computed using the non-linear estimator

$$d_1(\vec{v}, \vec{u}) = \sum_{i=1, v_i \neq u_i}^{m} \ln(|v_i - u_i|).$$

In this case, the method is equivalent to the one proposed by Zadeh and Handschuh (2014). Once computed, these similarity measures are used to weight candidate terms according to Equation 1.

3 Evaluation Materials and Parameters

The proposed method is evaluated using the GENIA terminological resource. Manually annotated term mentions from the GENIA corpus (Version 3.02) are collected to build a terminological resource. This resource's entries are distinct pairs of lexical units and their annotations. The annotations are employed to organize terms in a taxonomy similar to the one proposed by Kim et al. (2004) for evaluating bio-entity taggers. To keep the reports to a manageable size, we limit the evaluation task to the identification of terms belonging to the category of *proteins* (see Table 1).

Using the the obtained frequencies in the GENIA corps and c-value measure (i.e., a widely used method for ranking terms in ATR systems (Frantzi et al., 1998)) terms are ranked in a list. From this sorted list, the top 100 terms and their annotations are used to form a set of reference vectors (R_s). Consequently, in our evaluations, R_s contains 36 *protein* terms: terms that are annotated as co-hyponyms under the concept category of 'protein' from the GENIA Ontology. Figure 4 shows the distribution of protein terms in the obtained sorted list of terms using the c-value measure with respect to a random baseline. Except for a small number of terms at the top of the list, the proportion of protein terms in the c-value sorted list is similar to the random baseline. We use the c-value ranking as one baseline in our evaluations.

To show that R_s is not sufficient for developing an entity tagger, we verify the performance of a bio-entity tagger when the employed R_s is used for its training. Namely, we employ the ABNER system, an entity tagger designed for analysing biology text (Settles, 2005). It uses conditional random fields

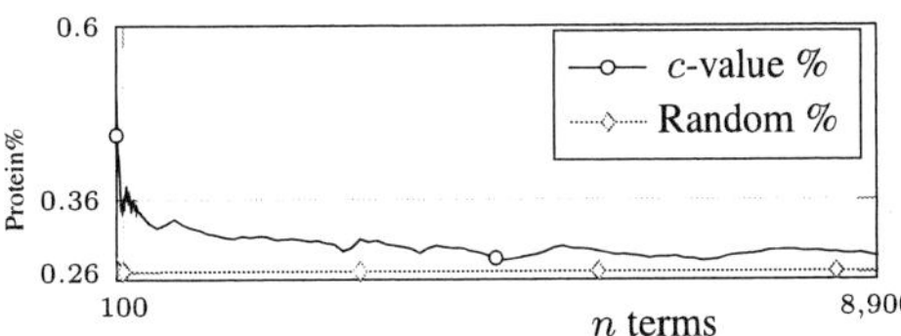

Figure 4: Proportion of protein terms in the top 8,900 terms, from lists of candidate terms sorted by the c-value measure and randomly.

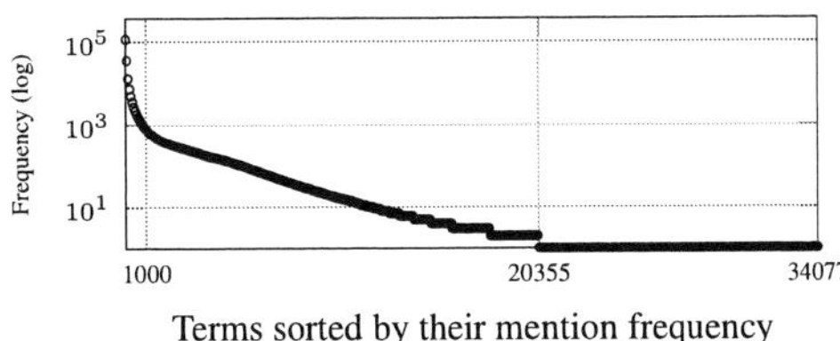

Figure 5: The frequency of terms in G_e.

and a variety of orthographic and contextual features to perform its task. If ABNER is trained using all the provided annotations for protein term mentions in the GENIA corpus, it achieves a reasonable performance (recall of 77.8 and precision of 68.1). However, if it is trained using the mentions of terms in R_s, the resulting model can only identify an additional 16 protein terms out of the remaining 8,864 terms. Put simply, the 1,321 mentions of the 36 protein terms in R_s are not sufficient to train ABNER.

Initially, we will construct vector spaces using the raw text from the GENIA corpus. Besides normalising text to lower-case letters and a simple Penn Treebank tokenisation, no other text pre-processing is performed. This pre-processing results in 490,941 tokens and a vocabulary size of 19,576. We then enlarge the corpus by fetching 223,316 abstracts from the PubMed repository, of which each abstract contains at least three of the terms in the terminological resource. The enlarged corpus has more than 55 million tokens and a vocabulary of size 881,040. Hereafter, we denote these two corpora by G_o (for the original GENIA corpus) and G_e (for the enlarged corpus). In this corpus, the terms employed in our experiments are mentioned more than 9 million times. As expected, only a small number of terms are frequent and the majority of terms are mentioned a few times. A large number of terms (i.e., about 40%) never appear in G_e (see Figure 5).

Using the method explained in Section 2, we use these two corpora to collect the co-occurrences and build vector space models. We perform our experiments with vector spaces that are constructed at the reduced dimension $m = 2000$. Considering the number of term vectors in the model (i.e., 34077), $m = 2000$ is a conservative choice that guarantees a small distortion in pair-wise distances between vectors. Similarly, because the vocabulary size $|\vec{w}| \geq 19576$, we use word vectors of 6 non-zero elements and 30 non-zero elements, respectively, for the construction ℓ_2 and ℓ_1-normed spaces. These values for the numbers of non-zero elements in word vectors are conservative choices that meet the criteria specified in Section 2 for the value of α in Equation 2.

The construction of vector spaces is carried out by collecting co-occurrence frequencies in context-windows that are configured differently regarding the direction and size in which they are stretched. Moreover, we investigate the influence of the inclusion of word order information in the model using the permutation technique described in Sahlgren et al. (2008). As suggested in research reports (see, e.g., Baroni et al. (2014) and Agirre et al. (2009)), narrow context-windows are more suitable to capture paradigmatic relations such as the one intended in this paper. Accordingly, we report the performance of the method for context-windows of $1 \leq \text{size} \leq 8$ tokens, for three directions of around (hereafter, denoted by A), only to the left (denoted by L), or to the right (denoted by R) of candidate terms. In addition, we construct vector spaces that encode information about the order of words in these context-windows. Hence, for each input corpus, 48 vector spaces are constructed to reflect each of the possible

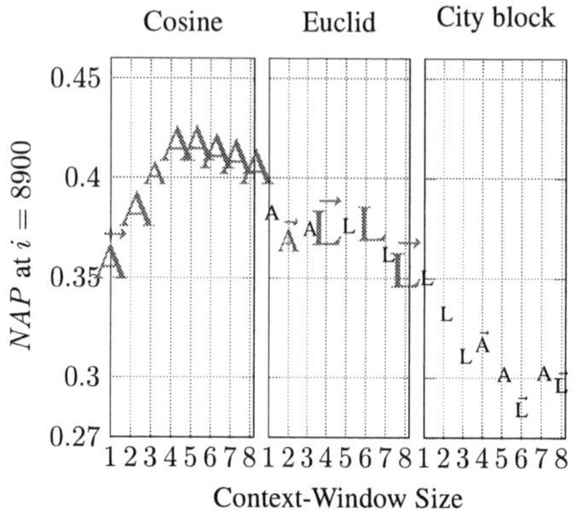
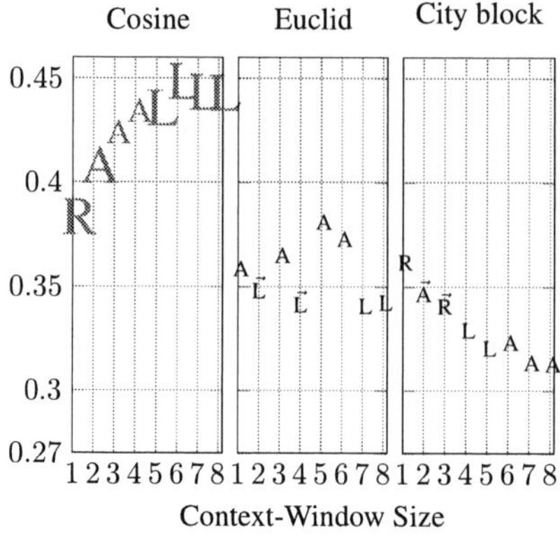

(a) Obtained performances from G_o (b) Obtained performances from G_e

Figure 6: The y-axis shows the observed NAP_i for $i = 8{,}900$ (i.e., recall 100%). For each of the employed similarity measures, the x-axis shows the size of context windows. The letters A, L, and R denote the direction in which context-windows are stretched (i.e., respectively, Around, Left, or Right side of the candidate terms). Models that encode word order information are denoted using the $\vec{\Box}$ on top. The size of letters, however, shows the value of k. The smallest size denotes $k = 1$ (black colour), while the largest size denotes $k = 25$ (grey colour); the medium size represents $k = 7$ (blue colour). In these experiments, the computed NAP over c-value ranked terms (i.e., the baseline) is 0.27. For the sake of readability, for each configuration of context-windows size and the employed similarity metric, we plot only the best observed results (complete plots are provided as supplementary materials).

configurations of context-windows, listed above.

The performance of the proposed k-nn technique is affected by the value of k. In the absence of a large training dataset, in the employed memory-based learning framework, a small value for k may lead to over-fitting and sensitivity to noise, while a large neighborhood estimation may reduce the discriminatory power of the classifier. Therefore, we report the performance of the method for three values of neighborhood size, i.e., $k \in \{1, 7, 25\}$. As stated earlier, term weighting in Equation 1 is performed by the help of three different measures: the cosine similarity, the Euclidean, and the city block distance.

4 Results

Following Schone and Jurafsky (2001), performance is measured and reported using the non-interpolated average precision at i:

$$NAP_i = \frac{1}{i} \sum_{n=1}^{i} P^n,$$

where P^n is the observed precision for extracting n protein terms. Figure 6 plots the performances that are measured by computing NAP at $i = 8900$ (i.e., 100% recall) in the obtained sets of terms that are ranked by the computed w_a (one for each of the constructed models). Independently of the size of the input corpus, the cosine similarity outperforms the Euclidean and city block distance. When the co-occurrence frequencies are collected from G_o, the best performance is obtained by using $k = 25$, in models that are built by collecting co-occurrence frequencies in context-windows of size 4 or 5 words that extend around terms. However, in experiments performed over G_e, using context-windows that expand to the left side of the candidate terms slightly outperform models that are built using context-windows that expand around the terms. As shown in Figure 6, encoding the word order information in context-windows often does not improve the performance.

Figure 7 plots the changes that are observed by enlarging the size of the input corpus. As shown, when the corpus size increases, the type of employed similarity measure plays an important role in determining the changes in the performances. When w_a weight are calculated using the cosine similarity,

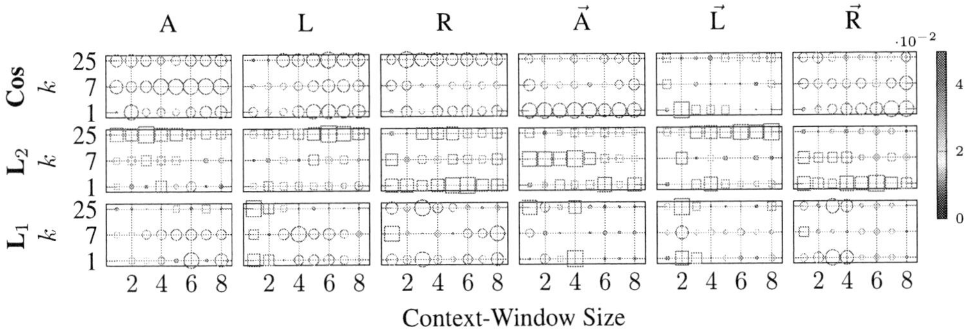

Figure 7: Changes in the performance of models caused by increasing the size of the input corps: the absolute value of the difference between the performance of a model constructed in G_e and G_o are shown. Squares denote negative impacts, while circles show improvements. The size/colour of shapes represents the amount of changes. The x-axis shows various configurations of context-windows (i.e., size, direction, and encoding word order information). The y-axis, however, represents classification parameters (i.e., the values of k and the employed measures for calculating similarities). For instance, when using the cosine similarity for classification in models constructed using context-windows that extend to the Left side of terms, size $= 6$ and $k = 25$, the performance in G_e is 0.448; the same parameters and configuration in G_o gives the performance of 0.40. This increase in the performance is shown by a wide circle in the plot.

enlarging the size of the corpus enhances the performance. Similarly, the city block distance shows a relatively better performance with larger input corpus. However, when similarities are measured using the Euclidean distance, an increase in the size of the corpus can drastically decline the performance. Using additional text, therefore, *does not guarantee* an improvement in the performance.

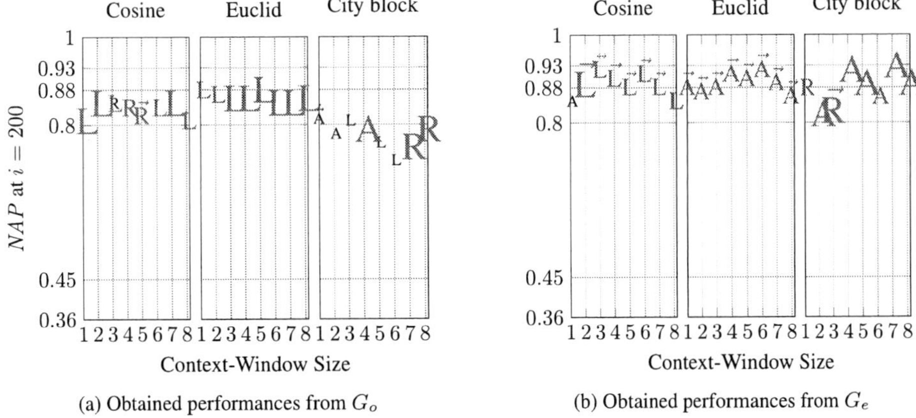

(a) Obtained performances from G_o

(b) Obtained performances from G_e

Figure 8: The observed performances when using NAP_i at $i = 200$ (i.e., approximately 2% recall). A notation similar to Figure 6 represents the results. In this plot, the minimum value of y-axis, i.e., 0.36, is the computed $NAP_{i=200}$ from the set of c-value ranked candidate terms (i.e., the baseline).

Figures 6 and 7 examine the method's performance for a large recall value. However, in a number of applications, we may be interested only in a small number of terms at the top of these ranked set of terms. Figures 8 and 9, similar to Figures 6 and 7, show the method's performance, however, when it is measured using NAP at $i = 200$ (i.e., for a small recall). In this case, increasing the size of the corpus can enhance or diminish the performance by 20%. Again, compared to the cosine and the city block distance, the Euclidean distance is more susceptible to changes in the corpus size. Specifically, for $k = 1$, the performance frequently drops when the corpus is enlarged.

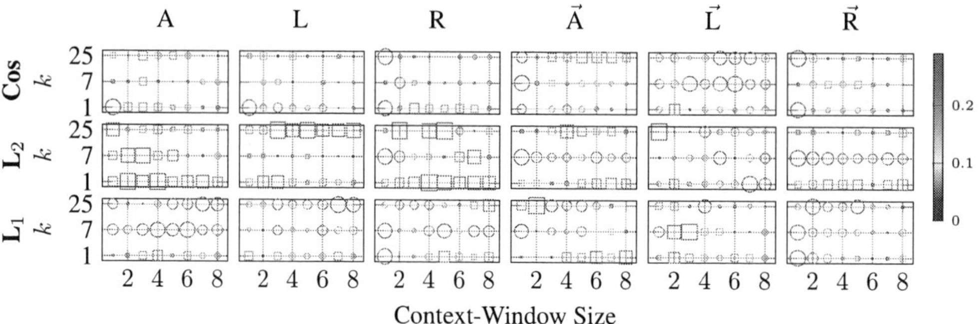

Figure 9: Differences in the performance based on the computed NAP at $i = 200$. The notation is similar to Figure 7.

5   Discussion

We investigated the use of a distributional method for finding co-hyponym terms using a memory-based classification technique. The method is useful when sufficient training data for developing an entity tagger is not available, e.g., when building a terminological resource with a taxonomic structure from scratch. Stable sparse random projections are employed to construct vector spaces directly at a reduced dimensionality. The models are then evaluated for term classification using a k-nn regression framework. We investigated the interplay between the size of the corpus that is used for the construction of the models, the configuration of context-windows (i.e., the way co-occurrence frequencies are collected), and metrics that are employed to measure similarity between vectors.

Our experiments showed that increasing the size of the input corpus for collecting co-occurrence frequencies can improve the performance of the proposed method if suitable configurations of context-windows and similarity metrics are used. We witnessed that the top performer parameters in the original corpus of a small size were not necessarily the top performers when the corpus size increases. In addition, we noticed that choosing the best performing parameters largely depends on the criteria set for the performance assessment. For instance, the city block distance showed a poor performance when the method is assessed at the 100% recall. However, at a small recall point, the city block showed a better performance than other metrics. These observations can perhaps justify a number of contradictory reports in the literature on the effect of the corpus size in the performance of distributional models.

On average, compared to the Euclidean and city block distance, cosine showed a better performance and a more positive and stable response to the increases in the size of the input corpus. This result can be expected intuitively, since cosine shows the degree of commonality between the elements of two vectors. Accordingly, we expect that the reported results can be improved further if, instead of normed-based metrics, a correlation coefficient measure is employed for computing similarities between vectors. Last but not least, a number of influential factors in the obtained results (e.g., the role of R_s and its size, the effect of using linguistic information or indirect co-occurrences) remained unexplored. The entries in specialized vocabularies are rare and less frequent than general vocabularies. For example, a handful of terms in the GENIA corpus (e.g., the term *physiologic cell lineage*) are so rare that they have appeared only once in the abstracts that are pulled out from the PubMed. It is interesting to design an experiment to study the reciprocal between the size of the corpus and the method's performance for the extraction of rare terms. The use of random projection matrix with standard distributions limits the use of common smoothing techniques such as the pointwise mutual information. These can be examined in future work.

Acknowledgments

We would like to thank reviewers for their constructive comments and criticisms. The author of this paper is funded by the Deutsche Forschungsgemeinschaft (DFG) through the 'Collaborative Research Centre 991 (CRC 991): The Structure of Representations in Language, Cognition, and Science'.

References

Eneko Agirre, Enrique Alfonseca, Keith Hall, Jana Kravalova, Marius Paşca, and Aitor Soroa. 2009. A study on similarity and relatedness using distributional and wordnet-based approaches. In *Proceedings of Human Language Technologies: The 2009 Annual Conference of the North American Chapter of the Association for Computational Linguistics*, NAACL '09, pages 19–27, Stroudsburg, PA, USA. ACL.

Sophia Ananiadou. 1994. A methodology for automatic term recognition. In *Proceedings of the 15th conference on Computational linguistics - Volume 2*, COLING '94, pages 1034–1038, Stroudsburg, PA, USA. Association for Computational Linguistics.

Marco Baroni, Georgiana Dinu, and Germán Kruszewski. 2014. Don't count, predict! a systematic comparison of context-counting vs. context-predicting semantic vectors. In *Proceedings of the 52nd Annual Meeting of the Association for Computational Linguistics (Volume 1: Long Papers)*, pages 238–247. Association for Computational Linguistics.

John A. Bullinaria and Joseph P. Levy. 2007. Extracting semantic representations from word co-occurrence statistics: A computational study. *Behavior Research Methods*, 39:510–526.

Scott Cederberg and Dominic Widdows. 2003. Using lsa and noun coordination information to improve the precision and recall of automatic hyponymy extraction. In *Proceedings of the Seventh Conference on Natural Language Learning at HLT-NAACL 2003 - Volume 4*, CONLL '03, pages 111–118, Stroudsburg, PA, USA. Association for Computational Linguistics.

Sunandan Chakraborty, Lakshminarayanan Subramanian, and Yaw Nyarko. 2014. Extraction of (key,value) pairs from unstructured ads. In *AAAI Fall Symposium Serie*.

Walter Daelemans and Antal Van Den Bosch, 2010. pages 154–179. Wiley-Blackwell.

Marie Dupuch, Laëtitia Dupuch, Thierry Hamon, and Natalia Grabar. 2014. Exploitation of semantic methods to cluster pharmacovigilance terms. *J. Biomedical Semantics*, 5:18.

Joe Ellis, Xuansong Li, Kira Griffitt, Stephanie M. Strassel, and Jonathan Wright. 2012. Linguistic resources for 2012 knowledge base population evaluations. In *Text Analysis Conference (TAC)*.

KaterinaT. Frantzi, Sophia Ananiadou, and Junichi Tsujii. 1998. The c-value/nc-value method of automatic recognition for multi-word terms. In *Research and Advanced Technology for Digital Libraries*, volume 1513 of *Lecture Notes in Computer Science*, pages 585–604. Springer Berlin Heidelberg.

James Gorman and James R. Curran. 2006. Scaling distributional similarity to large corpora. In *Proceedings of the 21st International Conference on Computational Linguistics and the 44th Annual Meeting of the Association for Computational Linguistics*, ACL-44, pages 361–368, Stroudsburg, PA, USA. Association for Computational Linguistics.

Benoit Habert, Adeline Nazarenko, Pierre Zweigenbaum, and Jacques Bouaud. 1998. Extending an existing specialized semantic lexicon. In Antonio Rubio, Navidad Gallardo, Rosa Castro, and Antonio Tejada, editors, *Proceedings First International Conference on Language Resources and Evaluation*, pages 663–668, Granada, may.

Kyo Kageura and Bin Umino. 1996. Methods of automatic term recognition: A review. *Terminology*, 3.2 (1996):259–289.

J. . D. Kim, T. Ohta, Y. Tateisi, and J. Tsujii. 2003. Genia corpus—a semantically annotated corpus for bio-textmining. *Bioinformatics*, 19(suppl 1):i180–i182.

Jin-Dong Kim, Tomoko Ohta, Yoshimasa Tsuruoka, Yuka Tateisi, and Nigel Collier. 2004. Introduction to the bio-entity recognition task at jnlpba. In *Proceedings of the International Joint Workshop on Natural Language Processing in Biomedicine and Its Applications*, JNLPBA '04, pages 70–75, Stroudsburg, PA, USA. Association for Computational Linguistics.

Marie-Claude L'Homme. 2014. Terminologies and taxonomies. *Oxford Handbooks Online*.

Ping Li. 2007. Very sparse stable random projections for dimension reduction in l_α $(0 < \alpha < 2)$ norm. In *Proceedings of the 13th ACM SIGKDD International Conference on Knowledge Discovery and Data Mining*, KDD '07, pages 440–449, New York, NY, USA. ACM.

James Mayfield, Paul McNamee, Craig Harmon, Tim Finin, and Dawn Lawrie. 2014. KELVIN: Extracting Knowledge from Large Text Collections. In *AAAI Fall Symposium on Natural Language Access to Big Data*. AAAI Press, November.

George A. Miller. 1995. Wordnet: a lexical database for english. *Commun. ACM*, 38(11):39–41, November.

Hiroshi Nakagawa and Tatsunori Mori. 2002. A simple but powerful automatic term extraction method. In *COLING-02 on COMPUTERM 2002: second international workshop on computational terminology - Volume 14*, COMPUTERM '02, pages 1–7, Stroudsburg, PA, USA. Association for Computational Linguistics.

Chikashi Nobata, Nigel Collier, and Jun ichi Tsujii. 1999. Automatic term identification and classification in biology texts. In *In Proc. of the 5th NLPRS*, pages 369–374.

Patrick Pantel, Eric Crestan, Arkady Borkovsky, Ana-Maria Popescu, and Vishnu Vyas. 2009. Web-scale distributional similarity and entity set expansion. In *Proceedings of the 2009 Conference on Empirical Methods in Natural Language Processing: Volume 2 - Volume 2*, EMNLP '09, pages 938–947, Stroudsburg, PA, USA. Association for Computational Linguistics.

Behrang QasemiZadeh and Siegfried Handschuh, 2015. *Random Indexing Explained with High Probability*, pages 414–423. Springer International Publishing, Cham.

Magnus Sahlgren, Anders Holst, and Pentti Kanerva. 2008. Permutations as a means to encode order in word space. In V. Sloutsky, B. Love, and K. Mcrae, editors, *Proceedings of the 30th Annual Conference of the Cognitive Science Society*, pages 1300–1305. Cognitive Science Society, Austin, TX.

Magnus Sahlgren. 2005. An introduction to random indexing. In *Methods and Applications of Semantic Indexing Workshop at the 7th International Conference on Terminology and Knowledge Engineering, TKE 2005*.

Patrick Schone and Daniel Jurafsky. 2001. Is knowledge-free induction of multiword unit dictionary headwords a solved problem? In *Proceedings of the 2001 Conference on Empirical Methods in Natural Language Processing*.

Burr Settles. 2005. ABNER: an open source tool for automatically tagging genes, proteins and other entity names in text. *Bioinformatics*, 21(14):3191–3192.

John Sinclair. 1996. Preliminary recommendations on corpus typology. Technical Report EAGLES Document EAG-TCWG-CTYP/P, EAGLES.

Peter D. Turney and Patrick Pantel. 2010. From frequency to meaning: vector space models of semantics. *J. Artif. Int. Res.*, 37(1):141–188, January.

Behrang Q. Zadeh and Siegfried Handschuh. 2014. Random manhattan integer indexing: Incremental l1 normed vector space construction. In *Proceedings of the 2014 Conference on Empirical Methods in Natural Language Processing (EMNLP)*, pages 1713–1723. Association for Computational Linguistics.

Pattern-based Word Sketches for the Extraction of Semantic Relations

Pilar León-Araúz
University of Granada
Department of Trans-
lation and Interpreting
Buensuceso, 11
18001 Granada (Spain)
pleon@ugr.es

Antonio San Martín
Maynooth University
Department of Spanish
and Latin American Studies
Arts Building, North Campus
Maynooth, Co. Kildare (Ireland)
antonio.sanmartin@nuim.ie

Pamela Faber
University of Granada
Department of Trans-
lation and Interpreting
Buensuceso, 11
18001 Granada (Spain)
pfaber@ugr.es

Abstract

Despite advances in computer technology, terminologists still tend to rely on manual work to extract all the semantic information that they need for the description of specialized concepts. In this paper we propose the creation of new word sketches in Sketch Engine for the extraction of semantic relations. Following a pattern-based approach, new sketch grammars are developed in order to extract some of the most common semantic relations used in the field of terminology: generic-specific, part-whole, location, cause and function.

1   Introduction

Terminological work is mostly based on corpus analysis because it is in texts where experts express knowledge and make it accessible (Bourigault and Slodzian 1999). The most basic way of using a corpus is by manually reading concordance lines containing a given term. However, this is time-consuming and inefficient, which has led to the development of new corpus-based methods and applications to analyze and extract information.

One of the most common approaches for the efficient extraction of information from a corpus is to search for knowledge-rich contexts (KRCs). A KRC is "a context indicating at least one item of domain knowledge that could be useful for conceptual analysis" (Meyer 2001). In order to find KRCs in corpora, knowledge patterns (KPs) are used, which are the linguistic and paralinguistic patterns that convey a specific semantic relation (Meyer 2001).

KPs have been successfully applied in many terminology-related projects that have led to the creation of knowledge extraction tools, such as Caméléon (Aussenac-Gilles and Jacques 2008) and TerminoWeb (Barrière and Agbago 2006). However, to the best of our knowledge, currently there are no user-friendly publicly available applications allowing terminologists to find KRCs in their own corpora with ready-made KPs. For this reason, terminologists still tend to rely on manual work to extract all the semantic information that they need for the description of specialized concepts.

In order to fill this void, we propose the creation of KP-based sketch grammars in the well-known corpus query system, Sketch Engine (Kilgarriff et al. 2004). This allows users to generate new word sketches that could be exploited by any terminologist, lexicographer or translator interested in the extraction of semantic relations.

Word sketches are automatic corpus-derived summaries of a word's grammatical and collocational behavior (Kilgarriff et al. 2004). Rather than looking at an arbitrary window of text around the headword – as occurs in previous corpus tools – Sketch Engine is able to look for each grammatical relation that the word participates in (Kilgarriff et al. 2004). The default word sketches provided by Sketch Engine represent different relations, such as verb-object, modifiers or prepositional phrases. However,

Proceedings of the 5th International Workshop on Computational Terminology,
pages 73–82, Osaka, Japan, December 12 2016.

with the exception of the recently implemented generic-specific word-sketches, they only represent linguistic relations. Therefore, we believe that the development of new sketch grammars focusing on the extraction of semantic relations is a timely contribution to the field of terminology, since a summary of the semantic behavior of concepts in the form of word sketches would allow terminologists to perform a more efficient conceptual analysis of any corpus uploaded to Sketch Engine.

The new sketch grammars presented in this paper have been developed for the extraction of some of the most common semantic relations used in the field of terminology, namely: generic-specific, part-whole, location, cause and function. Section 2 briefly reviews previous work on KPs and semantic relations; Section 3 shows the methodology followed to derive and formalize KPs; Section 4 presents our preliminary results; and Section 5 provides the conclusions derived from this work.

2 Semantic relations and knowledge patterns

The extraction of semantic relations from specialized corpora constitutes one of the most important tasks in terminology work, since many other tasks depend on them (i.e. conceptual modeling, definition elaboration). From a user perspective, the visualization of semantic relations is essential to comprehend how a concept interacts with others in a specialized domain (Faber, León-Araúz and Prieto Velasco 2009).

Thus, not surprisingly, the automatic retrieval of related term pairs has been explored for many years and from different perspectives. One of them is based on KPs, which are considered one of the most reliable methods for the extraction of semantic relations (Condamines 2002; Marshman, Morgan, and Meyer 2002; Marshman 2002; Barrière 2004; Bowker 2003; L'Homme and Marshman 2006; Cimiano and Staab 2005; Auger and Barrière 2008; Lefever, Kauter, and Hoste 2014; Marshman 2014; Lafourcade and Ramadier 2016). The term KP was coined by Meyer (2001) to refer to the lexico-syntactic patterns between the terms encoded in a proposition in real texts, but they were introduced much earlier by Hearst (1992). Since then, much has been written about them. Nevertheless, despite their popularity, KPs are still far from being fully studied and exploited, especially in specialized domains. Furthermore, as observed by Bowker (2003), there are still major problems with regard to noise and silence, pattern variation, anaphora, domain and language dependency, etc. Moreover, not all relations have been analyzed in the same depth.

Patterns conveying hyponymic relations are the most commonly studied since they play an important role in categorization and property inheritance (Barrière 2004). Some of the simplest examples of such KPs are *x is a kind of y, As include Bs, Cs and Ds* (Meyer 1994) and *comprise(s), consist(s), define(s), denote(s), designate(s), is/are, is/are called, is/are defined as, is/are known as* (Pearson 1998).

Meronymy, or part-whole relations, have also been previously researched (Berland and Chamiak 1999; Girju, Badulescu, and Moldovan 2003) and common patterns include *part of, constituent of, constituted by, made of, composed of, contains*, etc. These relations may be codified by prepositional phrases, possessives, and partitive verbs, but one of their main features is the fact that many KPs can be polysemic. For instance, *including* expresses both hyponymy and meronymy; and *formed by* expresses meronymy and causality (León Araúz 2014; León Araúz and Reimerink 2010).

Although to a lesser extent, other non-hierarchical relations have also been studied and implemented as KPs, each has their own peculiarities. For instance, unlike certain fairly clear-cut hierarchical relations, such as generic-specific, *cause* has many different subtypes (Marshman 2002). All studies dealing with causality affirm that there are many ways to express causation since it can be expressed by passive, active, subject-object, nominal or verbal propositions. Moreover, causes and effects have very diverse syntactic representations. More specifically, causation is not only expressed by constructions such as *due to* or *because of*, but also by causative nouns (*cause* or *consequence*) and verbs. Although there are many causative verbs (e.g. *cause, generate, lead, produce*, etc.), their syntactic behavior can also vary. As a result, one single grammar would not be sufficient to formalize their complementation structures (León Araúz and Faber 2012).

The above-mentioned patterns are only a simplification of what is actually found in a corpus. For instance, when formalizing the pattern *is a type of* we should also take into account all of its possible variants. The verb *to be* may be in its plural form or substituted by a comma; if it is in the plural, various hyponyms will be enumerated to the left of the pattern; the verb *to be* may be preceded by a modal verb; the word *type* may be preceded by an adjective and an adverb; and it may be substituted by other synonyms such as *kind, sort, example, group*, etc. This is in line with the types of KP identified by Meyer (2001): lexical patterns (literal strings); grammatical patterns (taking into account POS tags); and paralinguistic patterns (punctuation).

Therefore, these patterns can be useful as they are when manually querying a corpus. However, formalizing them in grammars requires finding the balance between precision and recall, and efficiency and complexity. This entails having to decide the number of possible paths that the same grammar may cover, how many elements will be optional or compulsory, whether the anchor points should be literal words or lemmas, POS tags or punctuation marks, while taking into account negative adverbs (*not, never, hardly*) that would give a false positive, etc.

3   Materials and methods

For this study, we used the English EcoLexicon corpus[1], which currently contains over 59 million words in English and is focused on the environmental domain. Although KPs have been tested in a domain-specific corpus, we believe that most of them could also be applied to other domains. Except for patterns such as *built for* or *built with*, which would only be activated in construction related domains, most of them are not domain-specific.

For corpus querying and the generation of word sketches, we employed Sketch Engine. Corpus querying in Sketch Engine is based on an extension of the CQL formalism (Schulze and Christ 1996), allowing for the formalization of grammar patterns in the form of regular expressions combined with POS-tags. CQL expressions in Sketch Engine can be used as one-time queries (giving access to matching concordance lines) or stored in a sketch grammar, which will produce word sketches.

As previously stated, the only semantic relation included in the default English sketch grammar so far is the hyponymic word sketch. Table 1 shows the resulting word sketch when querying *earthquake* in the general publicly available English Web 2013 (enTenTen13) corpus:

... is a "earthquake"		
	534	0.00
body	57	5.01
mind	46	5.15
event	41	3.92
heart	27	5.25
example	26	3.61

"earthquake" is a ...		
	1,295	0.00
disaster	80	7.72
event	75	5.01
result	74	3.65
part	57	1.04
time	48	2.20

Table 1. ...*is a* word sketch in Sketch Engine.[2]

The results in Table 1 would not be satisfactory for a terminologist. However, more sophisticated hyponymic KPs will soon be implemented in Sketch Engine in order to extract definitions (Kovář, Močiariková, and Rychlý 2016). Also, from a terminology perspective, Baisa and Suchomel (2015) have already explored hyponymy extraction by using sketch grammars in a specialized Czech corpus on the domain of land surveying. In line with our view, they acknowledge that apart from the term extraction function, terminologists need a function for placing the extracted terms in a tree structure.

Nonetheless, apart from placing terms in a tree structure, terms also need to be linked to others by means of other semantic relations. In what follows we explain our methodology for the extraction of generic-specific, part-whole, location, cause, and function relations.

Besides collecting the patterns mentioned by other authors (see Section 2), we also added our own based on our experience during the construction of EcoLexicon. All approaches seem to agree that the use of KPs for knowledge extraction involves a series of complementary steps. Nevertheless, the order of the steps differs depending on research objectives (e.g. identification of term pairs, discovery of

---

[1] This corpus was compiled by the LexiCon Research Group for the development of EcoLexicon (http://ecolexicon.ugr.es), a terminological knowledge base on the environment.
[2] The second column shows the number of occurrences and the third one the collocation strength score as calculated by Sketch Engine.

new KPs, searching for known KPs to discover new term pairs, etc.). In our case, we followed the following steps:

1. *Collection of KPs*: this first stage only includes the collection of patterns in plain English (no formalism or encoding language used).
   a. Patterns referenced by other authors.
   b. Patterns already known.
   c. Recursive method: term pairs linked by already known semantic relations are searched for to find new patterns. Then these patterns are used to find new term pairs, and so on.

2. *CQL encoding*: This second stage consists of translating the KPs collected during the first stage into CQL sketch grammars.
   a. Splitting or lumping: Some KPs collected in the first stage can be lumped into a single CQL sketch grammar, while others collected as a single KP need to be split.
   b. Addition of adverbs, punctuation, modal verbs, relative phrases, adjectives, determiners, etc.

3. *Validation, enrichment, refining*
   a. CQL patterns are validated trying to keep the balance between noise and silence.
   b. Enrichment: Testing the CQL patterns with additional optional elements to spot new variations of the pattern (for instance, the possibility of an adverb in a place where it was not previously accounted for). Validation of the new addition.
   c. Refining: Detection of erroneous concordance lines obtained with the CQL patterns. Analysis of the source of the error, and determination of whether it is appropriate to change the CQL pattern.

In the development of our sketch grammars (a total of 56), we have considered different issues that are specific to each relation. For instance, there are certain patterns that always take the same form and order (e.g. *such as*), whereas others show such a diverse syntactic structure that the directionality of the pattern must also be accounted for. We also had to take into account the fact that a single sentence could produce more than one term pair because of the enumerations that are often found on each side of the pattern (e.g. *x, y, z and other types of w*). This entails performing non-greedy queries in order to allow any of the enumerated elements fill the target term. However, this may also cause endless noisy loops. Sometimes it is necessary to limit the number of possible words on each side of the pattern. In this sense, we observed that enumerations are more often found on the side of hyponyms, parts, and effects than on the side of hypernyms, wholes, and causes. Consequently, the loops were constrained accordingly in the latter case. Table 2 shows a summarized and simplified version of the patterns included in each grammar according to the semantic relation conveyed.

<u>Generic-specific (18 sketch grammars):</u> HYPONYM ,|(|:|is|belongs (to) (a|the|…) type|category|… of HYPERNYM // types|kinds|… of HYPERNYM include|are HYPONYM // types|kinds|… of HYPERNYM range from (…) (to) HYPONYM // HYPERNYM (type|category|…) (,|() ranging (…) (to) HYPONYM // HYPERNYM types|categories|… include HYPONYM // HYPERNYM such as HYPONYM // HYPERNYM including HYPONYM // HYPERNYM ,|(especially|primarily|… HYPONYM // HYPONYM and|or other (types|kinds|…) of HYPERNYM // HYPONYM is defined|classified|… as (a|the|…) (type|kind|…) (of) HYPERNYM // classify|categorize|… (this type|kind|… of) HYPONYM as HYPERNYM // HYPERNYM is classified|categorized in|into (a|the|…) (type|kind|…) (of) HYPONYM // HYPERNYM (,|() (is) divided in|into (…) types|kinds|… :|of HYPONYM // type|kind|… of HYPERNYM (is|,|() known|referred|… (to) (as) HYPONYM // HYPONYM is a HYPERNYM that|which|… // define HYPONYM as (a|the|…) (type|category|…) (of) HYPERNYM // HYPONYM refers to (a|the|…) (type|category|…) (of) HYPERNYM // (a|the|one|two…) (type|category|…) (of) HYPERNYM: HYPONYM

Part-whole (17 sketch grammars): WHOLE is comprised|composed|constituted (in part) of|by PART // WHOLE comprises PART // PART composes WHOLE // PART is|constitutes (a|the|…) part|component|… of WHOLE // WHOLE has|includes|possesses (…) part|component|… (,|() (:|such as|usually|namely|…) PART // WHOLE has|includes|possesses (a|the|…) fraction|amount|percent… of PART // WHOLE part|component|… (,|() such as PART // part|component|… of WHOLE (,|() (:|such as|usually|namely|…) PART // (a|the|one|two|some|…) part|component|… of WHOLE is PART // (a|the|one|two|some|…) part|component|… of WHOLE (is) called|referred|… (to) (as) PART // PART (,|() (a|the|…) part|component|… of WHOLE // WHOLE is divided in|into (two|some|…) parts|components|… (,|() (:|such as|usually|namely|…) PART // WHOLE is divided in|into PART // WHOLE (is|,|() made|built|… (up) of|from|with PART // WHOLE contains PART // PART (is) contained in WHOLE // WHOLE consists of PART
Cause (10 sketch grammars): CAUSE (is) responsible for EFFECT // CAUSE causes|produces|… EFFECT // CAUSE leads|contributes|gives (rise) to EFFECT // CAUSE-driven|-induced|-caused EFFECT // EFFECT (is) caused|produced|… by|because|due (of|to) CAUSE // EFFECT derives|results from CAUSE // cause of EFFECT is CAUSE // CAUSE (is) (a|the|…) cause of EFFECT // CAUSE (,|() (a|the|…) cause of EFFECT // EFFECT is|,|(forms|formed by|from CAUSE
Location (4 sketch grammars): ENTITY (is) connected|delimited to|by PLACE // ENTITY (is) found|built|… in|on|… PLACE // ENTITY (is) formed|forms in|on|… PLACE // ENTITY (is) extended|extends (out) into|parallel|… (of|to) PLACE
Function (7 sketch grammars): ENTITY (has|provides|…) (a|the|…) function|role|purpose of FUNCTION // ENTITY is (built|designed|…) for|to FUNCTION // ENTITY is (useful|effective|…) for|to FUNCTION // ENTITY is (a|the|…) (…) built|designed|… for|to FUNCTION // ENTITY is (a|the|…) (…) used|employed|… for|as FUNCTION // use|employ|… ENTITY for|as|to FUNCTION // function|role|purpose of ENTITY is FUNCTION

Table 2. Simplified summary of knowledge patterns and semantic relations.

By way of example, Tables 3 and 4 show the actual CQL representation of a generic-specific KP and a causal KP respectively, followed by an explanation.

2:"N.*" [tag!="V.*"]{0,5} "MD"? [word!="not"]? [lemma="be|,|\\("] [word!="not"]? [word="defined|classified|categori.ed|regarded"] [word="as"] "DT.*|RB.*|JJ.*"* ([lemma="type|kind|example|group| class| sort|category|family|species|subtype|subfamily|subgroup| subclass|subcategory|subspecies"] [word="of"])? [tag!="V.*"]{0,2} 1:[tag="N.*" & lemma!="type|kind|example|group|class|sort|category|family|species|subtype|subfamily|subgroup|subclass|subcategory|subspecies"]	
2:"N.*"	The hyponym is a noun.
[tag!="V.*"]{0,5}	From 0 to 5 words that are not verbs. This allows to capture enumerations and allows for the presence of adverbs, prepositions, etc.
"MD"?	An optional modal verb
[word!="not"]?	Optional word that is not *not*. This filters out negative sentences.
[lemma="be|,|\\("]	The lemma *be,* comma or opening parenthesis.
[word!="not"]?	Optional word that is not *not*. This filters out negative sentences.
[word="defined|classified|categori.ed|regarded"]	The words *defined, classified, categorized, categorised* or *regarded*.
[word="as"]	The word *as*.
"DT.*|RB.*|JJ.*"*	From 0 to infinite determiners, adverbs or adjectives. This allows for phrases such as "the most important", "a very special", etc.

([lemma="type|kind|example| group|class|sort|category|family| species|subtype|subfamily| subgroup|subclass|subcategory| subspecies"] [word="of"])?	The lemma *type, kind, example, group, class, sort, category, family, species, subtype, subfamily, subgroup, subclass, subcategory* or *subspecies* followed by the word *of* (both optional).
[tag!="V.*"]{0,2}	From 0 to 2 words that are not verbs. This allows for the presence of determiners, adjectives, adverbs, etc.
1:[tag="N.*" & lemma!="type| kind|example|group|class|sort| category|family|species| subtype|subfamily|subgroup| subclass|subcategory|subspecies"]	The hypernym is a noun that does not have *type, kind, example, group, class, sort, category, family, species, subtype, subfamily, subgroup, subclass, subcategory* or *subspecies* as lemma.

Table 3. CQL representation of a generic-specific KP followed by its explanation.

2:"N.*" [tag!="V.*"]{0,7} [lemma="be|,|\("]? [tag="RB.*" & word!="not|never"]* [word="caused|produced|generated|provoked|induced|triggered|originated"] "RB.*"* ([word="by"]|[word="because"][word="of"] | [word="due"] [word="to"]) [tag!="V.*"]{0,7} 1:"N.*"	
2:"N.*"	The effect is a noun.
[tag!="V.*"]{0,7}	From 0 to 7 words that are not verbs. This allows to capture enumerations and allows for the presence of adverbs, prepositions, etc.
[lemma="be|,|\("]?	The lemma *be,* comma or opening parenthesis.
[tag="RB.*" & word!="not|never"]*	From 0 to infinite adverbs except *not* or *never*.
[word="caused|produced|generated|provoked|induced|triggered|originated"]	The word *caused, produced, generated, provoked, induced, triggered* or *originated*.
"RB.*"*	From 0 to infinite adverbs.
([word="by"]|[word="because"] [word="of"] | [word="due"] [word="to"])	The word *by*, the phrase *because of* or the phrase *due to*.
[tag!="V.*"]{0,7}	From 0 to 7 words that are not verbs.
1:"N.*"	The cause is a noun.

Table 4. CQL representation of a causal KP followed by its explanation.

These grammars combine our previously retrieved KPs, which act as anchor points, with certain constraints imposed by POS tags, punctuation or operators (i.e.?, *, {0,5}), which means that they include all types of KPs (lexical, grammatical and paralinguistic). Tables 4 and 5 show a sample of the concordances that can be extracted with several of our generic-specific and causal grammars:

bacteria , viruses, protozoans worms and other types of agents
Bacteria and protozoa are the major groups of microorganisms
bacteria are the main types of organisms
Clouds are classified into four families: high clouds, middle clouds, low clouds
materials are classified by grain size into clay, silt, sand, gravel, cobble, and boulder
Cumulonimbus is classified as a low cloud
weather phenomena such as local storms, tornadoes, hurricanes, or extra-tropical and tropical cyclones
sediment , usually sand but occasionally silt or clay
structures , namely headland breakwaters, nearshore breakwaters, and a groin field
sea stars, urchins, sea cucumbers, and other creatures

Table 5. Concordances extracted with generic-specific grammars.

earthquakes **can trigger massive** landslides
flooding **causes many** deaths **and much** damage
Pesticides **and commercial inorganic** fertilizers **cause air, water, and soil** pollution
cancers **caused by air** pollution
radiation **can lead to** cancer
erosion **results from** storms
damage **caused by severe** winds
tsunami **causes massive** destruction

Table 6. Concordances extracted with causal grammars.

4   Results

The combination of our sketch grammars with the statistics used in the Sketch Engine system has yielded encouraging results. To show the potential of this initial approach, we have selected different concepts showing word sketches for all types of relation and their inverse in Table 7. The results are sorted by frequency. Because of space constraints, only the first few results of each word sketch are shown.

"bacterium" is a type of...		
	1,007	0.12
organism	158	10.00
microorganism	88	10.92
micro-organism	28	9.64
agent	18	8.09
decomposer	15	8.83

"bacterium" is the generic of...		
	1,028	0.12
coli	17	8.94
plant	14	6.85
Pseudomonas	10	8.24
Escherichia	10	8.22
fungus	9	7.60

"rock" has part...		
	3,029	0.09
mineral	213	10.54
quartz	65	9.17
fragment	47	8.79
feldspar	45	8.79
plagioclase	41	8.67

"rock" is part of...		
	2,055	0.06
crust	44	9.09
soil	34	7.97
belt	27	8.52
continent	23	8.30
part	22	7.96

"volcano" is located at...		
	318	0.04
plate	17	10.11
island	14	9.42
boundary	11	9.38
Pacific	8	8.71
margin	7	8.87

"volcano" is the location of...		
	71	0.01
cone	7	11.10
ocean	3	8.23
type	3	6.74
area	3	6.59
precursor	2	9.66

"tsunami" is the cause of...		
	196	0.04
damage	18	7.54
destruction	12	8.74
erosion	7	6.70
devastation	6	9.08
death	6	6.67

"tsunami" is caused by...		
	1,057	0.20
earthquake	177	11.31
landslide	68	10.73
eruption	36	9.34
water	33	7.70
movement	23	8.65

"energy" has function...			"energy" is the function of...		
	2,151	0.03		999	0.02
water	57	8.71	fuel	23	8.96
produce	41	8.83	carbon	14	8.12
make	33	8.45	biomass	13	8.44
process	22	7.99	waste	13	8.20
electricity	21	8.17	light	12	8.28

Table 7. Examples of different word sketches obtained with our sketch grammars

There are several issues that still need to be dealt with in order to improve the outcome of these grammars. For instance, (1) there is still noise because the grammars need to be refined, especially that of function, where target terms may be nouns or verbs, and verbs are not always semantically relevant or self-contained (i.e. *make*, *produce*) and need an object to constitute a meaningful proposition; (2) most false positives (i.e. *fungus* or *plant* as a type of *bacterium*, or *type* as something located at a *volcano*, as shown in Table 5) are due to the imprecision of certain grammars or even to some mistakes derived from the POS tagger; (3) there is also pattern ambiguity that could only be solved by adding semantic constraints on the type of entities being linked (as done by Girju, Badulescu, and Moldovan 2003); (4) and semantic relations are also ambiguous, for example in the sense that distinguishing parts from locations is not always an easy task (i.e. *cone* could be a part of a *volcano* or be located in a *volcano*). Furthermore, of these issues there is one related to the processing of multiword expressions. So far, these word sketches only retrieve one-word terms, which is one of the causes of noise and lack of precision. This can be solved relatively easily (Kilgarriff et al. 2012), but poses the challenge of differentiating between multiword terms and usual collocations. For instance, in sentences (1) and (2) only *shield volcano* should take the role of the hyponym, whereas *huge* would only qualify as a simple modifier of *volcano*.

(1) "…monogenetic volcanoes are smaller than **polygenetic volcanoes**, *such as* **shield volcanoes**…"
(2) "…with igneous and **tectonic features** *such as* **huge volcanoes** and rift valleys…"

5   Conclusions and future work

In this paper we have shown how KPs can be converted into sketch grammars to generate new word sketches showing semantic relations. The resulting word sketches can be of great value to terminologists during the conceptual modeling of any domain. However, much remains to be done. First of all, the sketch grammars should be refined as new patterns are found and extended to include multiword terms. New grammars will also be needed to include other semantic relations, especially those related to process concept types, such as temporal relations. Precision and recall studies will be performed in order to improve the grammars and find the right balance between noise and silence. Finally, pattern disambiguation techniques are also needed for polysemic KPs.

References

Auger, Alain, and Caroline Barrière. 2008. "Pattern-Based Approaches to Semantic Relation Extraction: A State-of-the-Art." *Terminology* 14 (1): 1–19. doi:10.1075/term.14.1.02aug.

Aussenac-Gilles, Nathalie, and Marie-Paule Jacques. 2008. "Designing and Evaluating Patterns for Relation Acquisition from Texts with Caméléon." *Terminology* 14 (1): 45–73. doi:10.1075/term.14.1.04aus.

Baisa, Vít, and Vít Suchomel. 2015. "Corpus Based Extraction of Hypernyms in Terminological Thesaurus for Land Surveying Domain." In *Ninth Workshop on Recent Advances in Slavonic Natural Language Processing*, 69–74. Brno: Tribun EU.

Barrière, Caroline. 2004. "Knowledge-Rich Contexts Discovery." In *Seventeenth Canadian Conference on Artificial Intelligence (AI'2004)*, 187–201. London, Ontario: CSCSI. doi:10.1007/978-3-540-24840-8_14.

Barrière, Caroline, and A Agbago. 2006. "TerminoWeb: A Software Environment for Term Study in Rich Contexts." In *Conference on Terminology, Standardisation and Technology Transfer (TSTT 2006)*. Beijing. http://nparc.cisti-icist.nrc-cnrc.gc.ca/npsi/ctrl?action=rtdoc&an=8913210.

Berland, Matthew, and Eugene Charniak. 1999. "Finding Parts in Very Large Corpora." In *Proceedings of the 37th Annual Meeting of the Association for Computational Linguistics*, 57–64. Morristown, NJ: Association for Computational Linguistics. doi:10.3115/1034678.1034697.

Bourigault, Didier, and Monique Slodzian. 1999. "Pour Une Terminologie Textuelle." *Terminologies Nouvelles* 19: 29–32.

Bowker, Lynne. 2003. "Lexical Knowledge Patterns, Semantic Relations, and Language Varieties: Exploring the Possibilities for Refining Information Retrieval in an International Context." *Cataloging & Classification Quarterly* 37 (1-2): 153–71. doi:10.1300/J104v37n01_11.

Cimiano, Philipp, and Steffen Staab. 2005. "Learning Concept Hierarchies from Text with a Guided Agglomerative Clustering Algorithm." In *Proceedings of ICML 2005. Workshop on Learning and Extending Lexical Ontologies with Machine Learning Methods*, edited by Chris Biemann and Gerhard Paas. Bonn. http://citeseerx.ist.psu.edu/viewdoc/download?doi=10.1.1.59.7546&rep=rep1&type=pdf.

Condamines, Anne. 2002. "Corpus Analysis and Conceptual Relation Patterns." *Terminology* 8 (1): 141–62. doi:10.1075/term.8.1.07con.

Faber, Pamela, Pilar León Araúz, and Juan Antonio Prieto Velasco. 2009. "Semantic Relations, Dynamicity, and Terminological Knowledge Bases." *Current Issues in Language Studies* 1: 1–23.

Girju, Roxana, Adriana Badulescu, and Dan Moldovan. 2003. "Learning Semantic Constraints for the Automatic Discovery of Part-Whole Relations." In *Proceedings of the 2003 Conference of the North American Chapter of the Association for Computational Linguistics on Human Language Technology - NAACL '03*, 1:1–8. Morristown, NJ: Association for Computational Linguistics. doi:10.3115/1073445.1073456.

Hearst, Marti A. 1992. "Automatic Acquisition of Hyponyms from Large Text Corpora." In *Actes de COLING-92*, 2:539–45. Morristown, NJ: International Committee on Computational Linguistics.

Kilgarriff, Adam, Vít Baisa, Jan Bušta, Miloš Jakubíček, Vojtěch Kovář, Jan Michelfeit, Pavel Rychlý, and Vít Suchomel. 2014. "The Sketch Engine: Ten Years on." *Lexicography* 1 (1): 7–36. doi:10.1007/s40607-014-0009-9.

Kilgarriff, Adam, Pavel Rychlý, Vojtěch Kovář, and Vít Baisa. 2012. "Finding Multiwords of More Than Two Words." *Proceedings of the 15th EURALEX International Congress*, 1–7.

Kilgarriff, Adam, Pavel Rychlý, Pavel Smrz, and David Tugwell. 2004. "The Sketch Engine." In *Proceedings of the Eleventh EURALEX International Congress*, edited by Geoffrey Williams and Sandra Vessier, 105–16. Lorient: EURALEX.

Kovář, Vojtěch, Monika Močiariková, and Pavel Rychlý. 2016. "Finding Definitions in Large Corpora with Sketch Engine." In *Proceedings of the Ninth International Conference on Language Resources and Evaluation (LREC 2016)*, edited by Nicoletta Calzolari, Khalid Choukri, Thierry Declerck, Marko Grobelnik, Bente Maegaard, Joseph Mariani, Asuncion Moreno, Jan Odijk, and Stelios Piperidis. Portorož, Slovenia: European Language Resources Association (ELRA).

L'Homme, Marie-Claude, and Elizabeth Marshman. 2006. "Terminological Relationships and Corpus-Based Methods for Discovering Them: An Assessment for Terminographers." In *Lexicography, Terminology and Translation. Text-Based Studies in Honour of Ingrid Meyer*, edited by Lynne Bowker, 67–80. Ottawa: University of Ottawa Press.

Lafourcade, Mathieu, and Lionel Ramadier. 2016. "Semantic Relation Extraction with Semantic Patterns Experiment on Radiology Reports." In *Proceedings of the Ninth International Conference on Language Resources and Evaluation (LREC 2016)*, edited by Nicoletta Calzolari, Khalid Choukri, Thierry Declerck, Marko Grobelnik, Bente Maegaard, Joseph Mariani, Asuncion Moreno, Jan Odijk, and Stelios Piperidis, 4578–82. Portorož, Slovenia: European Language Resources Association (ELRA).

Lefever, E, M Van de Kauter, and V Hoste. 2014. "HypoTerm: Detection of Hypernym Relations between Domain-Specific Terms in Dutch and English." *Terminology* 20 (2): 250–78. doi:10.1075/term.20.2.06lef.

León Araúz, Pilar. 2014. "Semantic Relations and Local Grammars for the Environment." In *Formalising Natural Languages with NooJ 2013*, edited by Svetla Koeva, Slim Mesfar, and Max Silberztein, 87–102. Newcastle-upon-Tyne: Cambridge Scholars Publishing.

León Araúz, Pilar, and Pamela Faber. 2012. "Causality in the Specialized Domain of the Environment." In *Proceedings of the Workshop "Semantic Relations-II. Enhancing Resources and Applications" (LREC'12)*, edited by Verginica Barbu Mititelu, Octavian Popescu, and Viktor Pekar, 10–17. Istanbul: ELRA.

León Araúz, Pilar, and Arianne Reimerink. 2010. "Knowledge Extraction and Multidimensionality in the Environmental Domain." In *Proceedings of the Terminology and Knowledge Engineering (TKE) Conference 2010*. Dublin: Dublin City University.

Marshman, Elizabeth. 2002. "The Cause-Effect Relation in a Biopharmaceutical Corpus: English Knowledge Patterns." In *Proceedings of the 6th International Conference on Terminology and Knowledge Engineering*, 89–94. Nancy.

———. 2014. "Enriching Terminology Resources with Knowledge-Rich Contexts: A Case Study." *Terminology* 20 (2): 225–49. doi:10.1075/term.20.2.05mar.

Marshman, Elizabeth, Tricia Morgan, and Ingrid Meyer. 2002. "French Patterns for Expressing Concept Relations." *Terminology* 8 (1): 1–29. doi:10.1075/term.8.1.02mar.

Meyer, Ingrid. 1994. "Linguistic Strategies and Computer Aids for Knowledge Engineering in Terminology." *L'actualité terminologique/Terminology Update* 27 (4): 6–10.

———. 2001. "Extracting Knowledge-Rich Contexts for Terminography." In *Recent Advances in Computational Terminology*, edited by Didier Bourigault, Christian Jacquemin, and Marie-Claude L'Homme, 279–302. Amsterdam/Philadelphia: John Benjamins.

Pearson, Jennifer. 1998. *Terms in Context*. Amsterdam/Philadelphia: John Benjamins.

Schulze, Bruno Maximilian, and Oliver Christ. 1996. *The CQP User's Manual*. Stuttgart: Universität Stuttgart.

Constructing and Evaluating Controlled Bilingual Terminologies

Rei Miyata
The University of Tokyo
rei@p.u-tokyo.ac.jp

Kyo Kageura
The University of Tokyo
kyo@p.u-tokyo.ac.jp

Abstract

This paper presents the construction and evaluation of Japanese and English controlled bilingual terminologies that are particularly intended for controlled authoring and machine translation with special reference to the Japanese municipal domain. Our terminologies are constructed by extracting terms from municipal website texts, and the term variations are controlled by defining preferred and proscribed terms for both the source Japanese and the target English. To assess the coverage of the terms/concepts in the municipal domain and validate the quality of the control, we employ a quantitative extrapolation method that estimates the potential vocabulary size. Using Large-Number-of-Rare-Event (LNRE) modelling, we compare two parameters: (1) uncontrolled and controlled and (2) Japanese and English. The results show that our terminologies currently cover about 45–65% of the terms and 50–65% of the concepts in the municipal domain, and are well controlled. The detailed analysis of growth patterns of terminologies also provides insight into the extent to which we can enlarge the terminologies within the realistic range.

1 Introduction

In this study, we construct controlled terminologies for the municipal domain and evaluate them in terms of the coverage and the quality of the variation control. Term variation management is essential in helping with the consistent use of terminology by not only authors but also translators and machine translation (MT) (Daille, 2005). On Japanese municipal websites, the case in point, we can find a number of variant forms of the same referent, such as '印鑑登録証明書' and '印鑑証明書' (seal registration certificate). As the former might be a preferred term in the municipal domain, we can define the latter as a proscribed term. In the target language texts, we also encounter various translations that correspond to the source terms, such as 'personal seals registration certificate' and 'seal proof certificate'. To maintain the consistency of the terminology use on the target side, we need to prescribe authorised translations.

Since there are no bilingual municipal terminologies that are well maintained and easily available, focusing on the municipal life information, we construct Japanese-English controlled terminologies from scratch by extracting terms from municipal texts and controlling the variant forms. To facilitate the manual extraction of terms, we developed a simple platform in which laypeople can collect terms efficiently.

While many attempts have been made to conduct extrinsic evaluation of terminological resources such as MT output evaluation (Langlais and Carl, 2004; Thicke, 2011), the intrinsic status of terminology such as coverage has not been examined much. The methodological difficulty in validating the coverage, i.e. how much of the potential terminology in a given domain is covered by the current terminology, is due to the fact that the population size of the terminology to compare is rarely available.[1] Sager (2001, p.763) pointed out, however, that statistical means 'can be used to decide when the addition of more text does not produce any new terms'. We can tackle this issue by employing a statistical method proposed for inspecting the current status of the corpus (Kageura and Kikui, 2006). It is also difficult to assess the quality of controlled terminology, i.e. how well the term variations are managed and standardised. In this paper, we present the idea of comparing the controlled terminologies of multiple languages to validate the quality of control.

[1]If it is available, we no longer need to *evaluate* such a gold standard.

Proceedings of the 5th International Workshop on Computational Terminology,
pages 83–93, Osaka, Japan, December 12 2016.

2 Controlled Bilingual Terminology

2.1 Compiling Parallel Corpus

To build bilingual terminologies, we first compiled a parallel corpus by (1) extracting Japanese and English sentences from the municipal websites including body texts, headings and texts in tables, and (2) aligning the sentences between the languages.

We chose three website texts as sources: **CLAIR**,[2] **Shinjuku**[3] and **Hamamatsu**.[4] Each website covers a full range of categories for municipal life information such as residential procedures, tax payment and child care. The **CLAIR** website provides general purpose life information independent of particular municipalities, while the **Shinjuku** and **Hamamatsu** websites provide life information pertaining to the particular municipalities. It should be noted that the source texts of **Hamamatsu** are written in *Easy Japanese*, the lexicon and grammar of which are simplified in order to make the texts easier to read for non-native speakers of the language. We can reasonably assume that the three websites cover a wide range of content and linguistic phenomena.

We first extracted all sentences from the three sources, obtaining 16741 Japanese sentences and 15503 English sentences. We then manually aligned the Japanese and English sentences and obtained 15391 aligned sentence pairs,[5] from which we extracted bilingual term pairs.

2.2 Collecting Terms

2.2.1 Terms to be Collected

Our aim is to provide a practical terminology useful for authoring and (machine) translation. As Fischer (2010, p.30) pointed out, translators 'tend to consider terms in the broader sense, wishing to include everything which makes their work easier into a terminological database'. We thus decided to collect terms as widely as possible. The range of terms to be collected is defined as below.

1. Technical terms and proper nouns

   e.g. 外国人登録証明書/*gaikokujin-touroku-shomeisho* (alien registration card)
   e.g. JR 西日本/*JR-nishi-nihon* (JR West Japan)

2. More general words that refer to municipal services and activities

   e.g. 収入印紙/*shunyu-inshi* (stamp)
   e.g. 外交活動/*gaikou-katsudou* (diplomatic activity)

2.2.2 Extracted Terms

Ideally, the term extraction should be conducted by experts of the municipal domain. There is, however, a shortage of skilled municipal writers, and it is unrealistic to hire such experts. We thus employed four university students and asked them to manually extract bilingual term candidates from the parallel corpus. They are all native speakers of Japanese and have a sufficient command of English to correctly identify the translated terms.

In order to facilitate the extraction of terms, we developed a web-based platform to help with collaborative work. Figure 1 depicts the interface in which a pair of paralleled sentences is presented. This system enables users to capture the span of a term by clicking the starting word and the ending word.[6] At the bottom of the screen, terms that have been previously registered are also displayed. Registration of a pair of bilingual terms identical to an already identified pair is not allowed. These mechanisms support human decision-making and prevent duplicate registration, leading to improved efficiency of extraction.

---

[2]CLAIR (Council of Local Authorities for International Relations) Multilingual Living Information. `http://www.clair.or.jp/tagengo/`

[3]Shinjuku City, Living Information. `http://www.city.shinjuku.lg.jp/foreign/english/index.html`

[4]Hamamatsu City, Canal Hamamatsu. `https://www.city.hamamatsu.shizuoka.jp/hamaeng/`

[5]For some Japanese sentences, there were no corresponding English sentences, and vice versa.

[6]In this Figure, 'personal', the starting word of 'personal seal registration card', has been selected, and 'card', the ending word of the term, is about to be clicked.

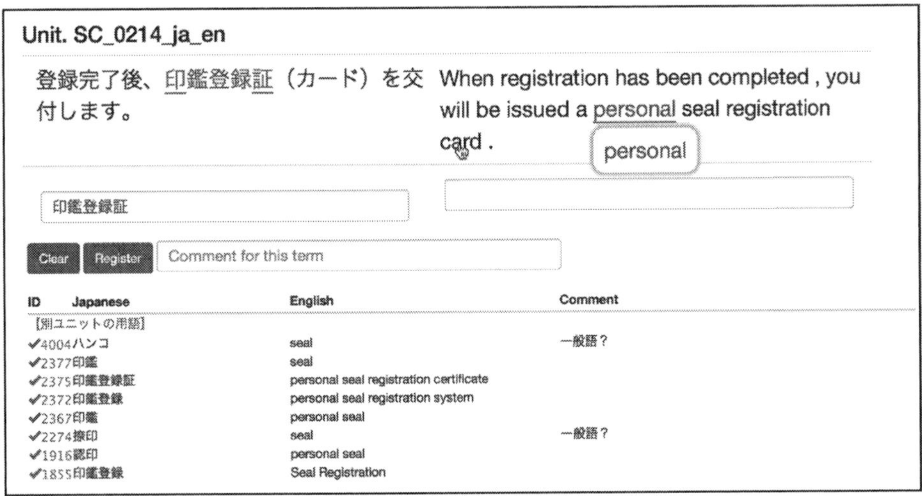

Figure 1: Term registration platform

Another important feature of this platform is that it is designed to facilitate collaborative term extraction and validation. As soon as a user adds a comment to each pair of paralleled sentences and/or to each term, other users can refer to the comments and a task manager can promptly respond to the comment if necessary. The status of the work progress as well as the extracted terms can be checked online at any time, which helps conduct the task smoothly.

The identification of terms is difficult even for experts (Frantzi et al., 2000). To alleviate the individual differences of term identification and ensure comprehensiveness, we instructed the students to extract the terms as widely as possible. Finally, we validated all the terms they extracted to improve the accuracy of the terms.

A total of 3741 bilingual term pairs were collected from 15391 aligned sentence pairs. The number of distinct Japanese terms is 3012, while that of English terms is 3465, suggesting that in general the translated English terms are more varied than the Japanese source terms. This can be explained by the general tendency of greater inconsistencies in the translated terms, i.e. 'terminology inconsistencies often increase in frequency in the translated version compared to the original, due to the fact that there can be several ways to translate a given term or expression' (Warburton, 2015, p.649). She also pointed out an important factor leading to the terminology inconsistencies as follows:

> When a document or a collection of documents is divided into smaller parts which are translated by several translators, terminology in the target language will be more inconsistent than when only one translator is involved.

We can reasonably assume that several translators took charge of translating the municipal texts (terms) we deal with here, as the organisations in charge (CLAIR, Shinjuku City and Hamamatsu City) are different. Besides, the unavailability of bilingual municipal terminologies they can consult can aggravate the problem of terminology inconsistencies.

2.3 Controlling Term Variations

The range of the term variations to be addressed is dependent on foreseen applications (Daille, 2005). In this study, from the point of view of controlled authoring and MT, we cover a wide range of variations, including not only morphological and syntactic variations, but also synonyms and orthographic variations (Jacquemin, 2001; Yoshikane et al., 2003; Daille, 2003; Carl et al., 2004).

Investigating all the term pairs extracted from the corpus, we identified 374 Japanese term variations (12.4% of 3012 Japanese term types) and 1258 English term variations (36.3% of 3465 English term types). What we need to do next is to define preferred terms and proscribed terms in both Japanese

	Term	Dic.	Freq.	Typology
1	**健康診査**/*kenkou shinsa*	✓	30	
2	健康診断/*kenkou shindan*	✓	5	
3	検査/*kensa*	✓	51	(A-1) omission
4	健診/*ken-shin*	✓	12	(C-1) initialism
1	health medical examination		1	(A-1) insertion
2	health check-up		17	(B-3) hyphen
3	medical check-up		3	(B-3) hyphen
4	medical examination	✓	10	
5	**health checkup**	✓	37	
6	check-up		14	(A-1) omission, (B-3) hyphen
7	health check		1	
8	physical check-up		2	(B-3) hyphen

Table 1: Examination of term variations

	(a) Uncontrolled types	(b) Controlled types	b/a	Tokens
Japanese	3012	2802	93.0%	15313
English	3465	2740	79.1%	15708

Table 2: The basic statistics of the controlled terminologies

and English (Warburton, 2014). We take into account the following three criteria to examine the variant terms:

Dictionary evidence: If a term is registered as an entry form in general dictionaries,[7] we regard it as preferable.

Frequency evidence: Higher frequency in the corpus is preferable.

Typological preference: The following types of variations are not preferable:[8] (A-1) omitting necessary information/inserting unnecessary information, (A-2) possessive case/personal pronouns, (B-1) emphasis symbols, (B-2) Kana characters, (B-3) hyphens, (C-1) initialisms/acronyms, (C-2) clipping and (D-1) transliteration.

Table 1 shows some examples of how each term meets each of the criteria. From this, we can define, for instance, '健康診査' as a preferred term since it is registered in the dictionary and also observed frequently (30 times) in the corpus, while the other three can be defined as proscribed terms. On the other hand, for the English translated terms, we can choose 'health checkup' as a standard translation. Though 'health check-up' (with a hyphen) is also frequently used in the corpus, we prefer 'health checkup' (without a hyphen) based on the typological preference policy (B-3) we adopted above.

Table 2 gives the basic statistics of our terminologies, showing the reduced number of term types after the variations were controlled. It can be noted that the number of English term types was reduced by about 20%, and the number of controlled term types in Japanese and in English became closer. This is not surprising because it is reasonable to assume that Japanese terminology and English terminology should contain the same size of *concepts* (or *referents*) in the parallel corpus. Controlling the variant forms of terms can be regarded as assigning one (authorised) linguistic form to one concept. We can estimate that the number of municipal concepts in our corpus is around 2700–2800.

We are now in the position to address the question: How do we evaluate the terminology and the controlled terminology we constructed? In the following sections, we propose a way to quantitatively evaluate the coverage of terminology and the quality of variation control, and evaluate our terminologies.

---

[7] In this study, we consulted the Sanseido Grand Concise Japanese-English Dictionary and the Kenkyusha New Japanese-English Dictionary.

[8] A: Syntax/morphology, B: Orthography, C: Abbreviation, D: Translation

3 Method for Evaluating Uncontrolled and Controlled Terminologies

To present the basic idea and framework of the evaluation, henceforth we use the following symbols based on Baayen (2001):

$V(N)$: number of distinct terms (number of types).
N: number of term occurrences in the corpus (number of tokens).
m: index for frequency class (m is an integer value).
$V(m, N)$: number of types that occur m times in the corpus.

3.1 Self-Referring Coverage Estimation

To estimate the coverage of the terminologies without using external terminologies, we employ the self-referring quantitative evaluation method proposed by Kageura & Kikui (2006). The basic idea is (1) to extrapolate the size of N to infinity using the observed data and estimate the saturation point, and (2) to evaluate the current status of the $V(N)$ in comparison with the saturation point.

While Kageura & Kikui (2006) estimated the coverage of the lexical items of a Japanese travel expression corpus, specifically focusing on the content words (nouns, verbs and adjectives), we assume this method can be applied to our task of estimating the coverage of the terms (mostly noun compounds) that appeared in our municipal corpus. They also emphasised that this method presupposes that the corpus qualitatively represents the whole range of relevant language phenomena in the given domain. Though the size of our municipal corpus itself is not large, it is possible to apply the method to our case, as the corpus focuses on a narrow domain (municipal life information) and covers a wide and well-balanced range of linguistic phenomena.

3.2 Conditions for Evaluation

We compare two parameters: (i) controlled and uncontrolled and (ii) Japanese and English. Thus, four conditions of terminology were prepared: (1) uncontrolled Japanese terminology, (2) uncontrolled English terminology, (3) controlled Japanese terminology, and (4) controlled English terminology.

To estimate the coverage of *terms*, we investigate the uncontrolled conditions. Our previous observations showed that uncontrolled English terminology is more varied than uncontrolled Japanese terminology, which may affect the population size of the terminologies. On the other hand, investigating the controlled conditions is important to see the coverage of *concepts* in the domain.

From the point of view of validating how well our terminologies are controlled, we explore the controlled conditions of the terminologies. Our hypothesis is that if the terminologies are well controlled, the estimated population number of Japanese and English term types become closer, as both represent the same set of concepts.

3.3 Expected Number of Terms

A number of methods have been proposed to estimate the population item size (Efron and Thisted, 1976; Tuldava, 1995; Baayen, 2001). Here we adopt Large-Number-of-Rare-Event (LNRE) modelling, which has been used in the field of lexical statistics (Khmaladze, 1987; Baayen, 2001; Kageura, 2012). We outline the computational steps behind the method, following Baayen (2001).

Let the population number of types be S and let each type be denoted by w_i ($i = 1, 2, ..., S$). With each w_i population probability p_i ($i = 1, 2, ..., S$) is associated. Using the binomial theorem, we can express the expected number of types that occur m times in a sample of N as follows:

$$E[V(m, N)] \;=\; \sum_{i=1}^{S} \binom{N}{m} p_i^m (1 - p_i)^{N-m} = \sum_{i=1}^{S} \frac{(Np_i)^m}{m!} e^{-Np_i}. \tag{1}$$

At the final step of (1), the Poisson approximation with parameter $\lambda = np$ is applied.

In order to express $E[V(N)]$, the expected number of types, we focus on the types that do not occur. Taking the complement of the probability that type w_i does not occur in the sample N tokens, we obtain the probability that w_i occurs at least once in the sample N. Hence, the $E[V(N)]$ is given as follows:

$$E[V(N)] = \sum_{i=1}^{S}(1 - \binom{N}{0}p_i^0(1 - p_i)^{N-0}) = \sum_{i=1}^{S}(1 - e^{-Np_i}). \tag{2}$$

Note that the Poisson approximation is used again in the last step of (2).

For mathematical convenience, we rewrite the Poisson models in integral forms using the structural type distribution $G(p)$, the cumulative number of types with probabilities equal to or greater than p, which is defined as follows: $G(p) = \sum_{i=1}^{S} I_{[p_i \geq p]}$, where $I = 1$ when $p_i \geq p$, and 0 otherwise. We can renumber the subscript of p for $p_j > 0$, such that $p_j < p_{j+1}$ ($j = 1, 2, ..., \kappa$). As $G(p)$ is a step function, jumps at the probabilities p_j, in other words, the number of types in the population with probabilities p_j, are given by $\Delta G(p_j) = G(p_j) - G(p_{j+1})$. We can now restate the equations (1) and (2):

$$E[V(m, N)] = \sum_{j=1}^{\kappa} \frac{(Np_j)^m}{m!}e^{-Np_j}\Delta G(p_j) = \int_0^{\infty} \frac{(Np)^m}{m!}e^{-Np}dG(p). \tag{3}$$

$$E[V(N)] = \sum_{j=1}^{\kappa}(1 - e^{-Np_j})\Delta G(p_j) = \int_0^{\infty}(1 - e^{-Np})dG(p). \tag{4}$$

Using some hypotheses about the form of distributions such as inverse Gauss-Poisson distribution, we can obtain models to extrapolate the $V(N)$ and $V(m, N)$ for $N \to \infty$.

3.4 Growth Rate of Terms

The constructed model also gives us insight into the growth rate, or how fast the number of types increases as we extract more terms from texts in the domain. The growth rate is obtained by taking the derivative of $E[V(N)]$ as follows:

$$\frac{d}{dN}E[V(N)] = \frac{d}{dN}\int_0^{\infty}(1 - e^{-Np})dG(p) = \frac{1}{N}\int_0^{\infty} Npe^{-Np}dG(p) = \frac{E[V(1, N)]}{N}. \tag{5}$$

4 Results and Discussions

4.1 Population Types and Present Status of Terminologies

Table 3 gives the estimated population number of term types $E[S]$, together with the coverage ratio $CR\ (= V(N)/E[S])$.

Though there are several models of LNRE, we chose the following two models, which were shown to be effective in this estimation task: Generalised Inverse Gauss-Poisson (GIGP) model (Sichel, 1975) and finite Zipf-Mandelbrot (fZM) model (Evert, 2004; Evert and Baroni, 2005).[9]

The lower χ^2-value and higher p-value indicate a better fit of the LNRE model, and Baayen (2008, p.233) remarks that a p-value above 0.05 is preferable. Though all of the p-values are below 0.05, the χ^2-values are not bad compared to the related work by, for example, Kageura (2012) or Baayen (2001), so we can reasonably assume that the estimation results are meaningful.

The estimated population size $E[S]$ ranges from 4299 to 7616, and the coverage ratio CR ranges from 42.7% to 64.0%. Though the values of $E[S]$ and CR depend on the models used,[10] we can observe several important points of the result.

Firstly, focusing on the uncontrolled terminologies, we recognise very different results between Japanese and English: the population number of types of Japanese, 5505 (GIGP) and 4626 (fZM), is much smaller than that of English, 7616 (GIGP) and 6083 (fZM). Consequently, the coverage ratio of Japanese is generally higher than that of English. This may reflect the higher diversity of the uncontrolled English terminology. As we have seen in Section 2.3, the ratio of variations in the English uncontrolled

---

[9]Though we tried two other LNRE models, the lognormal model (Carroll, 1969) and the Yule-Simon model (Simon, 1960), the fit of the models to our data was not good compared to the GIGP and fZM models, so we did not adopt these models.

[10]For all conditions, the fZM model produced higher values of $E[S]$ than the GIGP model.

		Model	$E[S]$	$V(N)$	$CR(\%)$	χ^2	p
Uncontrolled	Ja	GIGP	5505.3	2953	53.6	35.260	0.0008
		fZM	4626.2	2953	63.8	33.930	0.0012
	En	GIGP	7616.4	3255	42.7	23.857	0.0325
		fZM	6083.0	3255	53.5	28.197	0.0085
Controlled	Ja	GIGP	5111.9	2753	53.9	34.620	0.0010
		fZM	4299.0	2753	64.0	27.905	0.0093
	En	GIGP	5380.2	2611	48.5	35.354	0.0007
		fZM	4444.5	2611	58.7	36.525	0.0005

Table 3: Population types $E[S]$ and coverage CR

terminology is much higher than that in the Japanese one, which suggests the potential diversity of translated English terminology in the population.

Secondly, the controlled terminologies tend to exhibit a lower $E[S]$ and higher CR than the uncontrolled terminologies. For example, the CR of controlled terminology when fZM is adopted is 64.0% for Japanese and 58.7% for English, which means that around two thirds of the concepts in the domain are included in our terminologies. It is worth noting that the coverage of the controlled terminologies exceeds that of the uncontrolled ones. This result is fairly good as a starting point and encourages the practical use of the terminologies.

Finally, related to the second point, the differences of $E[S]$ and CR values between Japanese and English in the controlled conditions are much smaller than those in the uncontrolled conditions. In principle, the (population) size of the concepts in the parallel data of a given domain should be the same across the languages. The closer values of $E[S]$ between Japanese and English demonstrate that our constructed terminologies have a desirable nature. We should, however, remain aware that there are still differences between the Japanese and English controlled terminologies. We believe this is mainly because (1) the English translated sentences in the parallel corpus are sometimes not word-for-word translations of the original Japanese sentences, which may affect the distribution of terms in the corpus, and (2) the term variation control was performed solely by the authors of the paper, i.e. native speakers of Japanese, and there is still room for improvement in English term variation control.

4.2 Growth Patterns of Terminology

From the practical point of view, it is impossible to observe an infinite size of N within the limited textual data that is available. Our next question is to what extent we can enlarge the size of the terminologies and extend their coverage within the realistic range. To address this question, we take a closer look at the dynamic trends of the terminology growth.

We first observe how the expected number of term types $V(N)$ shifts as the number of term tokens N increases. Figure 2 draws for each LNRE model the growth curves of $V(N)$, as N grows to 100000, which is approximately 6.5 times as large as the present N.[11] The vertical dotted line indicates $N = 15000$, which is close to the present N.

Comparing the growth curves of the four conditions, we can easily recognize the general tendencies that conform to what we pointed out in Section 4.1. We summarise them as follows:

1. The English uncontrolled terminology grows more rapidly than the Japanese one.
2. The controlled terminologies shows more moderate growth than the uncontrolled ones.
3. The growth curves of the controlled Japanese and English align very closely.

The growth curves also enable us to visually grasp the shift of the growth rate. We can observe that all of the curves grow rapidly in the beginning and become gentler when N reaches around 30000, about twice the size of the present N. Although within the size of 100000, all the growth curves do

---

[11]Note that the actual present N is 15313 for Japanese and 15708 for English as shown in Table 2.

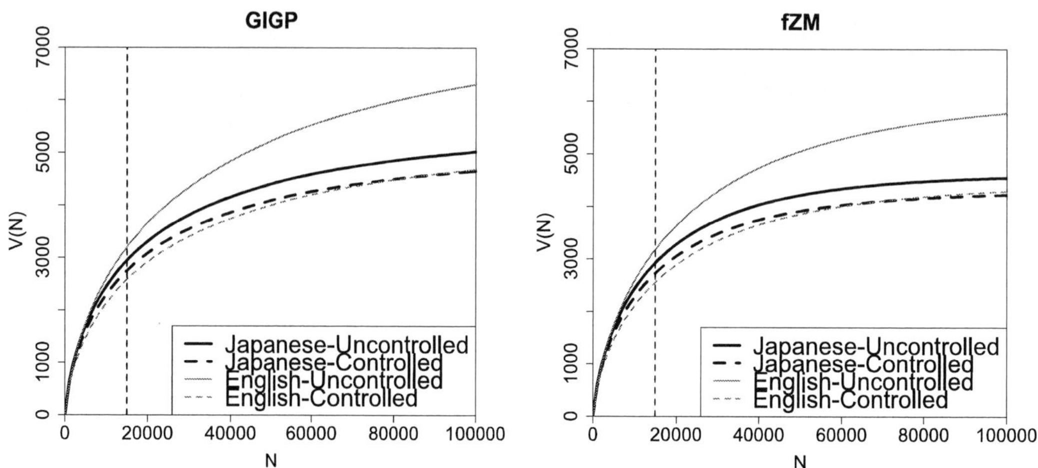

Figure 2: Growth curves of the terminologies

			0.5N		N		1.5N		2N		2.5N		3N	
			CR	GR	CR	GR	CR	GR	CR	GR	CR	GR	CR	GR
Uncont.	Ja	GIGP	39.0	0.144	53.9	0.082	63.2	0.055	69.8	0.040	74.6	0.030	78.4	0.024
		fZM	45.9	0.146	63.8	0.081	74.5	0.051	81.5	0.035	86.4	0.024	89.8	0.018
	En	GIGP	29.9	0.162	42.9	0.100	51.6	0.072	58.1	0.055	63.1	0.044	67.2	0.036
		fZM	37.2	0.163	53.5	0.099	64.2	0.069	71.8	0.050	77.4	0.038	81.8	0.030
Cont.	Ja	GIGP	39.4	0.133	54.2	0.075	63.4	0.051	69.9	0.037	74.7	0.028	78.4	0.022
		fZM	46.3	0.134	64.0	0.074	74.6	0.047	81.5	0.032	86.3	0.023	89.8	0.016
	En	GIGP	35.0	0.125	48.9	0.074	57.8	0.051	64.3	0.038	69.2	0.030	73.1	0.024
		fZM	41.9	0.126	58.7	0.073	69.3	0.049	76.5	0.035	81.8	0.025	85.7	0.019

Table 4: Shift in the coverage ratio (CR: %) and the growth rate (GR)

not seem flattened out, we can gain insight into how to effectively extend the size of the terminologies. Considering the difficulty in compiling bilingual (or multilingual) parallel municipal corpora on a large scale, we further restrict ourselves to a realistic size of N. Table 4 shows the shift in the estimated coverage ratio CR and the growth rate GR at $0.5N$ intervals up to $3N$ (about 450000 tokens). These two measures give us different perspectives for the terminology extension.

CR is a goal-oriented measure, which tells us how much addition of term tokens (or texts) is needed to attain a certain coverage of the potential terminology in the domain. If we double the token size N, we achieve nearly 80% coverage of the Japanese terms, 70% coverage of the English terms and 80% coverage of the concepts in the domain (when estimating by fZM), showing an increase of more than 15% compared to the original size N. If we treble N, we achieve an additional increase of at most 10% in the coverage ratio, with some of the values reaching nearly 90%. Setting goals for terminological (lexical) development is crucial in practical applications such as MT dictionary development (Dillinger, 2001; Kim et al., 2005). Using this measure, we can set the goal of terminology construction in terms of coverage.

GR is an ROI (return on investment)-oriented measure, which tells us how much addition of term tokens (or texts) is needed to obtain a new term or concept. At the current size of the terminologies, to obtain a new term type, 12 ($\approx 1/0.08$) term tokens should be added to the Japanese terminology, and 10 ($= 1/0.10$) to the English terminology. To obtain a new concept, 14 ($\approx 1/0.07$) term tokens should be added in the Japanese or English terminology. When we reach the token size of $2N$, to obtain a new term, 25 Japanese term tokens and 20 English term tokens should be added, showing the reduced efficiency in enlarging the terminologies as we examine more term tokens. This estimation enables us to decide when to stop collecting term tokens/texts in terms of cost effectiveness.

5 Conclusion and Future Work

In this study, we constructed controlled bilingual municipal terminologies and evaluated their status. The outcomes and contributions of this study are summarised as follows:

1. Using the term collection tool we developed, we efficiently extracted 3741 Japanese-English term pairs from a municipal text corpus. We then controlled the term variations by defining the preferred and proscribed terms to construct controlled bilingual terminologies.
2. The evaluation results showed that our terminology currently covers (1) about 55–65% (Japanese) and 45–55% (English) of the terms and (2) about 55–65% (Japanese) and 50–60% (English) of the concepts in the municipal domain. Also, the closer values of the population number of the term types and the similar shapes of the terminology growth curves for Japanese and English demonstrated that our terminologies are well controlled.
3. We proposed a method to evaluate the coverage of terminology. Though the self-referring method employed in this paper has difficulty in obtaining a good fit of the model for the observed data, we consider our method to respond to the practical need for estimating the potential size of terminology.

As future work, we plan to utilise the terminologies in our controlled authoring and MT environment, and evaluate their effectiveness and utility. We are now developing a real-time interactive terminology checker that detects term variations in the source text and suggests a preferred term (Miyata et al., 2016). The list of synsets of preferred terms and proscribed terms constructed in this study will be implemented in the checker. Furthermore, controlled authored source texts can be consistently translated by MT systems if their user dictionaries register pairs of preferred source and target terms.

We will also expand the size of our terminologies. Based on the estimation presented above, to achieve about 80–90% coverage of municipal terms and concepts, we need to check 15000–30000 more term tokens. At this stage, automatic term extraction (ATE) would be a viable option to efficiently collect term candidates (Itagaki et al., 2007; Macken et al., 2013; Aker et al., 2013; Kilgarriff et al., 2014). We also intend to adopt a 'generate and validate' method (Sato et al., 2013), which makes use of constituents of terms to obtain new term candidates. The terminologies constructed in this study enable us to employ this method.

Acknowledgements

This work was supported by JSPS KAKENHI Grant Number 16J11185, the Research Grant of Tokyo Institute of Technology, and the Research Grant Program of KDDI Foundation, Japan.

References

Ahmet Aker, Monica Paramita, and Robert Gaizauskas. 2013. Extracting bilingual terminologies from comparable corpora. In *Proceedings of the 51st Meeting of the Association for Computational Linguistics (ACL 2013)*, pages 402–411, Sofia, Bulgaria.

Harald Baayen. 2001. *Word Frequency Distributions*. Kluwer Academic Publishers, Dordrecht.

Harald Baayen. 2008. *Analyzing Linguistic Data: A Practical Introduction to Statistics using R*. Cambridge University Press, Cambridge.

Michael Carl, Ecaterina Rascu, Johann Haller, and Philippe Langlais. 2004. Abducing term variant translations in aligned texts. *Terminology*, 10(1):101–130.

John B. Carroll. 1969. A rationale for an asymptotic lognormal form of word-frequency distributions. In *Research Bulletin*. Educational Testing Service, Princeton, New Jersey.

Béatrice Daille. 2003. Conceptual structuring through term variations. In *Proceedings of the ACL 2003 Workshop on Multiword Expressions: Analysis, Acquisition and Treatment (MWE 2003)*, pages 9–16, Sapporo, Japan.

Béatrice Daille. 2005. Variations and application-oriented terminology engineering. *Terminology*, 11(1):181–197.

Mike Dillinger. 2001. Dictionary development workflow for MT: Design and management. In *Proceedings of the Machine Translation Summit VIII*, pages 83–88, Galicia, Spain.

Bradley Efron and Ronald Thisted. 1976. Estimating the number of unseen species: How many words did Shakespeare know? *Biometrika*, 63(3):435–447.

Stefan Evert and Marco Baroni. 2005. Testing the extrapolation quality of word frequency models. In *Proceedings of the Corpus Linguistics 2005*, Birmingham, UK.

Stefan Evert. 2004. A simple LNRE model for random character sequences. In *Proceedings of the 7es Journées internationales d'Analyse statistique des Données Textuelles (JADT 2004)*, pages 411–422, Louvain-la-Neuve, France.

Márta Fischer. 2010. Language (policy), translation and terminology in the European Union. In Marcel Thelen and Frieda Steurs, editors, *Terminology and Lexicography Research and Practice: Terminology in Everyday Life*, volume 13, pages 21–34. John Benjamins, Amsterdam.

Katerina Frantzi, Sophia Ananiadou, and Hideki Mima. 2000. Automatic recognition of multi-word terms: The C-value/NC-value method. *International Journal on Digital Libraries*, 3(2):115–130.

Masaki Itagaki, Takako Aikawa, and Xiaodong He. 2007. Automatic validation of terminology translation consistency with statistical method. In *Proceedings of the Machine Translation Summit XI*, pages 269–274, Copenhagen, Denmark.

Christian Jacquemin. 2001. *Spotting and Discovering Terms through Natural Language Processing*. The MIT Press, Cambridge.

Kyo Kageura and Genichiro Kikui. 2006. A self-referring quantitative evaluation of the ATR Basic Travel Expression Corpus (BTEC). In *Proceedings of the 5th International Conference on Language Resources and Evaluation (LREC 2006)*, pages 1945–1950, Genoa, Italy.

Kyo Kageura. 2012. *The Quantitative Analysis of the Dynamics and Structure of Terminologies*. John Benjamins, Amsterdam.

Estate V. Khmaladze. 1987. *The Statistical Analysis of Large Numbers of Rare Events*. Technical Report MS-R8804, Department of Mathematical Sciences, CWI, Amsterdam.

Adam Kilgarriff, Miloš Jakubíček, Vojtěch Kovář, Pavel Rychlý, and Vít Suchomel. 2014. Finding terms in corpora for many languages with the Sketch Engine. In *Proceedings of the Demonstrations at the 14th Conference of the European Chapter of the Association for Computational Linguistics (EACL 2014)*, pages 53–56, Gothenburg, Sweden.

Young-Gil Kim, Seong-Il Yang, Munpyo Hong, Chang-Hyun Kim, Young-Ae Seo, Cheol Ryu, Sang-Kyu Park, and Se-Young Park. 2005. Terminology construction workflow for Korean-English patent MT. In *Proceedings of the Machine Translation Summit X*, pages 55–59, Phuket, Thailand.

Philippe Langlais and Michael Carl. 2004. General-purpose statistical translation engine and domain specific texts: Would it work? *Terminology*, 10(1):131–153.

Lieve Macken, Els Lefever, and Véronique Hoste. 2013. TExSIS: Bilingual terminology extraction from parallel corpora using chunk-based alignment. *Terminology*, 19(1):1–30.

Rei Miyata, Anthony Hartley, Kyo Kageura, Cécile Paris, Masao Utiyama, and Eiichiro Sumita. 2016. MuTUAL: A controlled authoring support system enabling contextual machine translation. In *Proceedings of the 26th International Conference on Computational Linguistics (COLING 2016), System Demonstrations*, Osaka, Japan. (forthcoming).

Juan C. Sager. 2001. Terminology compilation: Consequences and aspects of automation. In Sue Ellen Wright and Gerhard Budin, editors, *Handbook of Terminology Management*, volume 2: Application-Oriented Terminology Management, pages 761–771. John Benjamins, Amsterdam.

Koichi Sato, Koichi Takeuchi, and Kyo Kageura. 2013. Terminology-driven augmentation of bilingual terminologies. In *Proceedings of the Machine Translation Summit XIV*, pages 3–10, Nice, France.

Herbert S. Sichel. 1975. On a distribution law for word frequencies. *Journal of the American Statistical Association*, 70(351a):542–547.

Herbert Simon. 1960. Some further notes on a class of skew distribution functions. *Information and Control*, 3(1):80–88.

Lori Thicke. 2011. Improving MT results: A study. *Multilingual*, January/February:37–40.

Juhan Tuldava. 1995. *Methods in Quantitative Linguistics*. Wissenschaftlicher Verlag Trier, Trier.

Kara Warburton. 2014. Developing lexical resources for controlled authoring purposes. In *Proceedings of LREC 2014 Workshop: Controlled Natural Language Simplifying Language Use*, pages 90–103, Reykjavik, Iceland.

Kara Warburton. 2015. Terminology management. In Sin-Wai Chan, editor, *Routledge Encyclopedia of Translation Technology*, pages 644–661. Routledge, New York.

Fuyuki Yoshikane, Tsuji Keita, Kyo Kageura, and Christian Jacquemin. 2003. Morpho-syntactic rules for detecting Japanese term variation: Establishment and evaluation. *Journal of Natural Language Processing*, 10(4):3–32.

Providing and Analyzing NLP Terms for our Community

Gil Francopoulo
Tagmatica
gil.francopoulo@wanadoo.fr

Joseph Mariani
LIMSI-CNRS
mariani@limsi.fr

Patrick Paroubek
LIMSI-CNRS
pap@limsi.fr

Frédéric Vernier
Paris-Sud U. - LIMSI-CNRS
Frederic.Vernier@limsi.fr.

Abstract

By its own nature, the Natural Language Processing (NLP) community is a priori the best equipped to study the evolution of its own publications, but works in this direction are rare and only recently have we seen a few attempts at charting the field. In this paper, we use the algorithms, resources, standards, tools and common practices of the NLP field to build a list of terms characteristic of ongoing research, by mining a large corpus of scientific publications, aiming at the largest possible exhaustivity and covering the largest possible time span. Study of the evolution of this term list through time reveals interesting insights on the dynamics of field and the availability of the term database and of the corpus (for a large part) make possible many further comparative studies in addition to providing a test field for a new graphic interface designed to perform visual time analytics of large sized thesauri.

1 Introduction

In the NLP community, we have tools, algorithms, resources, standards and common practices, but do we have a good knowledge of the terms that we use? The work we present here is an attempt at improving the situation. Our corpus contains articles from NLP conferences and journals about written, spoken and for a relatively small part, signed language processing, which is to our knowledge the largest ever collected in our field. It covers a time period from 1965 to 2015 and holds approximately 65,000 papers. Using OCR and PDF converters, we extracted the textual content of the documents and linked it into a database[1] with cleaned metadata about the associated events. After an NLP analysis of the content by means of lemmatizing, syntactic parsing, Named Entity recognition and various semantic lexical filtering with both large sized general language resources and some domain related ones, we produced a database of community specific terms which was manually checked. The result is a collection of terms annotated with various attributes like document-authors first appearance, alternative forms, occurrence statistics along different dimensions, including time, conferences etc. which is made available to the community along with the public part of the corpus for further comparative studies and enhancements. In the next two sections, we present related works and our corpus. Then we describe in detail the preprocessing applied to the corpus and the term extraction process. With the resulting term database, we present a study about "creation" (first appearance of a term in the corpus) and "impact" (relative dominance of a term in the last year of the time period covered by the corpus), introducing on this occasion a dedicated graphic interface designed for visual time analytics of large sized thesauri. Before concluding, we provide some interesting insights on the global dynamics of our field, revealed by the evolution of a few characteristic terms.

2 Situation with respect to other studies

The approach is to apply NLP tools on texts about NLP itself, taking advantage of the fact that we have a good knowledge of the domain ourselves. In the past, a similar methodology has been applied in the fields of applied linguistics (Nazar, 2011) and lexicography (deSchryver, 2012).

---

[1]The term database is freely available at `http://www.nlp4nlp.org/resultsOfRunsGlobal/allinnovators.html`

Proceedings of the 5th International Workshop on Computational Terminology,
pages 94–103, Osaka, Japan, December 12 2016.

Our work goes after the various studies initiated in the Workshop entitled: "Rediscovering 50 Years of Discoveries in Natural Language Processing" on the occasion of ACL 50th anniversary in 2012 (Radev et al., 2013) where a group of researchers studied the content of the corpus recorded in the ACL Anthology (Bird et al., 2008). Various studies, based on the same corpus followed, for instance (Bordea et al., 2014) on trend analysis and resulted in systems such as Saffron or the Michigan University web site. Other studies were conducted specifically on the speech-related ISCA archive (Mariani et al., 2013), and on the LREC archives (Mariani et al., 2016). More focused on resource usage is the study conducted by the Linguistic Data Consortium (LDC) team whose goal was, and still is, to build a language resource (LR) database documenting the use of the LDC resources (Ahtaridis et al., 2012).

3 Corpus

The corpus NLP4NLP[2] is made of the largest possible selection of NLP papers from conferences and journals, covering written, speech and for a limited part, sign language processing sub-domains; reaching out to a limited number of sub-corpora for which Information Retrieval and NLP activities intersect, reflecting the fact that we use NLP methods to process NLP content. It currently contains 65,003 documents coming from various conferences and journals. This is a large part of the existing published articles in our field, apart from workshop proceedings and published books. Despite the fact that they often reflect innovative trends, we decided not to include workshops as they may be based on various reviewing processes and because accessing their content is often difficult. The time period spans from 1965 to 2015. Broadly speaking and aside from the small corpora intersecting neighboring domains, one third comes from the ACL Anthology[3], one third from the ISCA Archive[4] and one third from IEEE[5]. The details are presented in table 1.

4 Preprocessing

Most of the papers are PDF documents and for a good part of them metadata are in various inconsistent formats. A phase of preprocessing is therefore needed to represent the various sources in a common format. We followed the organization of the ACL Anthology with distinct information groups for each document: the metadata and the content. For the former, we face four different types of sources with different format flavors and character encodings: BibTeX (e.g. ACL Anthology), custom XML (e.g. TALN), database downloads (e.g. IEEE) or HTML program of the conference (in general the program of the conference, e.g. TREC). The metadata (author names and title of each article) were normalized (java programs) into a common BibTeX format encoded in UTF8 and indexed by year and sub-corpus (conference or journal). Concerning the content, we face different possible formats, even inside the same sub-corpus as editing practices sometimes changed over time. Given that the amount of documents is huge, we cannot assign each file type individually by hand. Except for the small set of papers which where originally represented in raw text, we designed a type/subtype detection module as the first step in our normalization pipeline.

The vast majority of the documents are in PDF format of different sub-types. First, we use PDFBox[6] to determine the sub-type of the PDF content: text representation or bitmap image. For the first case, we use PDFBox again to extract the text, possibly with the use of the "Legion of the Bouncy Castle"[7] to extract encrypted contents. For the second case (bitmap image), we use PDFBox to extract the images and apply Tesseract OCR[8] to transform the images into a textual content. Note that we tested some commercial OCR but the quality improvement which was marginal did not justify its use. Then two filters are applied filter out degraded text content as sometimes the proceedings of conferences contains short abstracts of invited presentations or the OCR did not manage to extract proper content:

---

[2]http://www.nlp4nlp.org/
[3]http://aclweb.org/anthology
[4]www.isca-speech.org/iscaweb/index.php/archive/online-archive
[5]https://www.ieee.org/index.html
[6]https://pdfbox.apache.org/download.cgi
[7]https://www.bouncycastle.org
[8]https://code.google.com/p/tesseract-ocr

short name	# docs	format	long name	language	access to content	period	# venues
acl	4264	conference	Association for Computational Linguistics Conference	English	open access *	1979-2015	37
acmtslp	82	journal	ACM Transaction on Speech and Language Processing	English	private access	2004-2013	10
alta	262	conference	Australasian Language Technology Association	English	open access *	2003-2014	12
anlp	278	conference	Applied Natural Language Processing	English	open access *	1983-2000	6
cath	932	journal	Computers and the Humanities	English	private access	1966-2004	39
cl	776	journal	American Journal of Computational Linguistics	English	open access *	1980-2014	35
coling	3813	conference	Conference on Computational Linguistics	English	open access *	1965-2014	21
conll	842	conference	Computational Natural Language Learning	English	open access *	1997-2015	18
csal	762	journal	Computer Speech and Language	English	private access	1986-2015	29
eacl	900	conference	European Chapter of the ACL	English	open access *	1983-2014	14
emnlp	2020	conference	Empirical methods in natural language processing	English	open access *	1996-2015	20
hlt	2219	conference	Human Language Technology	English	open access *	1986-2015	19
icassps	9819	conference	IEEE International Conference on Acoustics, Speech and Signal Processing - Speech Track	English	private access	1990-2015	26
ijcnlp	1188	conference	International Joint Conference on NLP	English	open access *	2005-2015	6
inlg	227	conference	International Conference on Natural Language Generation	English	open access *	1996-2014	7
isca	18369	conference	International Speech Communication Association	English	open access	1987-2015	28
jep	507	conference	Journées d'Etudes sur la Parole	French	open access *	2002-2014	5
lre	308	journal	Language Resources and Evaluation	English	private access	2005-2015	11
lrec	4552	conference	Language Resources and Evaluation Conference	English	open access *	1998-2014	9
ltc	656	conference	Language and Technology Conference	English	private access	1995-2015	7
modulad	232	journal	Le Monde des Utilisateurs de L'Analyse des Données	French	open access	1988-2010	23
mts	796	conference	Machine Translation Summit	English	open access	1987-2015	15
muc	149	conference	Message Understanding Conference	English	open access *	1991-1998	5
naacl	1186	conference	North American Chapter of the ACL	English	open access *	2000-2015	11
paclic	1040	conference	Pacific Asia Conference on Language, Information and Computation	English	open access *	1995-2014	19
ranlp	363	conference	Recent Advances in Natural Language Processing	English	open access *	2009-2013	3
sem	950	conference	Lexical and Computational Semantics / Semantic Evaluation	English	open access *	2001-2015	8
speechc	593	journal	Speech Communication	English	private access	1982-2015	34
tacl	92	journal	Transactions of the Association for Computational Linguistics	English	open access *	2013-2015	3
tal	177	journal	Revue Traitement Automatique du Langage	French	open access	2006-2015	10
taln	1019	conference	Traitement Automatique du Langage Naturel	French	open access *	1997-2015	19
taslp	6612	journal	IEEE/ACM Transactions on Audio, Speech and Language Processing	English	private access	1975-2015	41
tipster	105	conference	Tipster DARPA text program	English	open access *	1993-1998	3
trec	1847	conference	Text Retrieval Conference	English	open access	1992-2015	24
cell total	67,937[5]					1965-2015	577

Table 1: Details of the sub-corpora. [5] In the global count of last line, for a joint conference (which is a rather infrequent situation), the papers are counted once (giving 65,003), so the sum of all cells in the table is slightly more important (yielding 67,937). Similarly, the number of venues is 558 when the joint conferences are counted once, but 577 when all venues are counted. Note that the * of the sixth column indicates inclusion in the ACL Anthology.

1. The content should be at least 900 characters.

2. The content should be of good quality. In order to assess text quality, the extracted content is analyzed by the morphological module of TagParser (Francopoulo, 2008), an industrial parser based on a broad English lexicon and Global Atlas —a knowledge base containing more than one million words from 18 Wikipedias —(Francopoulo et al., 2013) that computes deep parses of the sentences in order to detect out-of-the-vocabulary (OOV) words. We assume that the rate of OOV is a good indicator of the quality of a text and we retain a text only when it contains less than 9% of OOVs.

Then we apply a set of symbolic rules to extract the abstract, body and reference sections (in XML). Using our OOV text quality indicator we were able to test alternative strategies. The first experiment was to use ParsCit[9] (Council et al., 2008) with the original parametrization, but result were not satisfying, especially for accented Latin strings, or Arabic and Cyrillic characters because we did not have the time to retrain the software. We also tried Grobid[10], but we did not succeed to run it correctly with Windows operating system. We also considered Pdfminer[11], but it cannot deal with OCR and encrypted materials.

A semi-automatic cleaning process is applied on the metadata in order to avoid false duplicates[12] concerning middle names (e.g. for a three part name like X Y Z, is Y a second given name or the first part of the family name?). To answer this kind of question we dig into the metadata when it is in a specific BibTex format, which separates the given name from the family name with a comma. Then typographic variants (e.g. "Jean-Luc" versus "Jean Luc" or "Herve" versus "Hervé") were searched and false duplicates were normalized in order to be merged, resulting in 48,894 number of different authors. Let's add that figures are not extracted because we are unable to process and compare images. The majority (90%) of the documents comes from conferences, the rest from journals. The overall number of words is roughly 270M. Initially, the texts are in four languages: English, French, German and Russian. The number of texts in German and Russian is less than 0.5% , so they are detected automatically and discarded. The texts in French are a little bit more numerous (3%), and are kept with the same status as the English ones. This is not a problem since our pipeline is able to process both English and French.

5 Term extraction

The aim is to extract the domain terms from the bodies of the texts. We used a "contrastive strategy" where we contrast a specialized corpus with a non-specialized one using salient relative term frequency deviations from their expected mean value, along the same approach as in TermoStat (Drouin, 2004). The main idea is to discard words from "ordinary" language which are not interesting for our purpose and to retain only the domain terms. Two large non-specialized, corpora, one for English, one for French are parsed with TagParser. The English corpus is made of the British National Corpus (aka BNC), the Open American National Corpus (aka OANC), the Suzanne corpus release-5 and the English EuroParl archives (years 1999 until 2009) with 200M words. The French corpus is Passage-court with 100M words[13]. These results are filtered with the syntactic patterns presented in table 2, as follows.

type of condition	unigram pattern	bigram pattern	trigram pattern
sentence condition		the words of the term should belong to the same sentence.	the words of the term should belong to the same sentence.
syntactic condition	a noun phrase (NP), or a prepositional phrase (PP),	NP+NP, or Adjectival Phrase+NP, or NP+Adjectival Phrase	NP+NP+NP, or AdjectivalP+NP+NP, or AdjP+AdjP+NP, or NP+NP+AdjP
condition upon the head	the head should not be a pronoun	the heads should not be pronouns	the heads should not be pronouns
condition when a named entity	not a location, not an author name, not a conference name, not a numerical expression, not an URL-like expression (email address etc)		

Table 2: Syntactic patterns

A phase of filtering is then applied with a list of 800 unigram stop-words in order to discard various units and mathematical variables coming mainly from tables and formulas that are difficult to filter out. A small set of 30 bigram stop-words is also used to reject expressions like: "adjective adjective". The resulting parse trees are then flattened, retaining only lemmas and excluding punctuations. Finally two statistical matrices are built, one for each language. Texts from the NLP4NLP corpus are then parsed and contrasted with this matrix according to the same syntactic patterns and conditions. Afterwards, we

---

[9] https://github.com/knmnyn/ParsCit
[10] https://github.com/kermitt2/grobid
[11] https://pypi.python.org/pypi/pdfminer
[12] A false duplicates is when two occurences of the same name refer to two different people.
[13] http://atoll.inria.fr/passage/docs/CPCv2info.html

proceed in two steps: first, we extract the terms and we analyze the 2,000 most frequent ones in order to manually merge a small amount of synonyms which are not in the parser dictionary. Then the extraction pipeline is run a second time with the finalized term list to index all their occurences.

6 Basic results

There are 3.5M of different terms totalling 24M of occurrences of these terms. For all events, the proportion of single words terms is always less than the one of multiword terms (70% on average), with LREC exhibiting the largest difference between the two ratios (26.6% single words versus 73.5% multiwords). In general, there are common nouns, as opposed to rare proper names like "wordnet" or "wikipedia".

term	variants of all sorts	nb of occurrrences	rank
NP	NPs, noun phrase, noun phrases	1969140	1
HMM	HMMs, Hidden Markov Model, Hidden Markov Models, Hidden Markov model, Hidden Markov models, hidden Markov Model, hidden Markov Models,hidden Markov model, hidden Markov models	1950226	2
LM	LMs, Language Model, Language Models, language model, language models	1935840	3
SR	ASR, ASRs, Automatic Speech Recognition, SRs, Speech Recognition, automatic speech recognition, speech recognition	1928588	4
POS	POSs, Part Of Speech, Part of Speech, Part-Of-Speech, Part-of-Speech, Parts Of Speech, Parts of Speech, Pos, part of speech, part-of-speech, parts of speech, parts-of-speech	1864532	5
parser	parsers	1753427	6
annotation	annotations	1693523	7
classifier	classifiers	1642774	8
segmentation	segmentations	1173835	9
dataset	data-set, data-sets, datasets	1101070	10

Table 3: Basic results: the 10 most frequent terms over 1965-2015.

The 10 most frequent terms over the whole history are presented in table 3. We distinguish the classic notion of the occurrences of a term in a document from the notion of its presence, which is the number of documents holding at least one occurrence of the term. Not surprisingly, the most frequent term is "Noun Phrase" just followed by "Hidden Markov Model", since it is widely used by all NLP sub-communities, probably because of the linear aspect of written and spoken language.

7 Evolution over time

In the 60's and the 70's the number of documents per year was very low, but it went over 1,000 per year in the 90's to reach 3,000 in 2015 (see figure 1). The number of term occurrences followed more or less the same shapecurve, as presented in figure 2. We can notice also the regular biennial variation in the recent years due to the fact that COLING and LREC take place every even year.

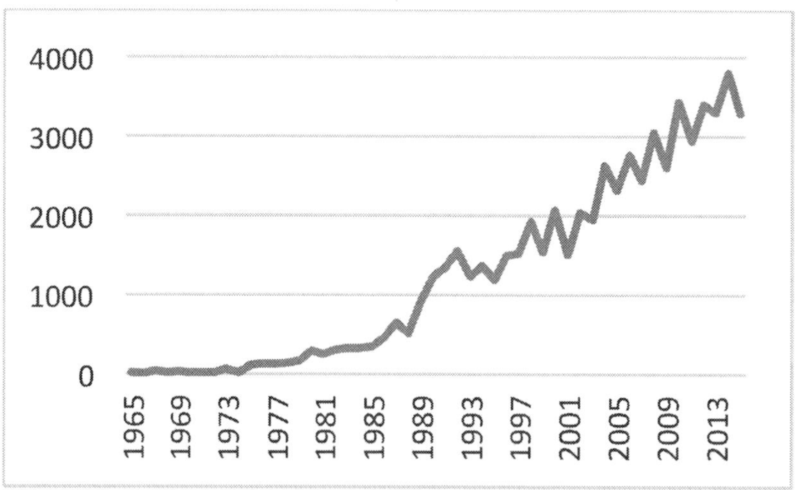

Figure 1: Document counts

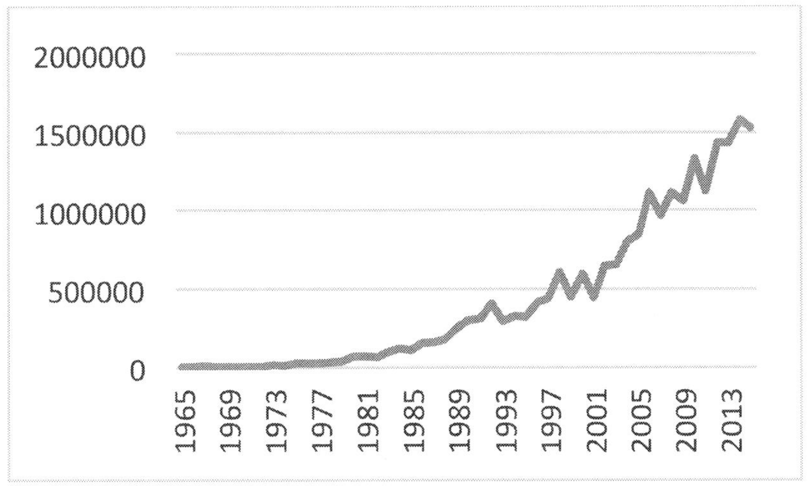

Figure 2: Occurence counts

8 Results according to creation and impact

These basic figures are computed over the whole history of our domain and are of course interesting for historical purposes but they also show which terms are ruling our community today. We consider that the year, in which we observe the apparition in the corpus of the first occurrence of a term, is the "innovation year"[14] for the term. Accordingly, all the authors who use that term in their articles during the innovation year are considered as the innovator(s) for the term. All the papers of the innovation year which hold at least one occurrence of the term are considered "innovative" papers for the term. We qualify as "external" the use of a term by authors other than the innovator(s). This distinction is important in order to exclude the overuse of particular program systems or resource names or systems specific to a particular group of people and to attribute more weight to the natural spreading of the given term rather than promote self-use by the innovator(s). The current impact of a term is defined as the number of external presences during the last year (i.e. 2015) divided by the number of innovative papers. Let's notice that for the 15 top ranking terms in impact value, the number of innovative papers is one, so the presence in the last year is equal to the impact. The impact is therefore the measure of the relative "importance" of a term today, which is used to compute an "innovation" factor for each author (Mariani et al., 2016). The 15 "technical" terms with top impact value are presented in table 4. Note that the present study considers for a single term all the observed form variations, but we assume that the term is used consistently throughtout the whole corpus with the same meaning, thus missing the possible cases of polysemy.

9 Visualization

Visualizing a large dataset is always a challenging task and our data raise several interesting questions. The term frequencies varies widely across time but no more than what is usually reported in other language studies. The first challenge is the aggregation of terms over different years because proceedings gather research contributions that are written many months before the official dates of the conferences, very often the year before in case of re-submissions. The second challenge is the huge numbers of specialized terms used by researchers. The third challenge is presented Zipf's law (very few terms appear frequently and most of the terms have small and comparable frequencies). However even low frequency terms remain of interest at every year because of the possible future evolution of their frequency.

---

[14]Note that "innovation" in the paper does not necessarily means "coining a new term", it refers to the fact that an author is the first to have used a term in a papers considering the vocabulary defined by the whole corpus.

Term	Year	Authors who introduced the term	Corpus	Document	External occurences in the last year	External presence in the last year	Impact
dataset	1966	Laurence Urdang	cath	cath1966-3	14026	1472	1472
classifier	1967	Aravind K Joshi, Danuta Hiz	coling	C67-1007	8213	999	999
optimization	1967	Ellis B Page	coling	C67-1032	3326	902	902
normalization	1967	Bruce A Beatie	cath	cath1967-16	2973	773	773
HMM	1980	Zoya M Shalyapina	coling	C80-1025	7658	687	687
SVM	1983	David D Sherertz, Mark S Tuttle, Marsden S Blois, Stuart Nelson	anlp	A83-1021	4333	644	644
GMM	1986	David D Mcdonald, James Pustejovsky	hlt	H86-1015	5520	589	589
filtering	1973	Eugenio Morreale, Massimo Mennucci	coling	C73-2024	1657	587	587
audio	1972	Victorine C Abboud	cath	cath1972-18	1787	553	553
ngram	1981	Gerd Willée, Wolfgang Kruase	cath	cath1981-6	4045	549	549
robustness	1972	Joel H Silbey	cath	cath1972-1	1347	542	542
clustering	1967	George L Cowgill	cath	cath1967-9	3168	538	538
cosine	1968	Harry B Lincoln	cath	cath1968-7	1864	536	536
regularization	1970	Charlotte L Levy, Jessica L Harris, Theodore C Hines	cath	cath1970-17	1964	510	510
test set	1975	Marvin R Sambur	taslp	taslp1975-34	1175	501	501

Table 4: Terms with highest impacts.

To tackle those three challenges we designed an interactive visualization called GapChart[15] where every term frequency is mapped in a graph where the x-axis represents time. GapChart uses the y-axis in a less traditional way. It mixes term frequency value (higher values displayed on top) and term ranking among other terms (lower rank displayed on top). The goal of the mix is to untangle terms with very similar frequencies on a particular year. Contribution of rank to the y-axis is computed in order to exactly spread the boxes of two consecutives terms and avoid overlapping. Gapchart provides a much cleaner view of dense/similar time series, the individual count and frequency values are not explicitly displayed but can be read by hovering the mouse pointer over a particular box. However the vertical gaps between boxes represent term frequency differences, consequently it is easy to identify visually which terms have a frequency higher than average. We added a set of interactive tools (sliders) to let the end-user zoom and move along the time axis and to control the box size, the links and the number of terms displayed. Terms can be selected by mouse click or search box and are then highlighted for analysis using a set of different colors. Also, we have added a checkbox to decide whether frequencies are normalized every year (between top and bottom of the view) or if they are normalized over the whole dataset. GapChart provides inherently cleaner display than line graphs, nevertheless the resulting visualization remained sometimes difficult to read since a small change of frequency between years can dramatically modify the ranking of a term. To solve this problem, we propose a last but not least feature: data smoothing. We first implemented a standard Gaussian blur processing where every value is replaced by a weighted average of the value and its neighbors. The system offers the possibility to manipulates the radius of the Gaussian kernel to let the user decide of the amount of smoothing applied. Pre-tests revealed that this feature is very powerful and efficient to unclutter the resulting view, but it may also hide many important features of the graph like peaks or yearly recurrent patterns. We thus found an interesting solution with a bilateral filtering, which is an improved Gaussian blur processing, also taking into account the difference of values using the same exponential formula. The second radius of this bell shaped kernel is also left adjustable to the end-user decision by means of a 5th slider.

10   Global analysis of the data

We analyzed the evolution of the terms over the period covered using the computation of the occurrences and presences and the GapChart visualization means. We first selected the terms we wanted to study, searched for their existence in the 50x200-boxes graph at some time over the 50-year timescale and allocated a different color for each of them. We then hid all other terms and reduced the time scope on the x-axis to the years when the terms occur and the ranking scope on the y-axis to the ranks of the terms according to their evolution. We then adjusted occurrence versus presence, ranking versus frequency or relative presence[16], and experimented data smoothing with standard or bilateral filtering Gaussian blur. Figure 3 gives an example for the set of terms "HMM" (Hidden Markov Models), "GMM" (Gaussian Mixture Models), "Neural Networks", "DNN" (Deep Neural Networks), "RNN" (Recurrent

---

[15]GapChart is available at `http://newcol.free.fr/rankvis/`

[16]The relative presence of a term is the percentage of documents in the corpus holding at least one occurrence of the term.

Neural Networks) and "dataset"[17], based on smoothed frequency with Gaussian blur.

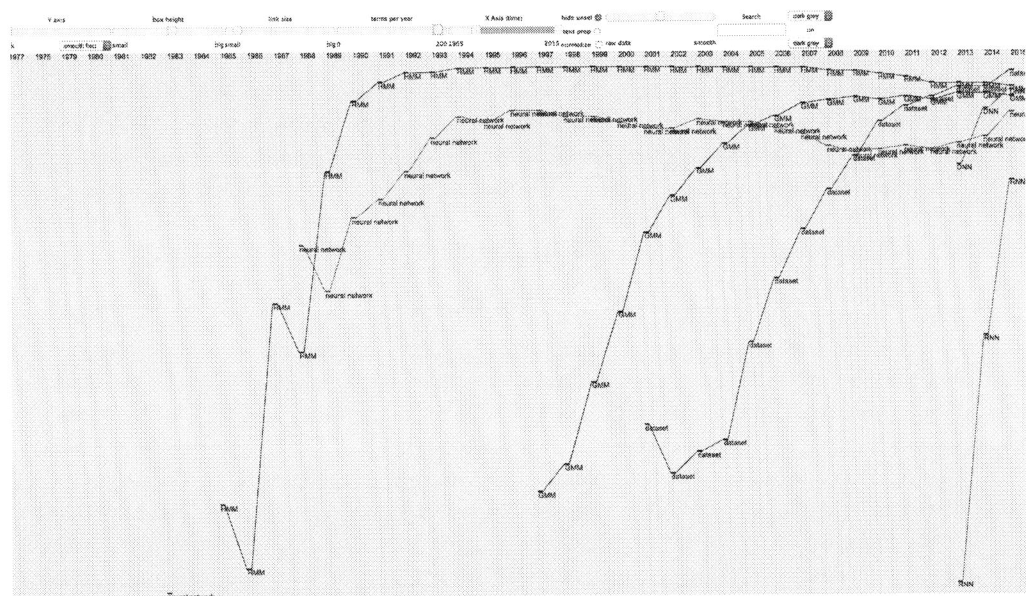

Figure 3: Evolution over time of the ranking of the terms HMM (red), GMM (blue), Neural Networks (dark green), DNN (light green), RNN (olive green) and dataset (purple) based on smoothed frequency with Gaussian blur.

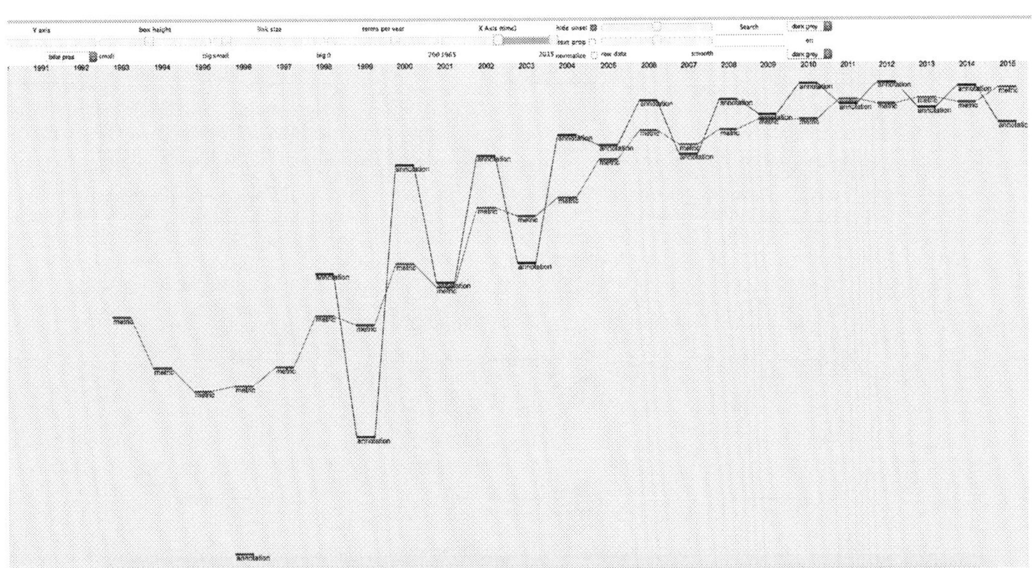

Figure 4: Evolution over time of the ranking of the terms "annotation" (red) and "metrics" (green) based on smoothed frequency with bilateral filtering Gaussian blur.

We see that the first apparitions of the term "HMM" among the 200 most frequent terms occurs in the mid 80'. The term became rapidly very popular and stayed as such until the early 2010'. It was rejoined by "GMM" at the turn of the century. Neural Networks came by the end of the 80' and became also

---

[17]Nowadays many would not consider dataset as a term but it was not the case 50 years before (Urdang, 1966).

popular but stayed below HMMs and then GMMs. Recently progress of computation and storage allowed for the development of Deep Neural Networks (DNN) which appeared abruptly and rapidly joined the highest rankings. Recurrent Neural Networks (RNN) are now following and the use of "datasets" accompanies those approaches. Interestingly, we found that the term "dataset" which has the highest impact was introduced in the NLP community in the "Computer & the Humanities" journal as early as 1966 by (Urdang, 1966), who mentions *The definitions were then divided into 158 subject fields, like physics, chemistry, fine arts, and so forth. Each unit of information—regardless of length–was called a dataset, a name which we coined at the time. (For various reasons, this word does not happen to be an entry in The Random House Dictionary of the English Language, our new book, which I shall refer to as the RHD.)"*. Another phenomenon may be analyzed on the terms "annotation" and "metrics" (figure 4). Here we ended using smoothed relative presence with bilateral filtering Gaussian blur.

We were surprised to see "annotation" fluctuating over the years, starting with a big increase in 1998 and reaching the highest rankings in agreement with the success of the data driven approaches and the necessity of disposing of annotated language resources. The highest rankings on those fluctuations appear on even years. A possible explanation is that it is due to the impact of the LREC conferences, which are devoted to Language Resources and Evaluation and happen on even years since 1998. Similarly the term "metrics", strongly attached to the evaluation of language technologies follows a similar evolution until it becomes a general term strongly attached to the research advances in the field and not only to the specific sub-field covered by LREC. Interestingly, the prediction of terms for future years predicts the continuation of the success of "Deep Neural Networks" and of the even years fluctuations of "annotation" (Francopoulo et al., 2016).

Instead of considering a set of names and all sub-corpora of NLP4NLP, another way to proceed is to select a term, starting from its first mention and to present its evolution, year after year, within the various corpora. Let's consider "WordNet", starting in 1991 in figure 5, which uses a classical visualization tool.

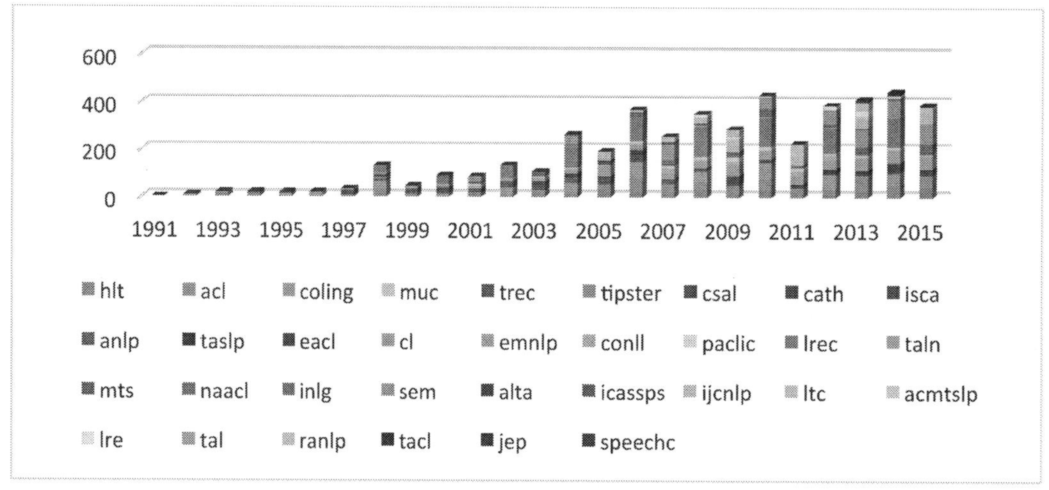

Figure 5: Evolution of "WordNet" presence in all corpora over time.

11   Conclusion

In this paper, we presented an experiment of terminology mining, by applying algorithms, resources, standards[18], tools and common practices of the NLP field to a large sized representative sample of the scientific literature of the NLP field itself. We have shown that NLP analysis of the text content of the scientific articles, extracted from the published electronic media, and associated with validated metadata can produce a term database with time information that provides useful insights about the dynamics of

---

[18]XML, UNICODE and ISO-24613 LMF.

the ongoing research in the community. In addition to showing the usefulness of lemmatizing, syntactic parsing, Named Entity recognition and various semantic lexical filtering with general and dedicated language resources for synthesizing information and saving manual cross-reference and normalization work, we have developped a specific graphic interface GapChart, especially designed for visual time analytics of large sized thesauri and delivered the terms of the domain of NLP covering both written and speech sub-domains and extended to a limited number of corpora, for which Information Retrieval and NLP activities intersect. We hope that the term database we have produced will be useful to our community for the point of view it offers upon our field and for providing the incentive to do further research on the terminology and language in NLP scientific publications.

References

Eleftheria Ahtaridis, Christopher Cieri and Denise DiPersio. 2012. LDC Language Resource Database: Building a Bibliographic Database. Proceedings of Eighth LREC, Istanbul, Turkey, ACL Anthology: L12-1549.

Steven Bird, Robert Dale, Bonnie J Dorr, Bryan Gibson, Mark T Joseph, Min-Yen Kan, Dongwon Lee, Brett Powley, Dragomir R Radev and Yee Fan Tan. 2008. The ACL Anthology Reference Corpus. A Reference Dataset for Bibliographic Research in Computational Linguistics. *Proceedings of the Sixth LREC*, Marrakech, Morocco, ACL Anthology: L08-1005.

Georgeta Bordea, Paul Buitelaar and Barry Coughlan. 2014. Hot Topics and schisms in NLP: Community and Trend Analysis with Saffron on ACL and LREC Proceedings. *Proceedings of the Ninth LREC*, Reykjavik, Iceland, ACL Anthology: L14-1697.

Issac G Councill, Giles C Lee and Min-Yen Kan. 2008. ParsCit: An open-source CRF reference string parsing package. *Proceedings of the Sixth LREC*, Marrakech, Morocco, ACL Anthology: L08-1291.

Patrick Drouin. 2004. Detection of Domain Specific Terminology Using Corpora Comparison. Proceedings of the Fourth LREC, Lisbon, Portugal, ACL Anthology: L04-1041.

Gil Francopoulo. 2008. TagParser: well on the way to ISO-TC37 conformance. *Proceedings of the First International Conference on Global Interoperability for Language Resources*, Hong Kong, PRC, pp 82-88.

Gil Francopoulo, Frédéric Marcoul, David Causse and Grégory Piparo. 2013. Global Atlas: Proper Nouns, from Wikipedia to LMF, in LMF Lexical Markup Framework Editor G. Francopoulo, ISTE Wiley.

Gil Francopoulo, Joseph Mariani and Patrick Paroubek 2016. Predictive Modeling: Guessing the NLP Terms of Tomorrow Proceedings of LREC 2016, 23-28 May 2016, Portorož, Slovenia.

Joseph Mariani, Patrick Paroubek, Gil Francopoulo and Marine Delaborde. 2013. Rediscovering 25 Years of Discoveries in Spoken Language Processing: a Preliminary ISCA Archive Analysis. *Proceedings of the Fourteenth Annual Conference of the International Speech Communication Association (Interspeech)*, Lyon, France.

Joseph Mariani, Patrick Paroubek, Gil Francopoulo and Olivier Hamon. 2016. Rediscovering 15+2 Years of Discoveries in Language Resources and Evaluation. Language Resources and Evaluation 50:165-220.

Rogelio Nazar 2011. Estudio diacrónico de la terminología especializada utilizando métodos cuantitativos: ejemplo de aplicación a un corpus de lingüística aplicada Revista Signos, vol.44 no.75 Valparaíso, Chile. http://www.scielo.cl/scielo.php?script=sci_pdf&pid=S0718-09342011000100005&lng=es&nrm=iso&tlng=es

Dragomir R Radev, Pradeep Muthukrishnan, Vahed Qazvinian, Amjad Abu-Jbara. 2013. The ACL Anthology Network Corpus. *Language Resources & Evaluation*, 47:919–944.

Gilles-Maurice de Schryver 2012. Lexicography in the Crystal Ball: Facts, Trends and Outlook R.V. Fjeld & J.M. Torjusen (eds.), Proc. of the 15th EURALEX International Congress, 7-11 August, 2012, Oslo: 93–163. Oslo: Department of Linguistics and Scandinavian Studies, University of Oslo. http://www.euralex.org/elx_proceedings/Euralex2012/pp93-163%20de%20Schryver.pdf

Laurence Urdang. 1966. The Systems, Designs and Devices Used to Process The Random House Dictionary of the English Language. Computer and the Humanities, p 31.

Evaluating a dictionary of human phenotype terms focusing on rare diseases

Simon Kocbek[1,2], Toyofumi Fujiwara[3], Jin-Dong Kim[3], Toshihisa Takagi[4], Tudor Groza[1,5]

[1]Kinghorn Center for Clinical Genomics, Garvan Institute of Medical Research, Australia
[2]Dept of Computing and Information Systems, The University of Melbourne, Australia
[3]Database Center for Life Science, ROIS, Tokyo, Japan
[4]Dept Biological Sciences, Gard School of Science, The University of Tokyo, Japan
[5]St Vincent's Clinical School, Faculty of Medicine, UNSW, Australia

```
skocbek@gmail.com, fujiwara@dbcls.rois.ac.jp,
jdkim@dbcls.rois.ac.jp, tt@bs.s.u-tokyo.ac.jp,
t.groza@garvan.org.au
```


Abstract

Annotating medical text such as clinical notes with human phenotype descriptors is an important task that can, for example, assist in building patient profiles. To automatically annotate text one usually needs a dictionary of predefined terms. However, do to the variety of human expressiveness, current state-of-the art phenotype concept recognizers and automatic annotators struggle with specific domain issues and challenges. In this paper we present results of annotating gold standard corpus with a dictionary containing lexical variants for the Human Phenotype Ontology terms. The main purpose of the dictionary is to improve the recall of phenotype concept recognition systems. We compare the method with four other approaches and present results.

1 Introduction

Human phenotype descriptions are the composite of one's observable characteristics/traits (e.g., renal hypoplasia, enlarged kidneys, etc.). These descriptions are important for our understanding of genetics and enable the computation and analysis of a varied range of issues related to the genetic and developmental bases of correlated characters (Mabee et al., 2007).

Concept Recognition (CR) is the identification of entities of interest in free text and their resolution to ontological terms with the aim of structuring knowledge from unstructured data. Linking from the literature to ontologies such as the Human Phenotype Ontology (HPO) has gained a substantial interest from the text mining community (e.g., Uzuner et al., 2012; Morgan et al., 2008). Although phenotype CR is similar to other tasks such as gene and protein name normalization, it has its specific domain issues and challenges (Groza et al., 2015). In contrast to gene and protein names, phenotype concepts are characterized by a wide lexical variability. As a result, simple methods like exact matching or standard lexical similarity usually lead to poor results. Additional challenges in performing CR on phenotypes include the use of abbreviations (e.g., *defects in L4-S1*) or of metaphorical expressions (e.g., *hitchhiker thumb*).

A fairly challenging task of phenotype concept recognizers is detecting lexical variants of tokens due to high variety of human expressiveness. For example, detecting similar words with classical similarity metrics such as the Levenshtein distance might group words with different meaning like *zygo-*

Proceedings of the 5th International Workshop on Computational Terminology,
pages 104–109, Osaka, Japan, December 12 2016.

matic (a cheek bone) and *zygomaticus* (cheek muscle) into one lexical cluster (even when using a high similarity threshold). On the other hand, less similar words with same meaning like, for example, irregular nouns (e.g., *phalanx* vs *phalanges,* or *femur* vs *femora*) might be grouped into different clusters.

Therefore, this paper presents results of experiments designed to evaluate a dictionary that tries to address the lexical variability of phenotype terms. Extending dictionaries with new terms has improved performance of, for example, gene phenotype recognizers (Funk et al., 2016). To help improve the performance (focusing on recall) of automatic phenotype CR process, we previously generated a dictionary of lexical variants for all HPO tokens (Kocbek and Groza, 2016), and here we present results of using this dictionary to annotate a gold corpus capturing text spans from 228 abstracts. The latter were manually annotated with Human Phenotype Ontology (HPO) concepts and harmonized by three curators (Groza et al., 2015).

We expect that adding lexical variants will improve the recall of the annotation process, however, we also try to measure the effect of parameter tuning on the precision of the system.

2   Methods

We used the dictionary of lexical variant clusters for all concepts and their synonyms in the HPO. Each HPO term and synonym was then extended with combinations of all words in the corresponding clusters. We automatically annotated the gold standard corpus and compared results of five different approaches.

2.1   The Human Phenotype Ontology and the gold standard corpus

The HPO (Köhler et al., 2014) is often used for the annotation of human phenotypes and offers a tool for large-scale computational analysis of the human phenotype, focusing on rare diseases. The HPO has been used in applications such as linking human diseases to animal models (Washington et al., 2009), describing rare disorders (Firth et al., 2009), or inferring novel drug indications (Gottlieb et al., 2011).

Most terms in the HPO contain descriptions of clinical abnormalities and additional sub-ontologies are provided to describe inheritance patterns, onset/clinical course and modifiers of abnormalities. Each term has a name and can have other synonyms (e.g., "Triangular head shape" is a synonym for "Trigonocephaly"). Each name and synonym may consist of several tokens (e.g., the term "synostosis of some carpal and tarsal bones" has 7 tokens).

Terms in HPO usually follow the Entity-Quality formalism where they combine anatomical entities with qualities (Mungall et al., 2007) For instance, the term "wide anterior fontanelle" describes an anatomical entity "anterior fontanelle" with the quality "wide". Entities can usually be grounded in ontologies such as the Foundational Model of Anatomy (Rosse and Mejino, 2003), while qualities usually belong to the Phenotype and Trait Ontology (Gkoutos et al., 2009). We have previously shown that rich lexical variability comes from the quality part of phenotype terms – due to their widespread usage in common English (Kocbek and Groza, 2016)

The manually annotated HPO gold standard corpus used in this study (Groza et al., 2015) comprises 1,933 annotations in 228 abstracts with an average length of 2,42 tokens per annotation. The gold standard was harmonized by three curators. The corpus covers 460 unique HPO concepts that include abnormalities of nervous system, neoplasms, abnormalities of the integument, and abnormalities of the skeletal system.

2.2   Dictionary construction

We used the HPO released in July 2016 to generate two dictionaries, i.e., collections of labels and their corresponding identifiers. In the first dictionary (Dict1), we extracted labels and their synonyms for each HPO term. This resulted in 25,603 unique dictionary entries that were used as a baseline in our annotation experiments described in Section 2.3. Each label and synonym belonging to the same HPO term were linked to the same corresponding HPO identifier adorned with a postfix. For example, the label "Sclerosis of 5th toe phalanx" and its synonym "Increased bone density in pinky toe bone" for the HPO term with identifier HP:0100929 would have identifiers HP:0100929_0 and HP:0100929_1 respectively.

For the second dictionary (Dict2), we developed a simple tokenizer that broke each name and synonym into series of lower case tokens. The following characters were removed: . / ( ) ' > < : ; and the space and backslash characters were then used as delimiters. We ignored numbers and short tokens (i.e., shorter than 3 characters). Then the NLM Lexical Variant Generator (LVG), 2016 release (The Lexical Systems Group, 2016) was used to create lexical variants for all HPO tokens. This way we created 29,602 variants grouped into 6,480 clusters with average size of 4.57 tokens per cluster. All combinations of token variants were then used to create the collection of lexical variants of the original term. Again, the identifiers were adorned with postfix. Figure 1 illustrates the process of creating Dict2. Please note that we generated lexical variants only for the 460 HPO terms annotated in the gold standard.

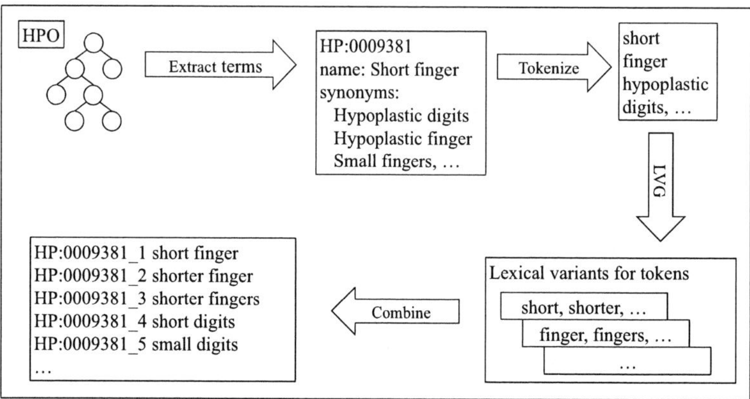

Figure 1: An example of lexical variants for the HPO term "HP:0009381 Short finger"

2.3   Annotation

To test the effectiveness of the created dictionary, we annotated the HPO gold standard corpus (Groza et al., 2015). For annotation with exact matching, we developed a simple annotator that compared lower case text against all terms in the developed dictionary. Common English stop word were ignored. Overlapping annotations with the same HPO identifier were considered as one annotation. The terms that were found in the text were annotated with text spans. For the similarity matching annotation we used the Jaccard coefficient, which is one of the commonly used metrics to measure similarity of two strings and is defined as the size of the intersection divided by the size of the union of the sample sets. For general performance of Jaccard coefficient in comparison with other approaches, readers are referred to (Cohen et al., 2003). Specifically we used PubDictionaries[1], a public service for text annotation using a dictionary (where the latter represent a collection of labels and their corresponding identifiers). A label is a natural language term that refers to the object identified by the corresponding identifier. PubDictionaries provides a REST service for text annotation using dictionaries which are plug-able, and it implements Jaccard coefficient for string similarity computation. The input to the REST services is the text, the type of the annotation, i.e., exact matching or similarity matching and the threshold coefficient in the case of the latter.

We have chosen to use PubDictionaries for our experiments not only because it eases our experiments with its pluggable dictionary system, but also by keeping the dictionaries in the public service, the experiments will remain replicable by any one. As PubDictionaries is an open source project, the experiments should be replicable. The following three similarity thresholds were used for annotation through PubDictionaries: 0.75, 0.85 and 0.95.

2.4   Evaluation

We defined true positive (TP), false positive (FP) and false negative (FN) concept annotations as follows. TPs were the annotations with the same HPO identifier found in both the dictionary and the gold standard corpus and an overlapping text span. For example, if in the following text: "A syndrome

---

[1] Available on: www.pubdictionaries.org

of brachydactyly (absence of some middle or distal phalanges)" the terms "brachydactyly" and "syndrome of brachydactyly" are both mapped to the same ID, they will represent the same annotation, since they overlap. On the other hand, when terms with the same identifier are found on different positions in the text, they represent different annotations. FP annotations were those detected with automatic annotator, but were not included in the gold standard corpus, while FN annotations represent annotations found in the gold standard and not detected with the automatic annotator.

Based on these three values, we evaluate the model with and report the Precision, Recall and F-Score values. Precision of positive class is the ratio of correctly annotated positive values to the number of all instances annotated as positive, this is also known as Positive Predictive Value. Recall of positive class is computed as the number of correctly annotated instances from the positive class divided by the number of all instances from the positive class; this is also known as sensitivity. F-Score is the weighted harmonic mean of Precision and Recall.

3   Results

Figure 2 summarizes results for five different approaches. One can notice that extending HPO terms with lexical variants in *Dict 2 E* reaches the highest F-Score (0.45), while it shares the highest Recall with the *Dict1 0.75* approach (0.45). The highest precision was achieved with *Dict1 0.95* (0.47).

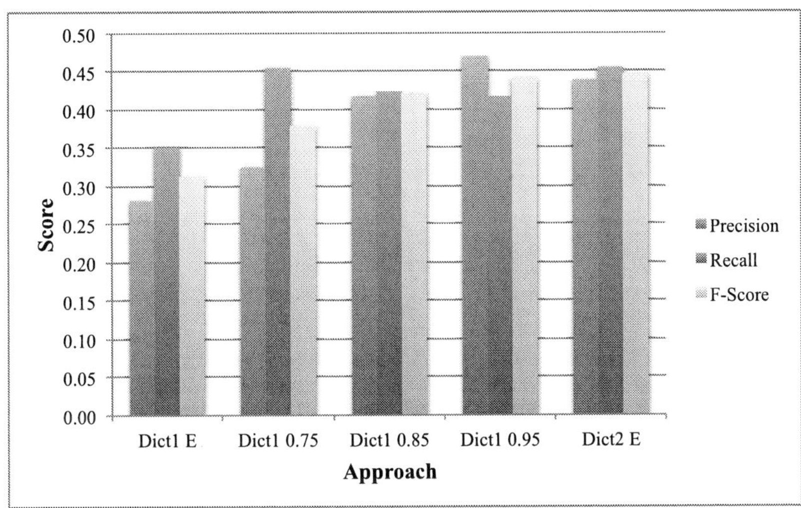

Figure 2: Precision, Recall and F-Score values for 5 different approaches: Dictionary 1 with Exact (E) matching and similarity matching (thresholds 0.75, 0.85 and 0.95), and Dictionary 2 with Exact matching.

Table 1 presents results of five different annotation combinations that were/were-not detected with different approaches. The term "syndrome of brachydactyly" is an example where a similarity metric with a low threshold preforms better than our approach with added lexical variants. Terms "autosomal dominant trait" and "synostosis of some carpal and tarsal bones" are examples where extending the dictionary with lexical variants works well, while the term "malformed pinna" was not detected with any approach.

Table 1: Some examples of annotations that were (Yes) or were not (No) detected with different approaches.

Annotation	Dict1 E	Dict1 0.75	Dict1 0.85	Dict1 0.95	Dict2 E
syndrome of brachydactyly	No	Yes	No	No	No
brachydactyly	Yes	Yes	Yes	Yes	Yes
autosomal dominant trait	No	Yes	Yes	Yes	Yes
synostosis of some carpal and tarsal bones	No	No	No	No	Yes
malformed pinna	No	No	No	No	No

4 Conclusion

We presented and evaluated a dictionary of human phenotype terms and their lexical variants. Using a gold standard HPO corpus we measured Precision, Recall and F-Score, and compared five different approaches. The results showed that extending HPO terms with their lexical variants significantly improves the Recall and F-Score values compared to the original dictionary with no lexical variants. However, the method did not achieve the highest Precision of the system. Depending on the task and application, one might consider using our dictionary when Recall plays a more important role than Precision. Please note that we also used a relaxed method for defining true positives as described in Section 2.4. In case of strict exact matching, the results would be affected.

In the current version of the dictionary, we extended only a small subset of all HPO terms. In the future we plan to extend also other terms, however, with the current approach this would result in a large number of irrelevant and incorrect terms (such as, for example, "low blooded pressure" for the original term "low blood pressure"). Therefore, we are planning to address this issue before generating the full dictionary. In addition, we are planning to consider other reference corpus in the evaluation step. The current version of the dictionary is publicly available through PubDictionaries (HP_Garvan).

Reference

William W. Cohen, Stephen E. Fienberg, Pradeep D. Ravikumar, and Stephen E. Fienberg. 2003. A Comparison of String Distance Metrics for Name-Matching Tasks. *Proceedings of IJCAI-03 Workshop on Information Integration on the Web*:73–78.

Helen V. Firth, Shola M. Richards, A. Paul Bevan, Stephen Clayton, Manuel Corpas, Diana Rajan, Steven Van Vooren, Yves Moreau, Roger M. Pettett, and Nigel P. Carter. 2009. DECIPHER: Database of Chromosomal Imbalance and Phenotype in Humans Using Ensembl Resources. *American Journal of Human Genetics*, 84(4):524–533.

Christopher S. Funk, K. Bretonnel Cohen, Lawrence E. Hunter and Karin M. Verspoor. 2016. Gene Ontology synonym generation rules lead to increased performance in biomedical concept recognition. *Journal of Biomedical Semantics*, 7:52.

Georgios V. Gkoutos, Chris Mungall, Sandra Dölken, Michael Ashburner, Suzanna Lewis, John Hancock, Paul Schofield, Sebastian Köhler, and Peter N. Robinson. 2009. Entity/quality-based logical definitions for the human skeletal phenome using PATO. In *Proceedings of the 31st Annual International Conference of the IEEE Engineering in Medicine and Biology Society: Engineering the Future of Biomedicine, EMBC 2009*, pages 7069–7072.

Assaf Gottlieb, Gideon Y Stein, Eytan Ruppin, and Roded Sharan. 2011. PREDICT: a method for inferring novel drug indications with application to personalized medicine. *Molecular systems biology*, 7(496):496.

Tudor Groza, S. Kohler, Sandra Doelken, Nigel Collier, Anika Oellrich, Damian Smedley, Francisco M. Couto, Gareth Baynam, Andreas Zankl, Peter N. Robinson, Sebastian Köhler, Sandra Doelken, Nigel Collier, Anika Oellrich, Damian Smedley, Francisco M. Couto, Gareth Baynam, Andreas Zankl, and Peter N. Robinson. 2015. Automatic concept recognition using the Human Phenotype Ontology reference and test suite corpora. *Database*, 2015(0):bav005-bav005.

Simon Kocbek and Tudor Groza. 2016. Building a dictionary of lexical variants for human phenotype descriptors. In *BioNLP Workshop*, pages 186–190. ACL.

Sebastian Köhler, Sandra C. Doelken, Christopher J. Mungall, Sebastian Bauer, Helen V. Firth, Isabelle Bailleul-Forestier, Graeme C M Black, Danielle L. Brown, Michael Brudno, Jennifer Campbell, David R. Fitzpatrick, Janan T. Eppig, Andrew P. Jackson, Kathleen Freson, Marta Girdea, Ingo Helbig, Jane A. Hurst, Johanna Jähn, Laird G. Jackson, et al. 2014. The Human Phenotype Ontology project: Linking molecular biology and disease through phenotype data. *Nucleic Acids Research*, 42(D1).

Paula M. Mabee, Michael Ashburner, Quentin Cronk, Georgios V. Gkoutos, Melissa Haendel, Erik Segerdell, Chris Mungall, and Monte Westerfield. 2007. Phenotype ontologies: the bridge between genomics and evolution. *Trends in Ecology and Evolution*, 22(7):345–350.

Alexander A Morgan, Zhiyong Lu, Xinglong Wang, Aaron M Cohen, Juliane Fluck, Patrick Ruch, Anna Divoli, Katrin Fundel, Robert Leaman, Jörg Hakenberg, Chengjie Sun, Heng-hui Liu, Rafael Torres, Michael Krauthammer, William W Lau, Hongfang Liu, Chun-Nan Hsu, Martijn Schuemie, K Bretonnel Cohen, et al. 2008. Overview of BioCreative II gene normalization. *Genome biology*, 9 Suppl 2(SUPPL. 2):S3.

Chris Mungall, Georgios Gkoutos, Nicole Washington, and Suzanna Lewis. 2007. Representing phenotypes in OWL. In *CEUR Workshop Proceedings*, volume 258.

Cornelius Rosse and José L V Mejino. 2003. A reference ontology for biomedical informatics: The Foundational Model of Anatomy. *Journal of Biomedical Informatics*, 36(6):478–500.

NLM The Lexical Systems Group. 2016. Lexical Tools, 2016, https://lexsrv3.nlm.nih.gov/LexSysGroup/Projects/lvg/2016/web/index.html, accessed June 2016

Özlem Uzuner, Brett R South, Shuying Shen, and Scott L DuVall. 2012. 2010 i2b2/VA challenge on concepts, assertions, and relations in clinical text. *Journal of the American Medical Informatics Association : JAMIA*, 18(5):552–6.

Nicole L. Washington, Melissa A. Haendel, Christopher J. Mungall, Michael Ashburner, Monte Westerfield, and Suzanna E. Lewis. 2009. Linking human diseases to animal models using ontology-based phenotype annotation. *PLoS Biology*, 7(11).

A semi automatic annotation approach
for ontological and terminological knowledge acquisition

Driss Sadoun
Laboratory MoDyCo / University of Paris-Ouest Nanterre.
`driss.sadoun@u-paris10.fr`

Abstract

We propose a semi-automatic method for the acquisition of specialised ontological and terminological knowledge. An ontology and a terminology are automatically built from domain experts' annotations. The ontology formalizes the common and shared conceptual vocabulary of those experts. Its associated terminology defines a glossary linking annotated terms to their semantic categories. These two resources evolve incrementally and are used for an automatic annotation of a new corpus at each iteration. The annotated corpus concerns the evaluation of French higher education and science institutions.

Key words : annotation, ontology, terminology, machine learning.

1   Introduction

For several years, French higher education and science institutions have been evaluated by an external institution. Most often this evaluation is conducted by the *High Council for the Evaluation of Research and Higher Education* (HCERES). Each year the HCERES recruits and trains academic experts participating in the evaluation of one or more institutions. These evaluations lead to the production of publicly accessible reports. These reports are rather standardized documents as their writing follows an established *evaluation template*. This *evaluation template* can be divided into ten *fields* : *Training, Governance, International Relations, Management, Piloting, Research, Student achievement, Scientific Culture* and *Valorization*. Each *field* may then be divided into several sub-fields (only twenty are explicitly named). Each report summarizes in its conclusion the strengths and weaknesses of the evaluated institution according to the *evaluation template*'s fields. Each year positive or negative assessments are manually classified by the HCERES experts according to the fields they refer to, in order to synthesise strengths and weaknesses of evaluated institutions over the same year.

In the reports, classifying an assessment means simultaneously identifying a term denoting a field and a term denoting an opinion. Sentences (1) and (2) below respectively contain a positive assessment on the field *training* and a negative assessment on the field *Valorization*. Sentences (3) and (4) contain more than one assessment, which is representative of the sentences of the conclusions. Thus, although sentences are generally well written, the aggregation of assessments can make them quite long and complex. Throughout this article, terms denoting a field appear in **bold** and terms denoting an opinion appear in *italic*.

Proceedings of the 5th International Workshop on Computational Terminology,
pages 110–120, Osaka, Japan, December 12 2016.

1. une **formation doctorale** *très attractive.* / (A *very attractive* **doctoral training.**)

2. une **politique de valorisation de la recherche** *peu lisible.* / (A **most unclear policy of research valorization.**)

3. Une **présidence** *forte* mais une **gouvernance** *à revoir.* / (A *strong* **presidency** but **governance** *must be overhauled.*)

4. Une *difficulté* de **prévision des recettes** et un *manque* d'**approche politique dans la construction du budget.** / (Some *difficulty* in **forecasting revenues** and a *lack* of a **political approach in budget drafting.**)

This work of classification is a long, complex and subjective task for a human being. Given the amount of work, experts have to restrict their annotation to the ten major fields. Moreover, the work has to be shared out among several academic experts, hence no expert can have a global view of all reports. Since the number of reports keeps increasing, it has becomes necessary to automate this classification task by training an opinion mining system. The main issue of the described work is the classification of opinions into fields and sub-fields. Indeed, it appeared that for the *HCERES* experts the ambiguity of term denoting a polarity as *fort (strong)* is almost nil.

Identifying fields and their associated terms is a prerequisite to training an opinion mining system. Due to the number and the diversity of the evaluated institutions, a comprehensive and consensual listing of all possible sub-fields appeared to be hardly feasible for the *HCERES* experts. Hence, we propose to identify and structure the different fields empirically by performing an annotation task, during which each expert is allowed to suggest new sub-fields when he feels the need. Suggested fields are then consensually validated or rejected. The resulting consensual annotations are used to automatically build an ontology conceptualising the fields validated during the annotation task as well as a terminology linking the annotated terms to the fields they refer to. These resources serve to train an automatic annotation system. Afterwards, a new corpus is automatically annotated before being submitted to the experts who may validate, correct or add missing annotations. This whole process represents one iteration. The resulting ontology, terminology and annotated corpus are available on request.

2 Related work

Structuring extracted terms from corpora has been a topic of interest for many years (L'Homme, 2004; Claveau and L'Homme, 2005; Toledo et al., 2012; Szulman, 2011; Marciniak et al., 2016). One issue is to choose between either a *onomasiological* based approach (relating the term to its concept) or a *semasiological* based one (relate the term to its meaning) (L'Homme, 2004) which may consist in choosing an ontology or a terminology as a means of representation.

Ontology and terminology building is often based on textual corpora because texts carry shared and stable knowledge (Mondary et al., 2008). Building an ontology or a terminology from text in a completely unsupervised manner is hardly feasible. This is due to the nature of natural languages, whose meaning depends as much on the formulated sentence as its context. Therefore, proposed methods and tools offer an assistance to reduce human effort (Cimiano et al., 2009). They require human intervention for validating or rejecting the automatically extracted terminological, onto-logical or termino-ontological resources from texts as *Text2Onto* (Cimiano and Völker, 2005), *OntoLT* (Buitelaar et al., 2004), *OntoGen* (Fortuna et al., 2007), *Terminae* (Szulman, 2011) or TermoPL (Marciniak et al., 2016). The validation may then depend only on a single person, which makes it subjective. Our aim is to minimise as much as possible the inherent human subjectivity.

To do so, we believe that the validation of identified resources has to be done consensually. Moreover, to reduce confusion and distinguish between the ontological and the terminological level to which a term can be related, we propose to use texts to build both a consensual representation of knowledge -formalized by an ontology- and a framework for interpreting terms in the context in which they appear -formalized by a terminology.

Identifying terms often depends on corpus annotation. When compared to the need and generally speaking, very few annotated corpora for opinion mining have been proposed and this regardless of language (Wiebe et al., 2005; Steinberger et al., 2014; Hammer et al., 2014; Wachsmuth et al., 2014; Croce et al., 2013; Mele et al., 2014; Daille et al., 2011; Lark et al., 2015). The lack of annotated corpus is due to the complexity of a human annotation which is notoriously difficult even for domain experts (Bernier-Colborne and Drouin, 2014). This observation is not recent and many works have proposed (semi-)automatic annotation approaches (Erdmann et al., 2000; Swift et al., 2004; Dufour-Lussier et al., 2012; Christen et al., 2015) most often based on the use of an ontology. Indeed, an ontology may be particularly helpful to help define and use complex annotation schemas (Ogren, 2006). In our approach, we propose an ontology and terminology evolution approach resembling those proposed in (Taleb et al., 2009; Toledo et al., 2012), which allows both resources to evolve while the corpus is iteratively annotated.

Empirical results have shown that using the syntactic structure of sentences to capture contexts of formulation in text is relevant for the task of opinion mining (Wu et al., 2009; Jiang et al., 2011; Lapponi et al., 2012). In addition, experiments have shown that methods based on dependency graphs may perform significantly better than the word-based methods (Hammer et al., 2014; Vilares et al., 2015). So, we chose to add to our semantically annotated corpus some annotations related to the syntactic features of the words involved in the annotated terms. In the remainder of this article, we discuss the practical value of such a choice for term identification.

3   Description of the corpus

Our corpus is made up of sentences extracted from the conclusions of the 34 evaluation reports published in 2013. More precisely sentences belong to the subsections detailing the *strong points*, the *weak points* and the *recommendations* addressed to evaluated institutions. The corpus contains 692 sentences, which represents around 20 sentences per report. The writing style is not standardized and depends on the writer. Sentences can be quite long and complex. Indeed, the number of words in the corpus is 12171, which means an average of 17 words per sentence. This length is due to the use of complex terms and to the conjunction of several nominal and verbal groups. Moreover, the majority of terms ($\simeq 73\%$) referring to a field or an assessment are complex terms, *i.e.* formed by multiple words such as **gestion des ressources humaines** (human resources management), **formation continue** (lifelong training) or *très bas* (very low). These terms may contain contiguous words, such as the term **sentiment d'appartenance** (sense of belonging) in sentence (1) or non contiguous ones like the same term in sentence (2). Each sentence may contain more than one opinion, as is the case in sentences (3) and (4). In the following sentences arrows in bold indicate the link between *head* words of terms denoting an assessment with *head* words of terms denoting a field. The light arrow indicates the link between non contiguous words belonging to the same complex term. In both cases, these arrows link words that are *heads of terms*. Among the words that form a term, the *head word* is the one that determines the syntactic features of the term. The other words that belong to a term can be designated as the *dependent words* in a syntactic sense. In a semantic sense they may be considered as *modifiers*. The addition or the deletion of dependent words does not change the syntactic distribution between *head words*. For example, sentence (5) highlights that deleting the words **d'appartenance** and *très* respectively from the terms **sentiment d'appartenance** and *très fort* does not modify the syntactic dependency between the terms *fort* and **sentiment**.

(1) Un *sentiment d'appartenance* **très fort** / A **very strong** *sense of belonging*

(2) Un *sentiment* **très fort** *d'appartenance* / A **very strong** *sense of belonging*

(3) Une *situation financière* **non maitrisée** et une **absence** de *sincérité budgétaire*. / A **non controled** *financial situation* and a **lack** of *budget honesty*.

(4) **Renforcer** le *pilotage* et le *contrôle de gestion* / **Reinforce** the *piloting* and the management control.

(5) Un *sentiment* **fort** / A **strong** *sense*

4   Semi-automatic term annotation

The aim of the semi-automatic term annotation is to bring out the shared vocabulary of the *HCERES* experts. First, a manual annotation involving the experts is performed and leads to a *consensual annotation*. Annotated terms and their associated fields are then used as a set for training an automatic annotation system. This system is based on the following automatically built resources : 1) an ontology structuring the evaluation fields ; 2) a terminology linking each annotated term to the field it refers to within the ontology and 3) syntactico-semantic patterns characterizing the features of the annotated terms. The trained system is used for the automatic annotation of a new corpus. The automatically annotated corpus is then submitted to a new manual annotation. This incremental process of the semi-automatic term annotation is illustrated in Figure 1.

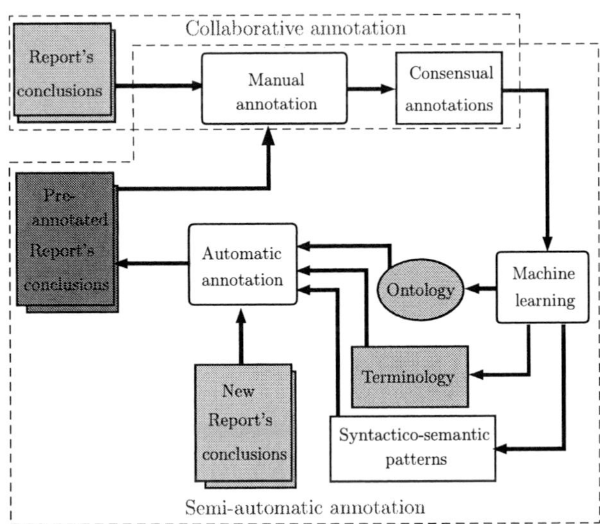

FIGURE 1 – The semi-automatic term annotation steps.

4.1 Experts' annotation

A total of 22 experts from the *HCERES* have participated in three successive annotations. They have been divided into six groups of 3 to 4 experts. Each group had a sixth of the corpus to annotate. The annotation has been done under the platform *Webanno* (Yimam et al., 2014) which enables online annotations. Many annotators can annotate the same corpus. Each annotator annotates their version of the corpus without viewing others' annotations. Then, elements of agreement and disagreement can be compared. Within *Webanno*, each annotation category may have an unlimited number of labels. In our framework, we defined the ten *main fields* as categories and their sub-fields as labels. Hence, the starting annotation tag set contained ten categories and twenty labels. To extend this tag set, annotators were allowed to offer new sub-fields for each major field when they felt it was necessary, *i.e.*, when the existing fields were not sufficient to characterize the terms to annotate. Indeed, *Webanno* authorizes the creation of new labels on the fly during annotation. When a new label is chosen, it is visible and usable by all other annotators. Moreover, if an expert identifies a new label which is better to annotate a term it can always change its previous annotations. At the end, each newly suggested sub-field can be validated or rejected, as it is based on the subjectivity of the annotator who proposed it.

Experts were all volunteers and motivated. However, as they had no previous annotation experience and due to their tight schedule, the first manual annotation took more than five weeks. Then, the use of a semi-automatic annotation approach quickly appeared as a need.

4.2 Inter-annotator agreement

Our annotation protocol is quite unusual since the tag set is not finite and evolves at each iteration as each annotator is able to propose a new label on the fly. As far as we know, there is no metric for calculating inter-annotator agreement (IAA) fitting that case. For the calculation of IAA, we then chose to calculate the F-measure by pairs of annotators of the same group. As expected, IAA for the first manual annotation was low ($\leq 40\%$). Hence, to reconcile divergent annotations, discussion sessions were organized. They took place between at least two annotators along with the authors of this article with the aim of finding common ground for each divergent annotation. In order to fit experts' schedules, each sessions duration was half an hour. Figure 2 is an example of a consensus reached on divergent annotations within the sentence 16. In this figure, the first line represents the consensual annotation, *i.e.* the one accepted by all. The next four lines correspond to the annotations of four different experts. A total agreement can be noted for the annotation of the term *développer* (develop) which refers to a *Recommendation*. However, concerning the term **sentiment d'appartenance** (sense of belonging) the associated sub-field differs for each expert. This highlights the subjectivity of the annotation task and by extension of the classification task. The annotation of *user-2* : **Identité** (Identity) is the one chosen, which is a sub-field **Gouvernance** (Governance). Once the consensual annotations are built they are used to build and change the ontology, the terminology as well as to train the automatic annotation system.

5 Automatic creation of the ontology

We chose to use an ontology to formalize the conceptual vocabulary of the *HCERES* experts as it is easily understandable by humans and readable by machines. It also allows experts to have a concise representation of their conceptual vocabulary. In addition, it offers the means to annotate its own elements in order to specify their meaning and give extra information and definitions about the set of semantic labels that will be used for the opinion classification.

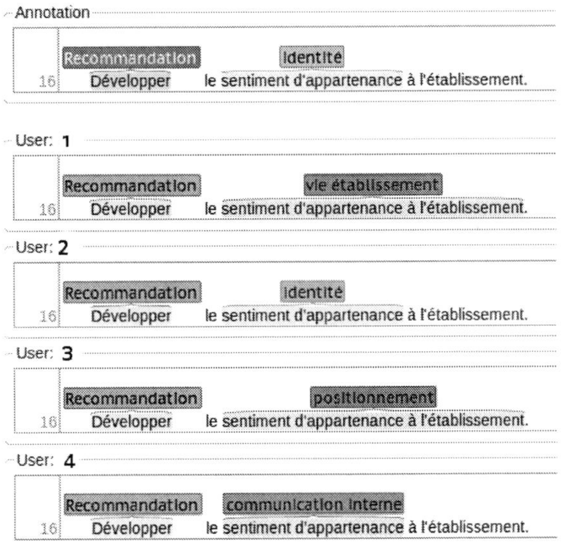

FIGURE 2 – A consensus on a divergent annotation.

After each annotation new sub-fields may be proposed by the annotators. Only fields that are agreed upon by the experts are kept i.e. added to the conceptual vocabulary. Each annotated corpus produced at an iteration is added to the collection of previously annotated ones. The whole annotated corpus is then analysed in order to automatically extract fields that have been used as annotation categories and labels. Each sub-field belongs to a field that is more general. Thus, a two-level hierarchy structure is extracted from the annotated corpus wherein a sub-field is a sub-concept of a field. This structure is represented in the form of an OWL ontology. This ontology is intended to serve the identification of opinions and their classification based on the several fields and types of assessments. Hence, the ontology also contains the concept *Assessment* and its three sub-concepts : *Positive*, *Negative* and *Recommendation*. Figure 3 is a fragment of the automatically built ontology. After a manual and two semi-automatic annotations, the ontology numbers 117 concepts including 113 fields. Among these fields, 83 are new sub-fields proposed and accepted by consensus by the experts during their collaborative annotation. These 83 new sub-fields are selected from over 100 proposed sub-fields over the three annotations.

The number of kept new sub-fields may appear high. It can be explained by the variety of evaluated institutions covered by the *HCERES* reports. This number tends to stabilize after the processing of the 34 evaluation reports published in 2013. However, it should increase (less significantly) in the future due to the particularity of certain *higher educational and scientific institutions* that reports were not yet annotated and the evolution of French institutions.

6 Automatic creation of the terminology

Opinion classification is largely based on the recognition of relevant terms in text and the conceptual categories they refer to. In order to link the linguistic knowledge to the conceptual vocabulary, we automatically create a terminology from the semi-automatic annotations. For higher recall, terms are stored in their lemmatized form. In addition, terms are linked to the sentences of the corpus they belong to. Thus, the terminology defines a glossary of the domain, with accompa-

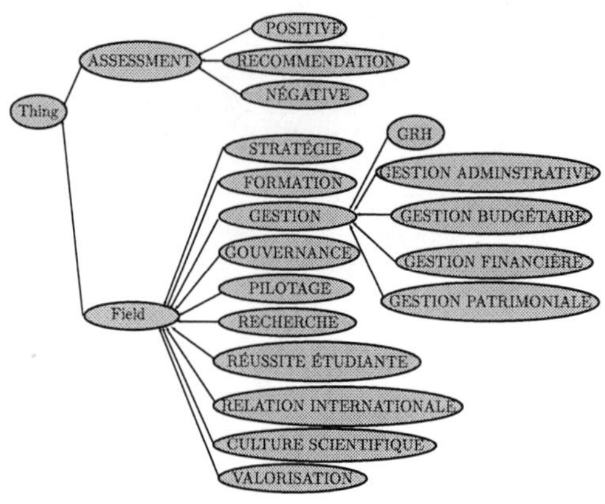

FIGURE 3 – A fragment of the ontology detailing the sub-fields of **GESTION**.

nying sentence examples for each term. For academic experts, this represents a precious resource for understanding the meaning behind the existing fields.

Term organization within the terminology is intended to allow the classification of opinions based on the organization of sub-fields within the ontology. For example, if the term *doctorate* is associated to the concept **Doctoral training** within the terminology while the concept **Doctoral training** is a sub-concept of the concept **Education**, then the identified opinion belongs to the field **Education**. If in the evolution of the ontology, the concept **Doctoral training** becomes a sub-concept of the concept **Research**, then the identified opinion will no longer belong to the field **Education** but to the field **Research**. Thus, the conceptual choices do not influence the way the opinion mining system is learned but only the opinions' classification. In practice, a sub-concept could be under two different Concepts. However, as the ontology hierarchy determines the distribution of opinions, at the moment, the choice has been made to avoid that kind of situation.

Throughout the three successive annotations, 1137 distinct terms were annotated then included in the terminology. Each was associated with the concept representing a sub-field of the ontology. When a term is not precise enough to be associated to a sub-field, it is associated directly to a field.

The ontology and the terminology do not prevent the portability of our approach. Indeed, in case they do not exist, they would be built from the first manual annotation and will evolve at each iteration. Otherwise, they will still evolve at each iteration.

7 Syntaxico-semantic pattern learning

The purpose of learning patterns is to capture the context of formulation of terms referring to a field or an assessment. These terms can be complex and contain non-contiguous words. Furthermore, words forming these terms may be subject to declension or conjugation. Hence, the characterization of these terms, must take into account both semantic and morpho-syntactic features. We propose to capture the formulation contexts of annotated terms using *syntactico-semantic patterns*. These patterns are used for automatic recognition of contiguous or non contiguous complex terms of the terminology. Constraining the identification of words based on their morpho-syntactic features, is meant to increase the accuracy of term recognition. To do so, at each iteration annotated sentences are analysed by the statistical dependency parser for French *Bonsai* (Candito et al., 2010). The syntactic features of sentences are then merged with their annotations. Figure 4

ID	FORM	LEMMA	CPOS	POS	FEATURES	HEAD	DEP	ANNOTATION	ANNOTATION LINK
1	Un	un	D	DET	g=m|n=s|s=ind	2	det	<>	<>
2	sentiment	sentiment	N	NC	g=m|n=s|s=c	0	root	<Identité[2, 5, 6] (Gouvernance)><>	
3	très	très	A	ADV	_	4	mod	< >	<>
4	fort	fort	A	ADJ	g=m|n=s|s=qual	2	mod	<Positive[3, 4] (Assessment)>	<>
5	d'	de	P	P	_	2	dep	< >	< 2]Suite_Gouvernance >
6	appartenance	appartenance	N	NC	g=f|n=s|s=c	5	obj	< >	< >

FIGURE 4 – A sentence annotated both syntactically and semantically.

illustrates the matching of syntactic and semantic features for the sentence : *Un sentiment très fort d'appartenance*. The first eight columns contain syntactic information while the last two columns come from the annotations. The 9th column contains the annotation features. For example, the feature *Identité[2, 5, 6] (Gouvernance)* means that the term (*sentiment d'appartenance*) composed of the words numbered 2, 5 and 6 has the annotation **Identité** which is a sub-field of **Gouvernance**. The 10th column contains the link with a previous part of a term containing non-contiguous words. For example, the feature *2]Suite_Gouvernance* of word number 5 (*d'*) means that this word is linked to word number 2 (*sentiment*) within an annotation of the field **Gouvernance**.

Annotations are represented on *head words* because syntactic dependencies linking terms referring to a field to those referring to an assessment are expressed on their *head nodes*. For example, the dependency *mod* between node 4 (*strong*) and its *head node* 2 (*sense*), which means that the term *very strong* modifies the term *sense of belonging*, is expressed over the head words *strong* and *sense*. The advantage of using syntactic dependency is that regardless of the order of words in the sentence, whether terms are simple or complex, or contiguous or not, the dependencies between head nodes remain unchanged. This property is very useful in our context in which most terms are complex and almost 15% are non contiguous. Semantic and syntactic levels are complementary without being interdependent. Thus, opinion mining system training, can be based on either the semantic level or the combination of both levels.

Syntactico-semantic patterns are acquired using an algorithm which calculates the shortest dependency path between two terms. They contain word lemmas, morpho-syntactic categories, morphological features and syntactic dependencies to check that identified words are syntactically linked to form a complex term of the terminology. For example, the pattern bellow represents the shortest dependency path between the terms *sentiment d'appartenance* (words of nodes 29,30 and 31) and *réel* (*real*). The involved dependency is *mod* (for modifier) that links the nodes of the terms *sentiment* (node number 29) and *réel* (node number 28).

mod({sentiment,sentiment,29,N,NC,g=m\|n=s\|s=c,26,Identité[29,30,31] (Gouvernance)},
{réel,réel,28,A,ADJ,g=m\|n=s\|s=qual,29,Positive[28] (Appreciation)})

Acquired syntactico-semantic patterns cover 116 semantic categories (3 types of assessment, 10 fields and 103 sub-fields). A total of 776 syntactico-semantic patterns are acquired. Among them, 728 are for complex term covering all the semantic categories and 48 are for simple terms covering only 37 semantic categories. These last numbers show how large the proportion of complex terms is in our corpus.

8   Semi-automatic term acquisition

The automatic term acquisition is guided by the ontology, the terminology and the syntactico-semantic patterns. Each combination of words of a sentence is checked looking for a match within the terminology. Terms that match a syntactico-semantic pattern are then annotated with the concept they are linked to within the terminology. Then, the automatically annotated corpus is submitted to the experts who may validate, correct or add missing annotations. Among the semi-automatic annotations, we distinguish three kinds of annotated terms :
- added ($\simeq$43%) : terms newly annotated by the experts.
- validated ($\simeq$32%) : terms automatically annotated that were kept by the experts.
- expanded ($\simeq$25%) : terms annotated by experts based on automatic annotations. For example, the annotated term **pilotage de la formation** (piloting of education) contains the two automatically annotated terms *pilotage* (piloting) and *formation* (education).

Almost a third ($\simeq$32%) of term annotations are automatic annotations and more than half ($\simeq$57%) of the annotations are based on the semi automatic annotations. Annotators confirmed that the automatic pre-annotation considerably eased and sped up their task. Indeed, at each new iteration annotators are less required to act as terms that have been consensually annotated once do not have to be manually annotated again. Moreover, automatic annotations serve as real examples for the annotators. These results show that automatic pre-annotation provides valuable assistance for expert annotators. In addition, automatic annotation reflects the consensual agreements between annotators, thus making it less subjective. After three iterations of the semi-automatic annotation, 1792 terms have been annotated : 932 terms referring to a field and 860 terms referring to an assessment.

9   Conclusion

We proposed a semi-automatic method for the acquisition of ontological and terminological knowledge. This method relies on incrementally building and tuning up these domain resources thanks to previous expert's annotations i.e. consensually approved knowledge. At each iteration these resources serve the automatic annotation of new corpora to ease and speed up experts' annotation work, decreasing the inherent subjectivity of such a task. The annotated corpus, the ontology and the terminology are built to train an opinion mining system for the evaluation of higher education and science institutions. In our method, domain dependent resources are built from scratch if they do not exist and evolve incrementally. So, we believe that it can be applied to other domains.

References

Gabriel Bernier-Colborne and Patrick Drouin. 2014. Creating a test corpus for term extractors through term annotation. *Terminology. International Journal of Theoretical and Applied Issues in Specialized Communication*, 20(1) :50–73.

Paul Buitelaar, Daniel Olejnik, and Michael Sintek. 2004. A protégé plug-in for ontology extraction from text based on linguistic analysis. In *The Semantic Web : Research and Applications*, volume 3053, pages 31–44.

Marie Candito, Benoît Crabbé, and Pascal Denis. 2010. Statistical French Dependency Parsing : Treebank Conversion and First Results. In *Proceedings of the Seventh International Conference on Language Resources and Evaluation (LREC'10)*, may.

Victor Christen, Anika Groß, Julian Varghese, Martin Dugas, and Erhard Rahm, 2015. *Annotating Medical Forms Using UMLS*, pages 55–69.

Philip Cimiano and Johanna Völker. 2005. Text2onto - a framework for ontology learning and data-driven change discovery. In *Proceedings of the 10th International Conference on Applications of Natural Language to Information Systems (NLDB)*, volume 3513, pages 227–238.

Philipp Cimiano, Alexander Mädche, Steffen Staab, and Johanna Völker. 2009. Ontology learning. In *Handbook on Ontologies*, pages 245–267.

Vincent Claveau and Marie-Claude L'Homme. 2005. Structuring terminology using analogy-based machine learning. In *Proceedings of the 7th International Conference on Terminology and Knowledge Engineering, TKE*.

Danilo Croce, Francesco Garzoli, Marco Montesi, Diego De Cao, and Roberto Basili. 2013. Enabling Advanced Business Intelligence in Divino. In *Proceedings of the 7th International Workshop on Information Filtering and Retrieval co-located with the 13th Conference of the Italian Association for Artificial Intelligence*, pages 61–72.

Béatrice Daille, Estelle Dubreil, Laura Monceaux, and Matthieu Vernier. 2011. Annotating opinion-evaluation of blogs : the Blogoscopy corpus. *Language Resources and Evaluation*, 45(4) :409–437.

Valmi Dufour-Lussier, Florence Le Ber, Jean Lieber, Thomas Meilender, and Emmanuel Nauer. 2012. Semi-automatic annotation process for procedural texts : An application on cooking recipes. *CoRR*.

Michael Erdmann, Alexander Maedche, Hans-Peter Schnurr, and Steffen Staab. 2000. From manual to semi-automatic semantic annotation : About ontology-based text annotation tools. In *Proceedings of the COLING - Workshop on Semantic Annotation and Intelligent Content*.

Blaz Fortuna, Marko Grobelnik, and Dunja Mladenic. 2007. Ontogen : semi-automatic ontology editor. In *Proceedings of the 2007 conference on Human interface : Part II*, pages 309–318.

Hugo Lewi Hammer, Per Erik Solberg, and Lilja Øvrelid. 2014. Sentiment classification of online political discussions : a comparison of a word-based and dependency-based method. In *Proceedings of the 5th Workshop on Computational Approaches to Subjectivity, Sentiment and Social Media Analysis*, pages 90–96.

Long Jiang, Mo Yu, Ming Zhou, Xiaohua Liu, and Tiejun Zhao. 2011. Target-dependent twitter sentiment classification. In *Proceedings of the 49th Annual Meeting of the Association for Computational Linguistics : Human Language Technologies - Volume 1*, pages 151–160.

E. Lapponi, J. Read, and L. Ovrelid. 2012. Representing and Resolving Negation for Sentiment Analysis. In *Data Mining Workshops (ICDMW)*.

Joseph Lark, Emmanuel Morin, and Sebastián Peña Saldarriaga. 2015. CANÉPHORE : a French corpus for aspect-based sentiment analysis evaluation. TALN 2015.

Marie-Claude L'Homme. 2004. A lexico-semantic approach to the structuring of terminology. In *Proceedings of the 3rd Computerm*, pages 7–14.

Malgorzata Marciniak, Agnieszka Mykowiecka, and Piotr Rychlik. 2016. Termopl - a flexible tool for terminology extraction. In *Proceedings of the Tenth International Conference on Language Resources and Evaluation (LREC)*.

Francesco Mele, Antonio Sorgente, and Giuseppe Vettigli. 2014. An Italian Corpus for Aspect Based Sentiment Analysis of Movie Reviews. In *First Italian Conference on Computational Linguistics CLiC-it*.

Thibault Mondary, Sylvie Després, Adeline Nazarenko, and Sylvie Szulman. 2008. Construction d'ontologies à partir de textes : la phase de conceptualisation. In *Actes des 19èmes Journées Francophones d'Ingénierie des Connaissances (IC'08)*, pages 87–98.

Philip V Ogren. 2006. Knowtator : a plug-in for creating training and evaluation data sets for biomedical natural language systems. In *Proceedings of the 9th International Protégé Conference*, pages 73–76.

Josef Steinberger, Tomáš Brychcín, and Michal Konkol. 2014. Aspect-Level Sentiment Analysis in Czech. In *Proceedings of the 5th Workshop on Computational Approaches to Subjectivity, Sentiment and Social Media Analysis*.

Mary D Swift, Myroslava Dzikovska, Joel R Tetreault, and James F Allen. 2004. Semi-automatic syntactic and semantic corpus annotation with a deep parser. In *Proceedings LREC*.

Sylvie Szulman. 2011. Une nouvelle version de l'outil terminae de construction de ressources termino-ontologiques. In *22èmes journées francophones d'Ingénierie des Connaissances (poster)*, page 3 pages.

Nora Taleb, Sellami Mokhtar, and Michel Simonet. 2009. Knowledge acquisition for the construction of an evolving ontology : Application to augmented surgery. In *Proceedings of World Academy of Science, Engineering and Technology*.

C. M. Toledo, O. Chiotti, and M. R. Galli. 2012. An ontology evolution approach for information retrieval strategies with compound terms. In *Informatica (CLEI), 2012 XXXVIII Conferencia Latinoamericana En*, pages 1–10.

David Vilares, Miguel A. Alonso, and Carlos Gómez-Rodríguez. 2015. On the usefulness of lexical and syntactic processing in polarity classification of Twitter messages. *Journal of the Association for Information Science and Technology*.

Henning Wachsmuth, Martin Trenkmann, Benno Stein, Gregor Engels, and Tsvetomira Palakarska. 2014. A Review Corpus for Argumentation Analysis. In *Computational Linguistics and Intelligent Text Processing*, volume 8404, pages 115–127.

Janyce Wiebe, Theresa Wilson, and Claire Cardie. 2005. Annotating Expressions of Opinions and Emotions in Language. *Language Resources and Evaluation*, 39(2-3) :165–210.

Yuanbin Wu, Qi Zhang, Xuanjing Huang, and Lide Wu. 2009. Phrase Dependency Parsing for Opinion Mining. In *Proceedings of the 2009 Conference on Empirical Methods in Natural Language Processing : Volume 3*, pages 1533–1541.

Seid Muhie Yimam, Richard Eckart de Castilho, Iryna Gurevych, and Chris Biemann. 2014. Automatic Annotation Suggestions and Custom Annotation Layers in WebAnno. In *Proceedings of the 52nd Annual Meeting of the Association for Computational Linguistics. System Demonstrations*, pages 91–96.

Understanding Medical free text: A Terminology driven approach

Santosh Sai Krishna
gsk.krishna@gmail.com

Manoj Hans
manojhans1989@gmail.com

Abstract

With many hospitals digitalizing clinical records it has opened opportunities for researchers in NLP, Machine Learning to apply techniques for extracting meaning and make actionable insights. There has been previous attempts in mapping free text to medical nomenclature like UMLS, SNOMED. However, in this paper, we analyzed diagnosis in clinical reports by mapping into ICD10 codes. We propose a lightweight approach with real-time predictions by introducing concepts like WordInfo, root word identification. We were able to achieve 68.3% accuracy over clinical records collected from qualified clinicians. Our study would further helps the healthcare institutes in organizing their clinical reports based on ICD10 mappings and derive numerous insights to achieve operational efficiency and better medical care.

1 Introduction

A vast amount of non-standardised clinical reports are available which are rich in information about patient care and disease progression. These clinical reports rarely follow any standards and have minimal grammatical correctness. These reports are usually documented by qualified practitioners about patient's medical history. However, increasing demand for accessing clinical data in industry needs a process for extracting structure and meaning out of the available clinical reports.

There are two major problems for extracting insights from clinical reports. One is unavailability of structured medical data and other is available data is highly varied in terms of terminology for any given phenomenon in the medical field. The main reason for this discrepancy is different information systems in clinics and hospitals. All of these systems have their own separate rules and terminologies to record medical data. This lack of consistency between data from different information systems has reduced interoperability across health care organisations. In order to improve interoperability, the data must be represented using standard terminologies.

The present work proposes a goal to develop a system of mapping free text such as patients clinical report and diagnosis with an ICD-10 code for a disease.

2 Related Work

Some known systems for mapping free text to UMLS are SAPHIRE (Hersh et al., 1995), MetaMap (Aronson, 2001), IndexFinder (Zou et al., 2003), and NIP (Huang et al., 2005). The SAPHIRE system uses a lexical approach and maps text to UMLS terms. Later, IndexFinder added Semantic and Syntactic filtering to improve performance of lexical mapping. NIP uses sentence boundary detection, noun phrase identification and parsing, all of these are computationally expensive processes.

MetaMap is another approach to map free text to a terminology like UMLS. This approach uses a three step process, where a free text is first broken down to simple noun phrases using the Specialist minimal commitment parser. After this, variant of phrases and mapping candidates are generated using UMLS source vocabulary. Then for all of these candidates, a score is generated to evaluate the best fit

Proceedings of the 5th International Workshop on Computational Terminology,
pages 121–125, Osaka, Japan, December 12 2016.

medical concept of each term. MetaMap is also computationally expensive therefore unsuitable for real time processing.

The work done by (Hazlehurst et al., 2005) is on mapping free text to UMLS by generating all the synonyms of each word of the input. All these words and synonyms are used to find the best possible combination among them, which matches a concept in UMLS. This process matches 1 concept every 20 seconds or longer thereby unsuitable for real-time concept mapping.

SNOMED CT also offers a huge potential for standardising clinical reports into medical concepts. One of the known research by (Patrick and Wang, 2007) uses augmented lexicon, term composition and negation detection to come up with phrases that have a potential match of concepts from SNOMED CT. The idea is to come up with medical concepts which can properly describe a given clinical note. The major limitation for this approach is that it is not considering various possible order of words that can be used while writing a report. It is expecting user to write reports according to the rules and standards used in SNOMED CT.

We are offering an approach which considers multiple combination of noun phrases, ordered by its entropy and which can be used in free writing. It is computationally inexpensive and can be used in real time systems to map free text to a disease code in ICD-10

3 Architecture

Given a clinical report on a patient history, we need to map the diagnosis into ICD10 code(s). As the clinical reports are filled by Doctors, who have numerous reports to fill in a day, there are chances of human errors in spelling variants and sometimes the order of words. Before we even map the individual words to the most descriptive ICD10 code, we need to clean and normalise the words. Furthermore, the resulting ICD10 codes needs to be ranked based on their relevancy to the diagnosis and also the irrelevancy with the remaining words in a ICD10 code. All the above steps put together fall into a pipelined approach as detailed below:

3.1 Preprocessing

With any error in spelling it would be easy to miss the optimal ICD10 code. If someone types "acute gastrtis" instead of "acute gastritis", then we would be left with ICD10 codes that match only the word "acute". We lost the primary context of "gastritis" and this results in a misleading classification to "acute". Hence, it is crucial to resolve the spelling mistakes. To resolve the misspelling, all unique words mentioned in all ICD10 codes are collected and a Trie data structure is built on the characters of each word. The resulting spell correction algorithm is able to suggest correct words in less than 1ms with a maximum edit distance of 2. After spell correction, the text is cleaned by removing non alphanumeric characters, any ICD codes and later followed by lemmatization.

3.2 Finding Primary and Secondary words

To match a diagnosis with an ICD10 code it is often difficult and not necessary to match the entire diagnosis text, it would be enough to match the context, e.g., "dengue fever" can be matched with a concept having "dengue" rather than looking for both the words to be matched. This means that we need to identify the root word for every medical word. In our example, "dengue" is_a "fever" . If such a mapping can be derived, then every diagnosis free text can be split into two sets of words, i.e., primary (must match) and secondary (should match). The primary list follows a must match criteria whereas the secondary list doesn't follow a strict criteria however any code that contain words from the secondary list will be ranked higher.

- **Deriving root words** : Understanding the terminology of ICD10 gives us a great context of the organisation of diseases. For example, the concept "K12" which talks about "stomatitis (inflammation in mouth)" has its ancestors concept as "K00-K14" that elaborate "Diseases of oral cavity, salivary glands and jaws". This ancestor mapping provides an insight of hypernym relation (root words) like "stomatitis" is_a "disease", "stomatitis" is_a "oral cavity", etc. Any hypernym relation which appears above 80% of all ancestor mappings is considered as a root word.

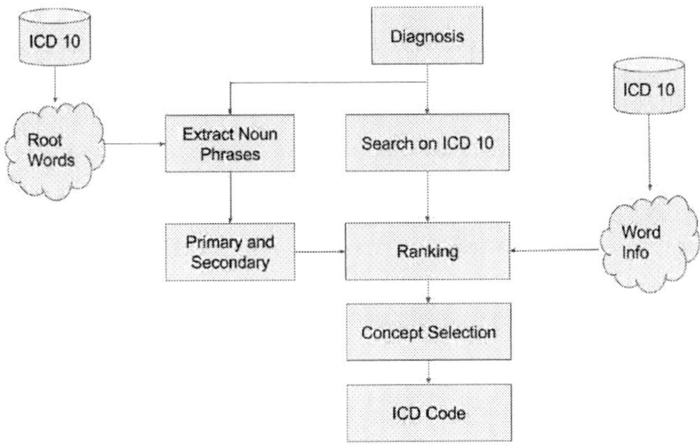

Figure 1: Architecture Components

- **Finding the Primary/Secondary split** : With the diagnosis text preprocessed, all noun phrases are extracted using the nltk package in python. Within each noun phrase, any possible root words will be extracted using the mappings extracted from the above step. All the root words are considered as Secondary and all the specific (non-root) words are considered as Primary. The remaining words of the diagnosis are added to the Secondary list. For example, "dengue" (non-root) would map to "fever" (root), which makes "dengue" as primary and "fever" as secondary.

3.3 Word Informativeness

You shall know a word by the company it keeps (Firth, J. R.). If a word like "other" is often seen and with different words, then it carries very less information, compared to a word like "cardiac" which is often used in the very specific context of heart-related diseases. The WordInfo is a metric derived from the randomness associated with a word. It defines how random a word is based on the number of unique words seen in its surrounding context. This helps in ranking ICD10 codes when multiple codes are matched with the terms in diagnosis. It derives from the idea that an ICD10 mapping should be as specific about the diagnosis as possible and as generic as possible in terms of the remaining words of that code.

The WordInfo is calculated in two steps as detailed below:

- **Calculating PMI scores** : The PMI scores are calculated using the below formula

$$PM1(x, y) = \log(\frac{P(x, y)}{P(x).P(y)})$$

The above equation helps us in deriving the pointwise mutual information between any two specific words. A higher PMI score indicates a closer association between two words. However, we want to capture the randomness of an individual word.

- **The Skewness of PMI scores** : For common words like "other", there would be high number of co-occurring words with varying PMI scores. We had assigned WordInfo to be the third moment (skewness) of PMI scores because we have observed that common words share a skewness below zero compared to words like "cardiac". This is attributed to the fact that a number of infrequent words are being associated with common words and hence resulting in a left-skewed distribution of PMI values.

3.4 Search and Rank

An inverted index is built over all ICD10 codes. A boolean OR query is performed on the tokens extracted from a diagnosis to retrieve all ICD10 codes that mention one or more of the diagnosis tokens. The retrieved concepts need to be ranked based on their relevancy to the diagnosis. Ideally, we want the retrieved codes topic to be matching with the diagnosis and doesnt contain any other topic. Based on these two factors, the ranking algorithm is designed as follows

- **Likelihood of unique Primary words** : After segregating a diagnosis text into primary and secondary, the extent of context overlap between the diagnosis and the code can be identified with the likelihood of finding unique Primary words in the code terminology.

$$P(\text{Unique Primary}) = \frac{\text{No. of unique primary matched}-}{\text{No. of total unique primary words in query}}$$

- **Total likelihood of Primary words** : This measures the probability of finding a Primary word in the definitions of a Code.

$$P(\text{Total Primary}) = \frac{\text{No. of primary words matched}}{\text{No. of total words in a code}}$$

- **Likelihood of unique Secondary words** : After having observed the Primary words, this measure evaluates the relevancy of a Code based on the overlap of Secondary terms.

$$P(\text{Unique Secondary}) = \frac{\text{No. of unique secondary words matched}}{\text{No. of total unique secondary words in query}}$$

- **Total likelihood of Secondary words** : Among the remaining terms, the probability of visiting a Secondary word is calculated with this measure.

$$P(\text{Total Secondary}) = \frac{\text{No. of secondary words matched}}{\text{No. of total words in a code}}$$

- **Randomness associated with the remaining non-query words** : To evaluate if a Code is elaborating other concepts along with the diagnosis we need to understand the information provided by the non-query words. Using the WordInfo metric calculated for each word as described in section above, we will be able to call out the codes that do not match the context in a diagnosis.

3.5 Concept Selection

The retrieved Codes are ranked based on a linear weighted combination of above metrics with weights being assigned on a descending priority of above order. However, the task is to assign Code(s) to a diagnosis. This assignment problem is achieved by a greedy approach. The top ranked Code will be first assigned to a diagnosis. All the Primary words appeared in the assigned Code are removed from the diagnosis and the assignment step is repeated until all Primary words are found in the assigned Code(s).

4 Results

It is hard to compile data sources providing the gold standard of mapping for a given free text. However, we evaluated our algorithm using a dataset gathered from clinical hospitals. The dataset consists of clinical reports written by qualified professional doctors after examining a patient mentioning the case history, diagnosis with its corresponding ICD10 code and a few other details. We extracted diagnosis with its ICD10 code for our evaluation study. Out of the 5823 total case reports available, there were 4902 records that had a non-empty diagnosis and ICD10 code.

As the entire architecture is built on a knowledge base approach which does not rely on supervision of ICD10 codes, we used the entire 4902 samples for evaluating the algorithm. The evaluation metrics

	Elasticsearch	Preprocess + Search + Primary/Secondary	+ WordInfo
Accuracy	25.5	64.2	68.3

used here is Accuracy. We compared the results against a basic approach which used search and ranking capabilities of Elasticsearch.

As per the results mentioned in Table 1, it is evident that our approach is performing better than a basic search algorithm. It can also be seen that the impact of WordInfo scores introduced in this paper is significantly improving the results. With all modules included, our algorithm was able to assign an ICD10 code for a diagnosis with an average time of 25ms.

5 Conclusion

It has been an acknowledged fact that understanding clinical records is crucial in improving the medical care. This paper is an attempt at understanding the diagnosis provided by qualified doctors by mapping them to a standard nomenclature like ICD10. We were able to achieve an accuracy of 68.3% over 4902 records. These results can be attributed to algorithms introduced like the identification of root words, deriving WordInfo values along with a probabilistic ranking approach. However, this work can be further extended by adding synonyms to diagnosis terms, or improving their representation using deep learning models like word2vec, GloVe and also by expanding any abbreviations.

References

Patrick J, Wang Y, Budd P. 2007 *An automated system for conversion of clinical notes into SNOMED clinical terminology.* Proceedings of the 5th Australasian Symposium on ACSW Frontiers, Ballarat, Australia

Hersh, W. R. and D. Hickam 1995 *Information retrieval in medicine: The SAPHIRE experience.* Journal of the American Society for Information Science 46(10): 743-747

Aronson, A. R. 2001 *Effective mapping of biomedical text to the UMLS Metathesaurus: the MetaMap program.* Proc AMIA Symp 17: 21.

Zou, Q., W. W. Chu, et al. 2003 *IndexFinder: A Method of Extracting Key Concepts from Clinical Texts for Indexing.* Proc AMIA Symp 763: 7.

Huang, Y., H. J. Lowe, et al. 2005 *Improved Identification of Noun Phrases in Clinical Radiology Reports Using a High-Performance Statistical Natural Language Parser Augmented with the UMLS Specialist Lexicon* American Medical Informatics Association.

Hazlehurst, B., H. R. Frost, et al. 2005 *MediClass: A System for Detecting and Classifying Encounter-based Clinical Events in Any Electronic Medical Record* American Medical Informatics Association.

Author Index